POSTCARD HISTORY SERIES

Orange

A POSTCARD GUIDE TO ITS PAST

ORANGE TRANSCRIPT

OR-OPT-OPEN-OPINE-OPINER

POSTCARD HISTORY SERIES

Orange

A POSTCARD GUIDE TO ITS PAST

Don and Marietta Dorflinger

ARCADIA
PUBLISHING

ISBN 978-0-7385-0317-2

Published by Arcadia Publishing
Charleston SC, Chicago IL, Portsmouth NH, San Francisco CA

Printed in the United States of America

Library of Congress Catalog Card Number: 2007924960

For all general information contact Arcadia Publishing at:
Telephone 843-853-2070
Fax 843-853-0044
E-mail sales@arcadiapublishing.com
For customer service and orders:
Toll-Free 1-888-313-2665

Visit us on the Internet at www.arcadiapublishing.com

Dedication

To our fathers,
Edmund A. Dorflinger and Dr. Mario V. Pizzi,
Native Orangeites
Who would have enjoyed seeing this book in print.

On the front cover: "Greetings From Orange NJ" is a typical postcard from the *c.* 1908 era. (Author's collection.)

On the back cover: See page 119. (Author's collection.)

CONTENTS

ACKNOWLEDGMENTS

When we began collecting Orange, New Jersey postcards and ephemera several years ago, we never realized what fruits our labors would ultimately bear. With the advent of Internet auction services, our collection began to grow rapidly. Then, in the spring of 1999, we received an email from a Connecticut postcard collector and former Essex County resident, Hoby Van Deusen, who noticed that we were gobbling up "Orangeiana." Hoby's collection of over 600 Orange cards was available for sale, and when we saw it, we knew immediately that we had to have it! The idea became quite simple: the collection would form the nucleus for an Arcadia book, and the proceeds from the book would finance the collection.

Thank you Hoby, for your lifetime efforts in amassing a collection of Orange postcards that could never be duplicated today!

Our thanks also to the following groups and individuals:

Bob Reed of the First Presbyterian Church, who gave generously of his time, expertise, and materials.

Doris Walker's Reference Staff at the Orange Public Library, who bore with me patiently as they dredged up a truckload of musty old files from the archives.

Marty DeMarzo, Deputy Chief of the Orange Fire Department, who provided all of the Fire Department photographs and information.

David L. Pierson (1865–1938), Orange's "Official" Historian, whose three volumes published in 1921 proved indispensable.

Frank P. Jewett, Master Photographer of Orange, who recorded many of the images in this work.

. . . and Virginia Pizzi, lifelong Orangeite and aunt of the author, whose recollections helped make sense of it all.

INTRODUCTION

The postcard was the electronic mail of its era. Posted in the morning in the days of twice-daily delivery, it could easily reach its intended local recipient by the same afternoon, frequently conveying such timely information as, "I'll meet you for dinner at 5 o'clock," or, "Prudence will be arriving at the Lackawanna Depot at 3:15." Its simplicity and innocence long ago vanished into a past replete with horse and carriage, summer picnics, band concerts, railroad excursions, and dips in the lake at the local park. It was the hallmark of a quieter age devoid of today's fast cars, airplanes, computers, and people ruled by speed and efficiency.

The postcard was also an historical record of the evolution of villages, towns, and cities. Often the only photographic view of a particular bucolic scene, it holds an intense value for both the historian and the collector. In a city of 35,000 residents like Orange, New Jersey, nearly one

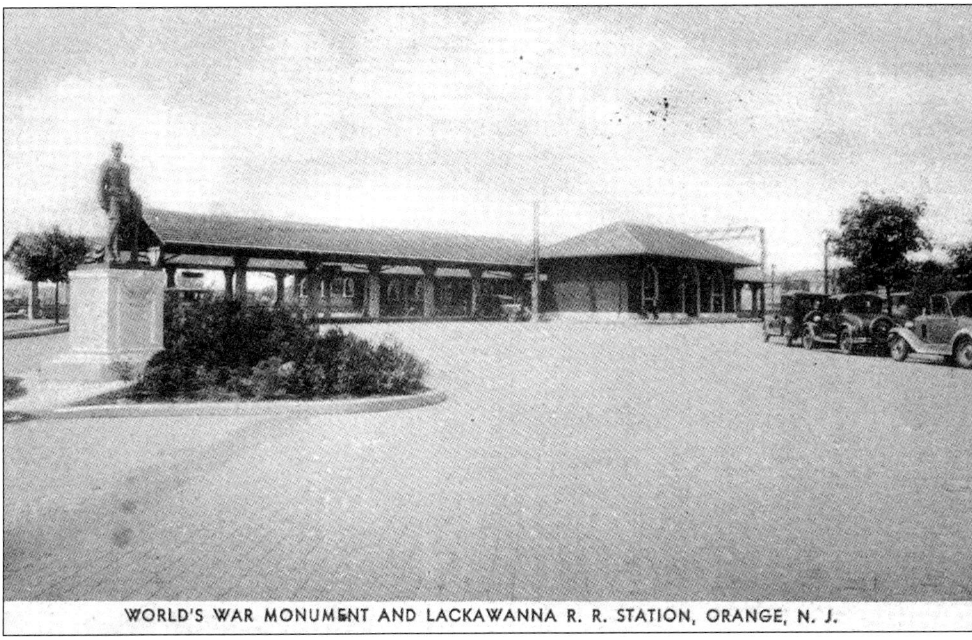

WORLD'S WAR MONUMENT AND LACKAWANNA R. R. STATION, ORANGE, N. J.

thousand different postcard views probably exist, taken at various times from the turn of the century until the present. With a "meager" collection of only 650, we are not discouraged, but delighted that we have at least 300 more yet to discover!

The postcard views in this book, with minor exceptions, provide a vignette of Orange as it existed between 1905 and 1920. (In a few instances, photographs were utilized where postcards were unavailable.) Interestingly, many scenes remained relatively unchanged into the 1950s. Therefore, baby boomers may easily identify with much of what they see, and younger Orange residents can virtually look through a window in time to view the heritage that has passed into history.

Orange, New Jersey, had its origins in Connecticut's New Haven Colony. In 1666, barely three decades after settling there, 30 of New Haven's families took the perilous journey by water to found "a town on the Passayak" River. They arrived on territory now encompassing Newark, the four Oranges, and several other municipalities. The area was situated in the northeast portion of a land grant conveyed by King Charles II of England to his brother James, Duke of York. In 1664, James conveyed the land to two proprietors, Lord John Berkeley and Sir George Carteret. Since Carteret had been Royal Governor of the Isle of Jersey, the territory became known as "New Jersey."

Orange was initially a part of the city of Newark, and remained such until November 27, 1806, when the territory now encompassing all of the Oranges was detached. On April 13, 1807, the first government was elected, but not until March 13, 1860, was Orange officially incorporated as a city. Immediately, the new city began fragmenting into smaller communities, primarily because of local disputes about the costs of establishing paid police, fire, and street departments. South Orange was organized on January 26, 1861, Fairmount (later to become part of West Orange) on March 11, 1862, East Orange on March 4, 1863, and West Orange (including Fairmount) on March 14, 1863.

Orange lay on the Mt. Pleasant Turnpike, the main road from Newark to Morristown, and ultimately to Easton, Pennsylvania. Therefore, the town became a busy thoroughfare for travelers, and hotels abounded. Initially, the stagecoach was the primary method of transportation. Omnibuses of the Eclipse and the Morris & Newark Lines serviced Orange. The Morris & Essex Railroad arrived in Orange in November 1836, its first cars drawn by horses. On October 2, 1837, the first steam locomotive appeared, and the horses were, with minor exception, relegated to pasture. The "M&E" later became a vital part of the Delaware, Lackawanna, & Western Railroad (DL&W) and survives today as NJ Transit's busy Morristown Line. Trolley cars appeared much later, with the Orange and Newark Horse Car Railroad Company running its first car up Main Street in May 1862. The Orange Crosstown Line, eventually extending from Morris Street, Orange, to Bloomfield, was started in June 1888. (The first electric trolley in the State of New Jersey operated over a section of this line.) Eventually all of the trolleys, and the buses that replaced them, became part of the sprawling Public Service Coordinated Transport System.

Orange was an industrial city from the outset. Early settlers found a profuse growth of hemlock trees, an ideal supply of tannic acid for the tanning industry, and boot and shoemaking factories soon flourished. Hat making was the essential industry, and can be traced to 1792. By 1892, 21 firms were engaged in that trade, employing over 3,700 people in plants valued at nearly $1.1 million. Nearly 4.8 million hats left Orange that year alone, bound for all four corners of the globe. By 1921, however, only five firms were left, and by 1960, all had departed for places such as Norwalk and Danbury, Connecticut.

Beer was a major revenue producer in Orange beginning in the 1890s when the three Winter Brothers of Pittsburgh, Pennsylvania, arrived in the city and built the first brewery. The Orange Brewery was constructed in 1901 at a reported cost of $350,000. The production of beer ceased with prohibition in 1920, and after the repeal of the Volstead Act in 1933, the brewery was sold to John F. Trommers of Philadelphia. Trommers brewed beer under that label until 1950, when the concern was again sold to Liebmann Breweries, Incorporated, which bottled Rheingold. Eventually, after several additional owners, the plant was closed for good in 1977.

Other notable firms located in Orange were the Monroe Calculating Company, manufacturers of the patented adding machines of the same name, and the Bates Manufacturing Company, producers of office accessories such as staplers and stampers. The United States Radium Company was a notorious resident of Orange. This firm refined ore and extracted radium used to make luminous paint for dials and hands of watches and other indicators. It was only years later that the terrible carcinogenic effects of this material became known, and the polluted site of the factory became a thorn in the side of the city.

Orange has produced such notables as baseball's Monte Irvin and Heavyweight Boxer Tony Galento. Actor William Bendix lived and worked here for a short while. It was once the hat-making capital of the United States, as several brothers founded the "No-Name Hat Company," before one of them moved on to make fedoras in Philadelphia under the family name, "Stetson." Presidents, presidential candidates, and governors visited. Orange threw the biggest party of all on its 100th anniversary and another when it turned 150.

Orange is our hometown. Our grandparents operated businesses here. Our fathers were both born here. We went to school here, graduating from the now closed Our Lady of the Valley High School, and we were married in June 1970, in that parish's church. Our daughters, Jennifer and Karen, first saw the light of day at Saint Mary's Hospital. Marietta's mother still resides in the same house where Marietta grew up, and her brother is a lieutenant on the Orange Police force. Don's mother, father, and brother are buried in Rosedale Cemetery. Despite having moved from Orange nearly 30 years ago, we still consider it our hometown. In short, our lives have always been, and continue to be, to some degree, tied to Orange.

In 1982, citizens voted overwhelmingly to change the designation of Orange from a city to a township, thereby making it eligible for National Revenue Sharing funds. In 1985, the State of New Jersey named Orange as a State Urban Enterprise Zone, creating tax breaks and investment incentives. As Orange is perched on the brink of its brighter future, we hope that a look at its past can provide some valuable lessons.

This book is a labor of love. Orange is building renewed civic pride as the millennium approaches, and we hope that this volume will help in that effort.

One

Getting Around

A panorama of Main Street, looking west from South Center Street in 1907, shows a variety of transportation conveyances. The open air trolley in the left foreground with the crowd clinging to the side is headed for Newark, while the more distant car hurries its passengers toward the West Orange Loop near the Erie Railroad Station. The third car, an Orange Crosstown, sits between the First Presbyterian Church (whose spire dominates the scene) and the Bijou Theatre, on opposite corners of Day Street. Automobiles have yet to dominate this scene, so horses with buggies and wagons are prevalent. The white milk wagon of Henry Becker is at the curb in the right foreground. Becker's Dairy of Livingston was a fixture in the area for decades, and was the last farm to ship its milk via the Lackawanna Railroad. The closing of his creamery at Straders, New Jersey, in the 1960s was a contributing factor in the abandonment of the DL&W Sussex Branch. The bunting and flags are in place for the Centennial Celebration of the Oranges.

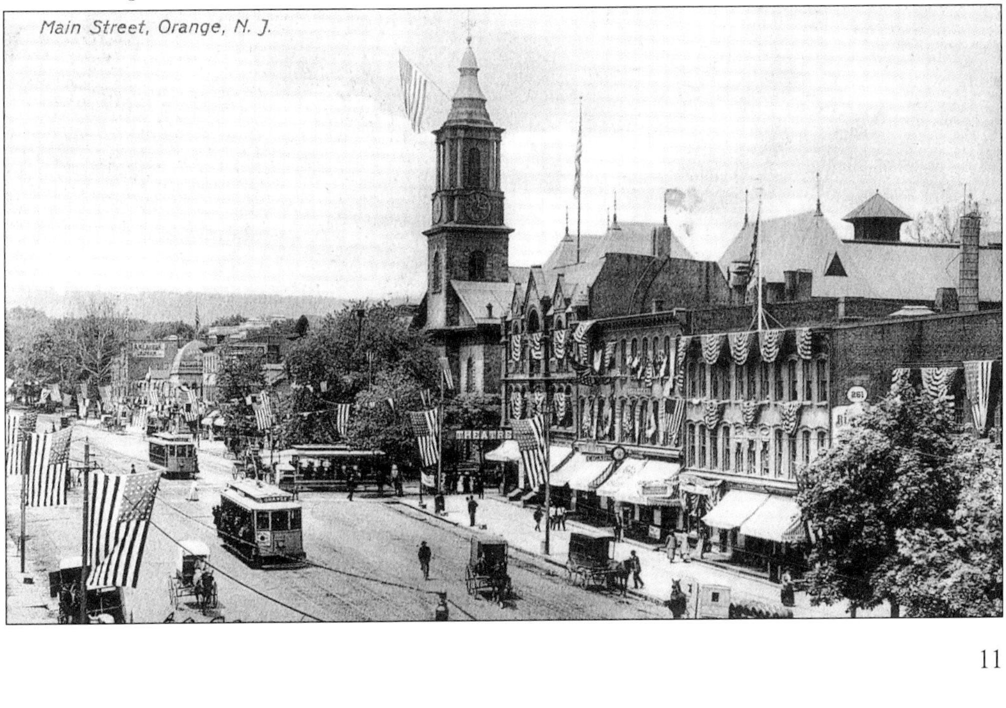

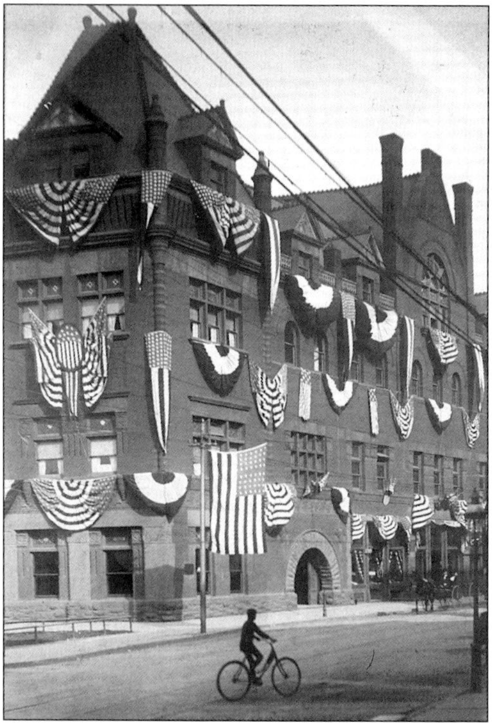

A solitary bicyclist makes his way along the street past the Orange Theatre. Cycling was a popular means of individual transportation in the early part of the 20th century. The theatre is bedecked in bunting and flags for the Centennial Celebration of the Oranges in 1907.

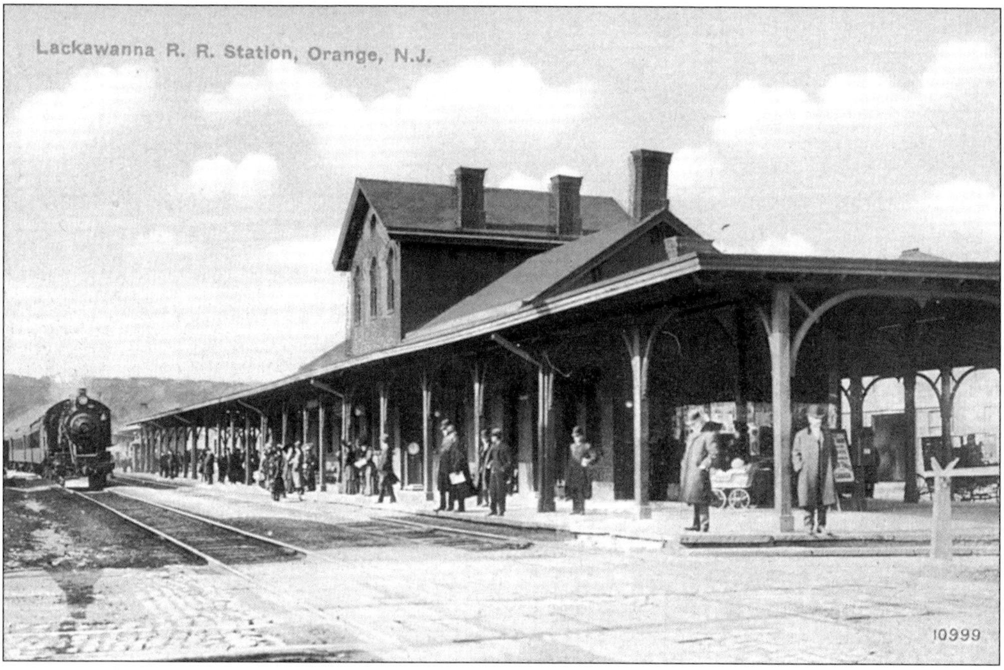

A group of New York commuters anxiously awaits the arrival of the morning train at Orange's principal station on the Lackawanna Railroad. This station was located between Day Street and Essex Avenue on the westbound side of the tracks. The station boasted the third largest yard on the DL&W in New Jersey. The building would later be demolished during a track reconstruction program in 1916–1918.

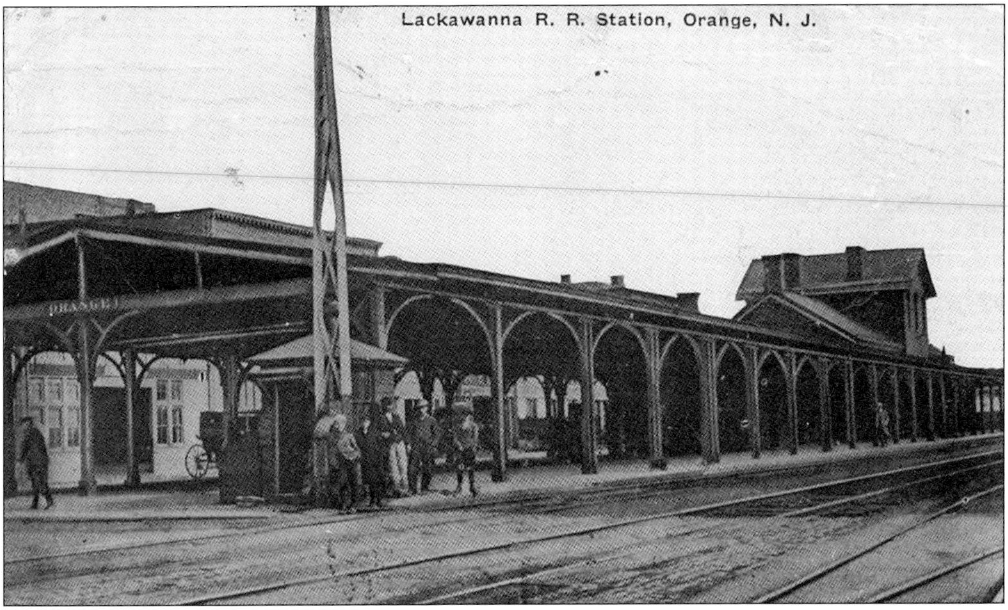

The Lackawanna Railroad rebuilt and elevated much of its line though the Oranges between 1916 and 1918 in order to eliminate grade crossings and modify curvatures and gradients. The track was realigned slightly to reduce the sharpness of the Orange Curve, necessitating demolition of this building. A new brick station was constructed just west of this site. In this view, local boys find the gateman's shanty a good place to congregate.

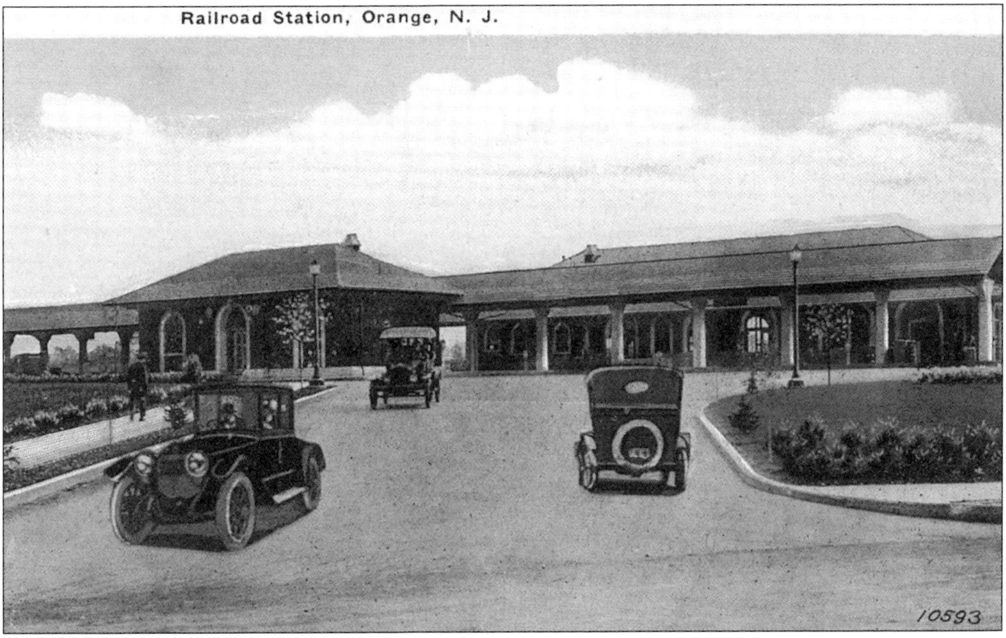

The new Orange station featured landscaped lawns and wide driveways, as seen in this view from the westbound side. Vintage Fords dominate this picture of the new building, which features the smaller, unmanned waiting room constructed of red brick. Platform canopies were formed of poured concrete (the Lackawanna's favored construction method) and structural steel.

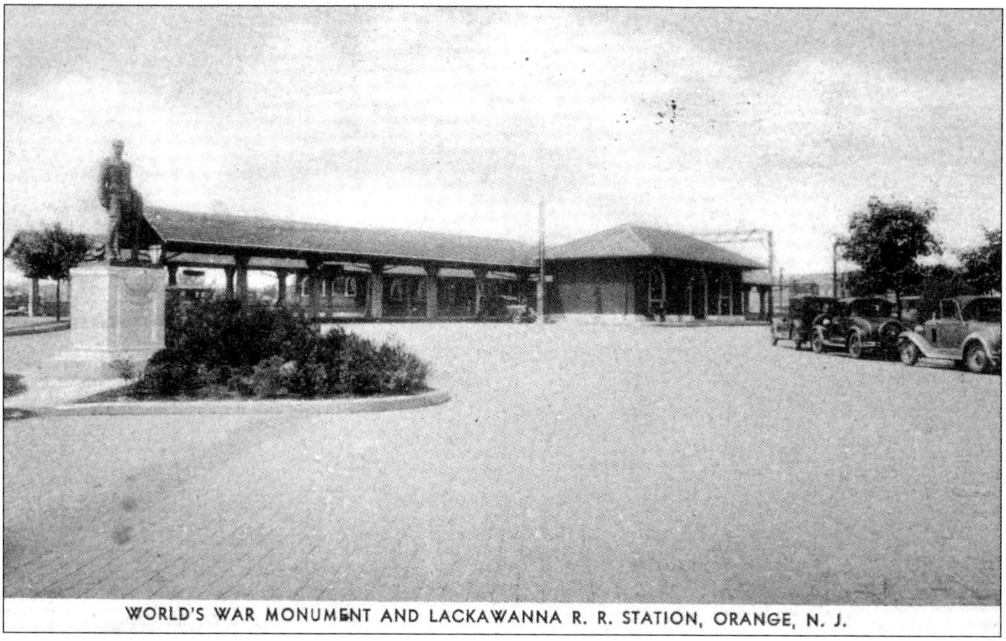

The ticket agency and baggage room were on the eastbound side of the new station, and the freight house situated a block west at Lincoln Avenue. The spacious road in the foreground is Lackawanna Plaza (today Tony Galento Plaza). The statue on the island commemorates casualties suffered by sons of Orange in World War I. Catenary poles behind the station reveal that this photo was taken after the completion of the DL&W's 1931 electrification project.

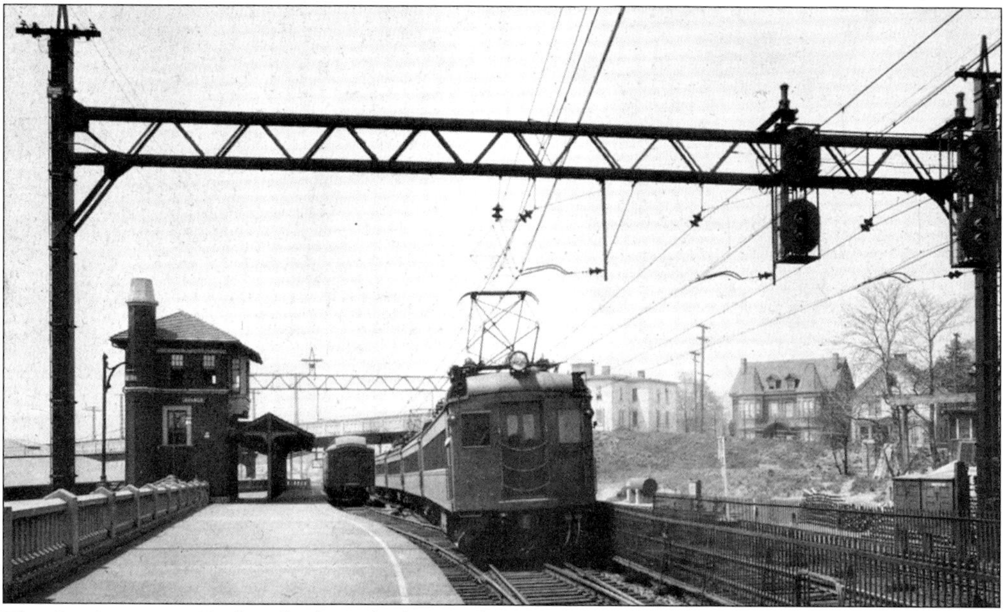

The Lackawanna Railroad electrified its suburban service in 1930–31 to eliminate smoke pollution and reduce congestion at its Hoboken Terminal. Here, on May 6, 1931, a four-car multiple-unit eastbound electric train eases to a stop at the Orange station. The tower in the background controlled switches and signals in the area. A baggage car is sitting at the Railway Express Agency platform located above the freight house, which was down on street level.

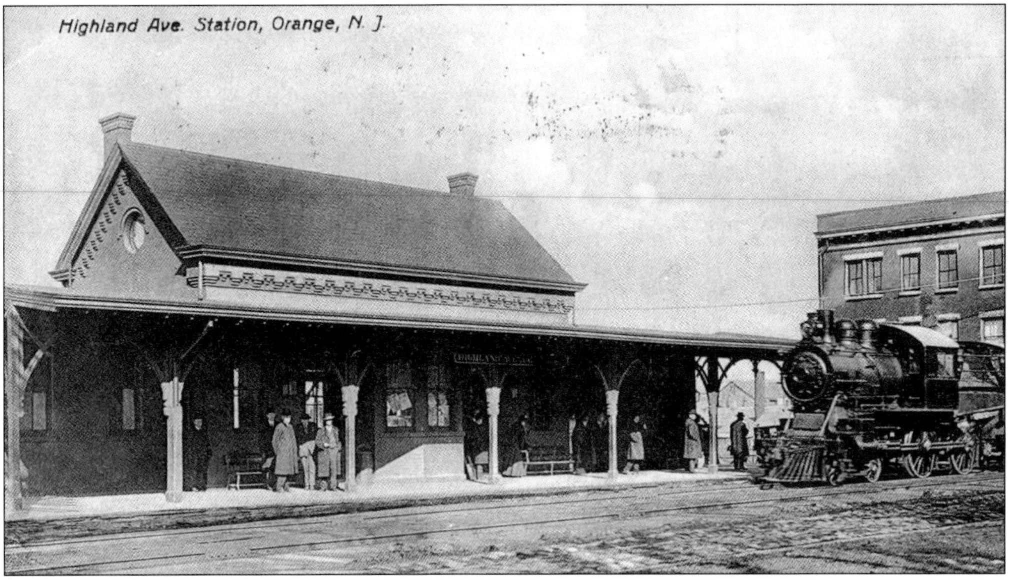

An unidentified camelback-type *4-4-2* locomotive of the DL&W eases a westbound train into Highland Avenue Station on a sunny morning around 1910. This second stop in Orange was originally called Orange Valley, but the name was changed around 1890. Built in about 1905, this station survived only about 12 years before it was demolished during the 1916–18 grade separation project. A new station was then constructed on the eastbound side.

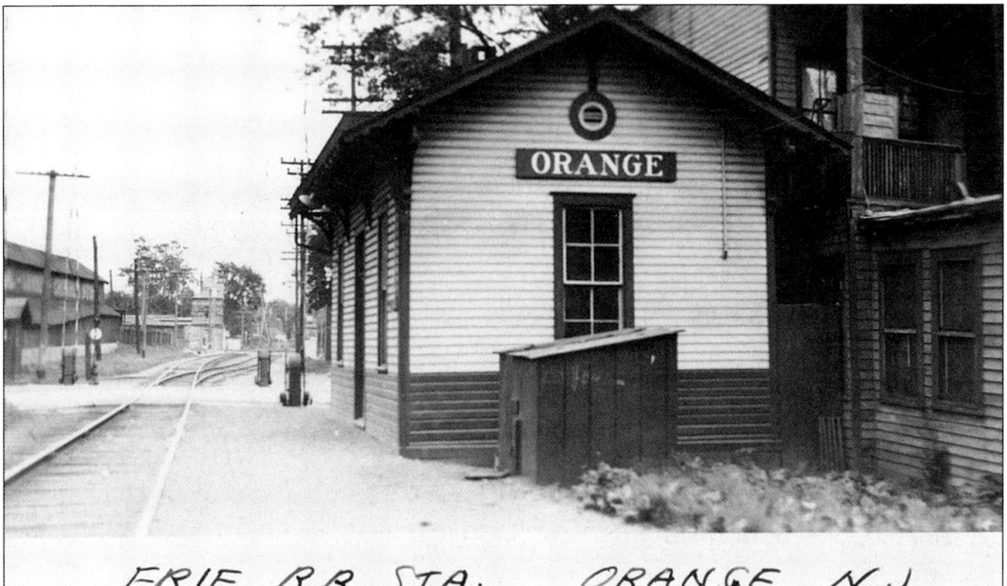

The Erie Railroad Company "crept" into Orange through the back door by purchasing the New York & Greenwood Lake and Watchung Railways. It took a circuitous route through East Orange's Doddtown and eventually terminated at Main Street by the West Orange border. In doing so, it passed over the border into Orange just long enough to build this small shelter at the Washington Street crossing. This 1930 scene, complete with neatly painted clapboards, manual gates, and small watchman's shanty belied the futility of the line. Commuters generally preferred the Lackawanna, and Erie passenger service was gone by April 1955.

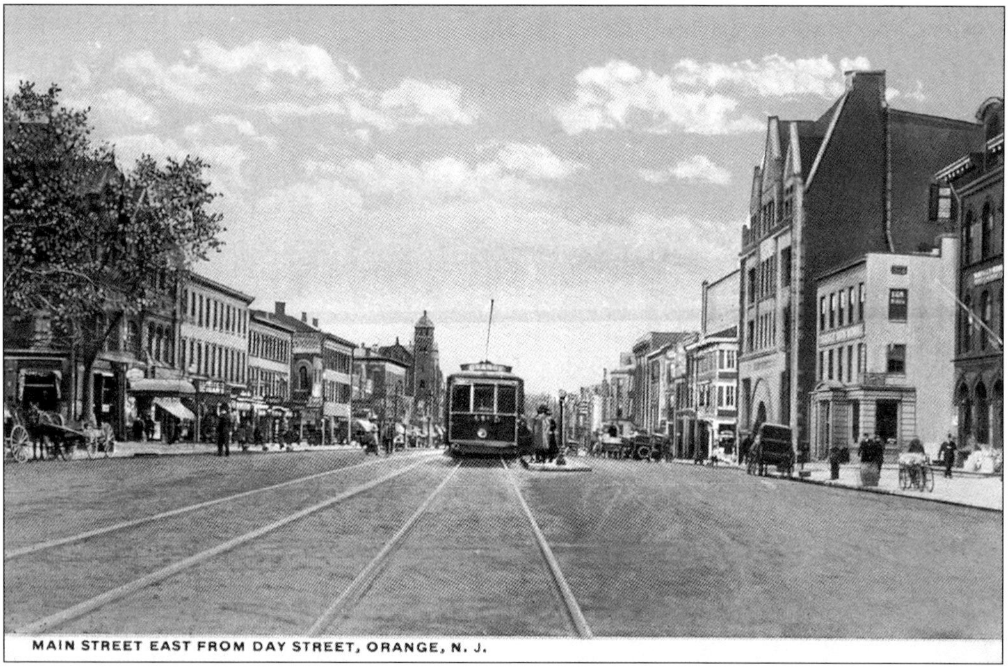

The arrival of automobiles on the streets of Orange made mid-road trolley hopping a bit more challenging. To alleviate the inherent danger, the city of Orange added small safety islands to the middle of Main Street at critical stops. Here, a sprinkling of travelers boards the eastbound car for Newark.

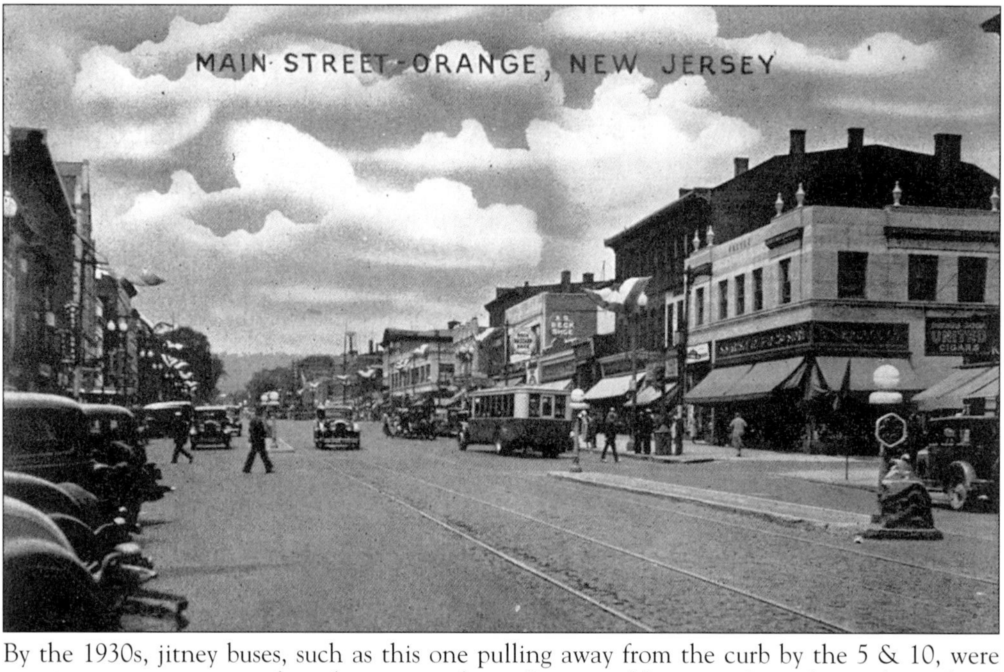

By the 1930s, jitney buses, such as this one pulling away from the curb by the 5 & 10, were carrying more customers than the traction lines. Buses could go anywhere the road wandered and were not constrained by an overhead wire. On March 1, 1951, streetcar operations on the Orange Line ceased. Central Avenue's trolleys had already vanished December 13, 1947.

Two

MAIN STREET

Every town has a "Main Street," and Orange is no exception. Its major thoroughfare stretches 1.2 miles between its borders with East and West Orange, and was home to countless businesses and residences. This busy view, looking west from just below Center Street, shows an amalgam of activity, including east and westbound trolleys, wagons, carriages, buckboards, and a beautiful new touring car. Its lucky owner in driving togs, this car, parked in front of Miller's store, is likely one of the earliest automobiles in the city, as the card is postmarked November 7, 1904.

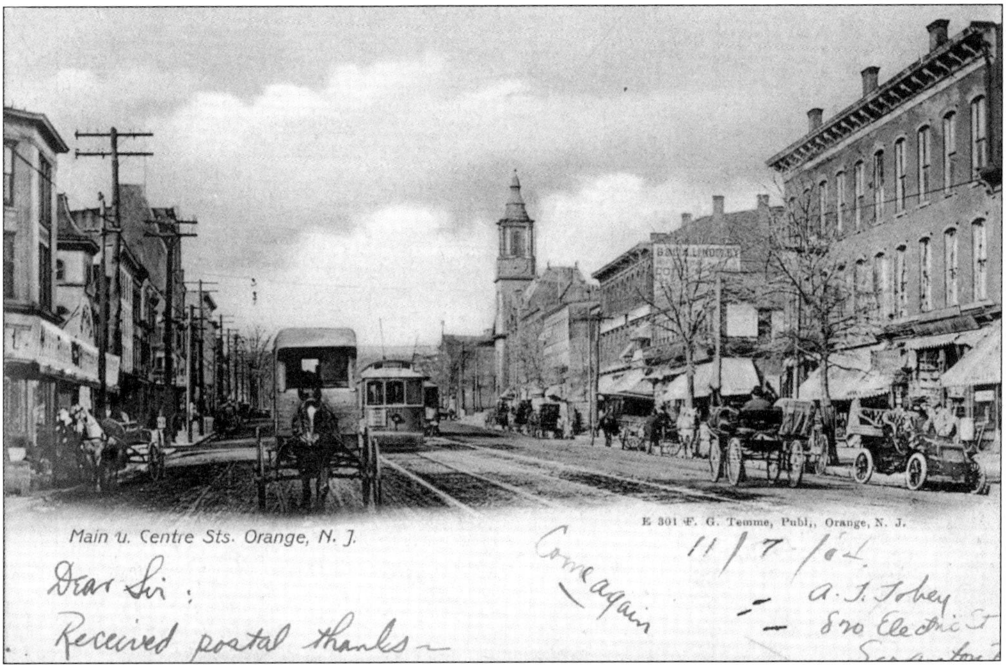

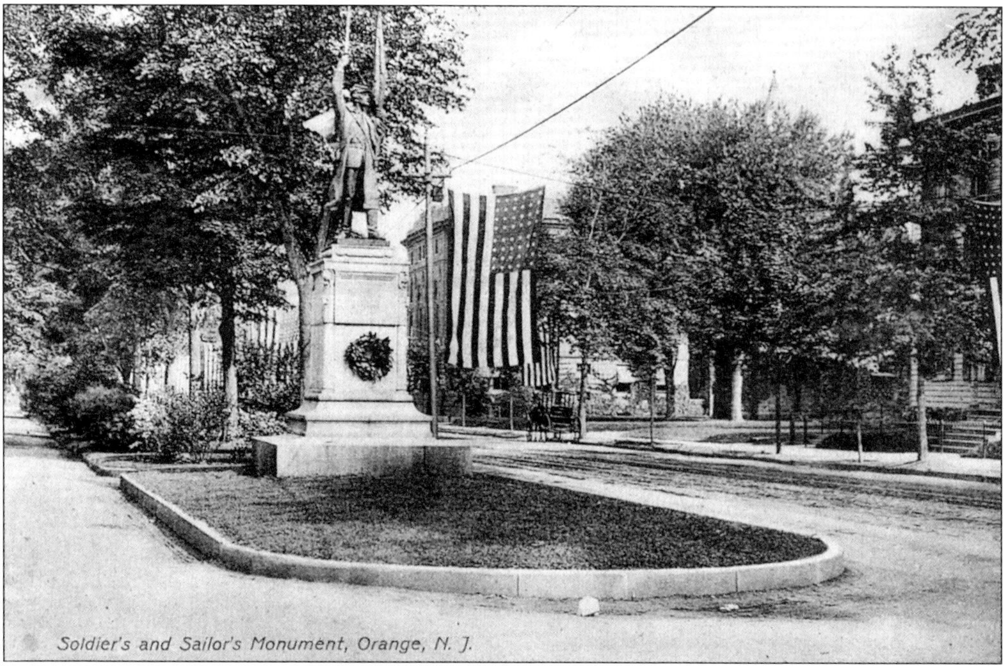

The Soldiers' and Sailors' Monument at the east end of Military Common was designed and sculpted by W. Granville Hastings. This bronze memorial to Federal troops killed during the Civil War was dedicated Memorial Day, May 30, 1899. The Uzal Dodd Post of the Grand Army of the Republic inspired the subscription of $6,000 for the 8-foot-high likeness of a color-sergeant and its 15-foot granite pedestal.

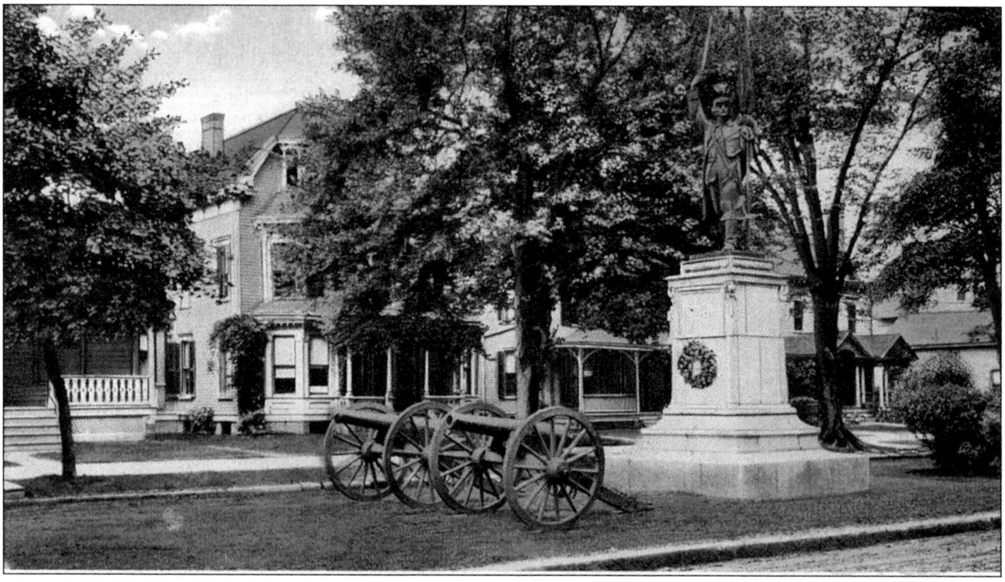

The dedication of the monument was preceded by a grand parade from Lincoln Avenue to the Commons and included various dignitaries. Members of the Dodd Post were escorted by Gatling Gun Company A of East Orange. As Elizabeth Bradford Pierson unveiled the statue, Company A fired a 21-gun salute. At the conclusion of the ceremonies, the thousands assembled joined in singing *America*, and there undoubtedly wasn't a dry eye in the house.

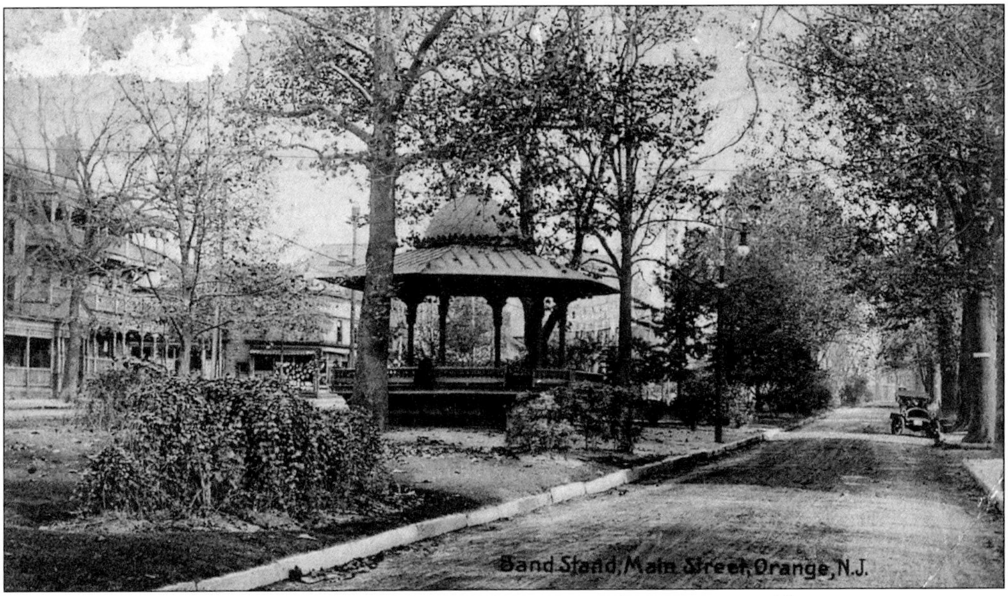

The bandstand in Military Commons was the scene of many enjoyable summer concerts. On October 26, 1900, William Jennings Bryan, the great orator and candidate for President running against incumbent William McKinley, visited Orange and delivered a 30-minute speech from this location to a crowd estimated at ten thousand. McKinley still carried the town.

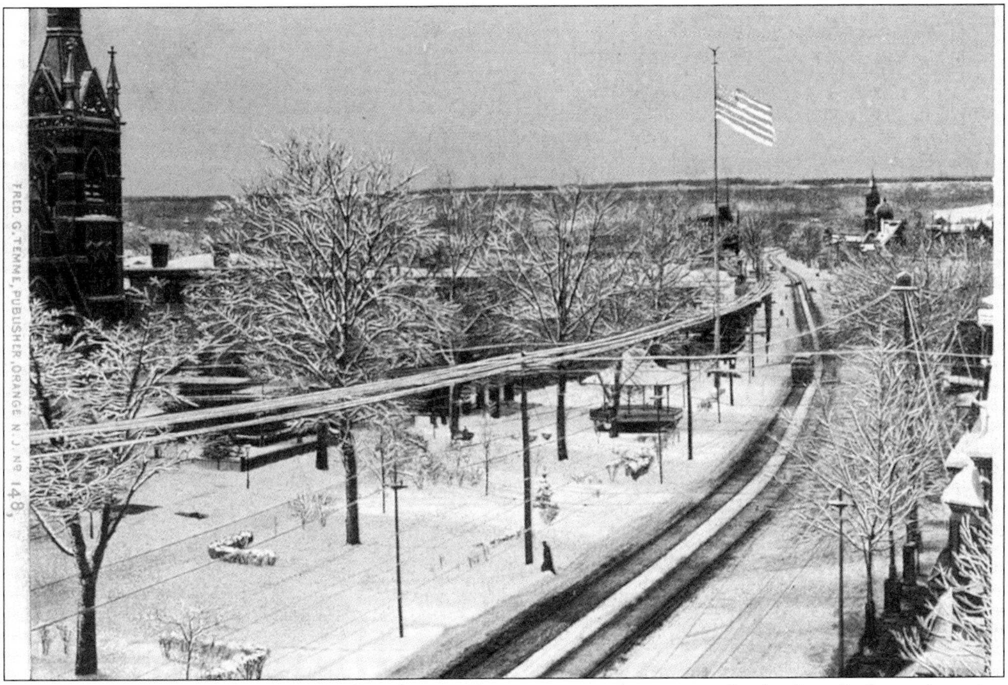

A view of lower Main Street and Military Commons in the winter looked so forlorn that the artist felt compelled to add an enormous American flag to the barren pole. The trolley company has cleared its tracks and an eastbound car can be seen approaching. This photo was probably taken from the roof of the Young Men's Christian Association (YMCA).

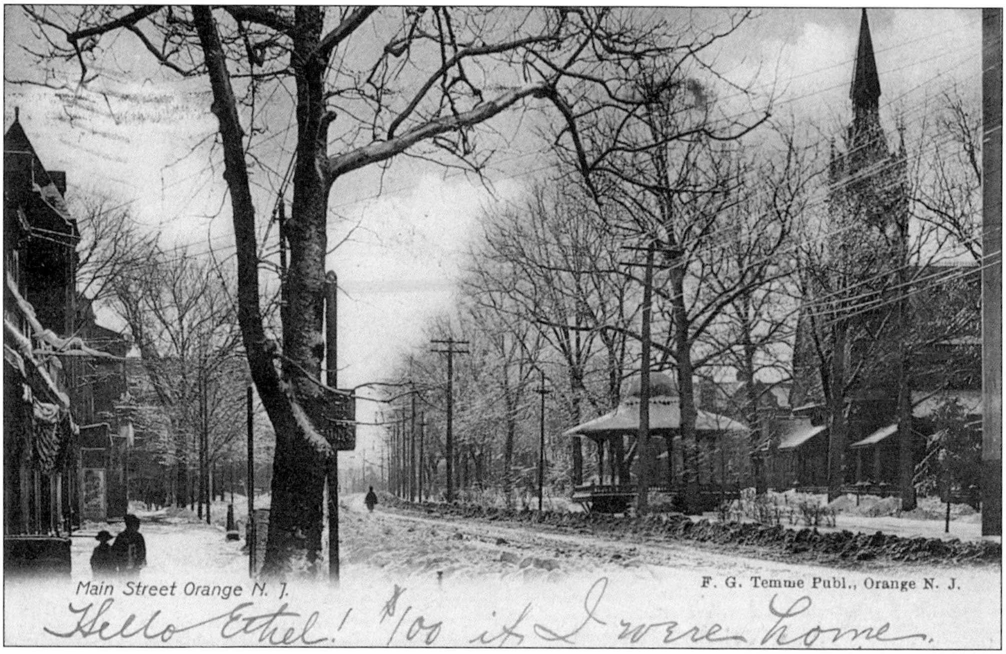

Another view of the Military Commons in winter shows a lonely bandstand with the North Orange Baptist Church in the background. Only a few hearty souls have dared to brave the elements on this day.

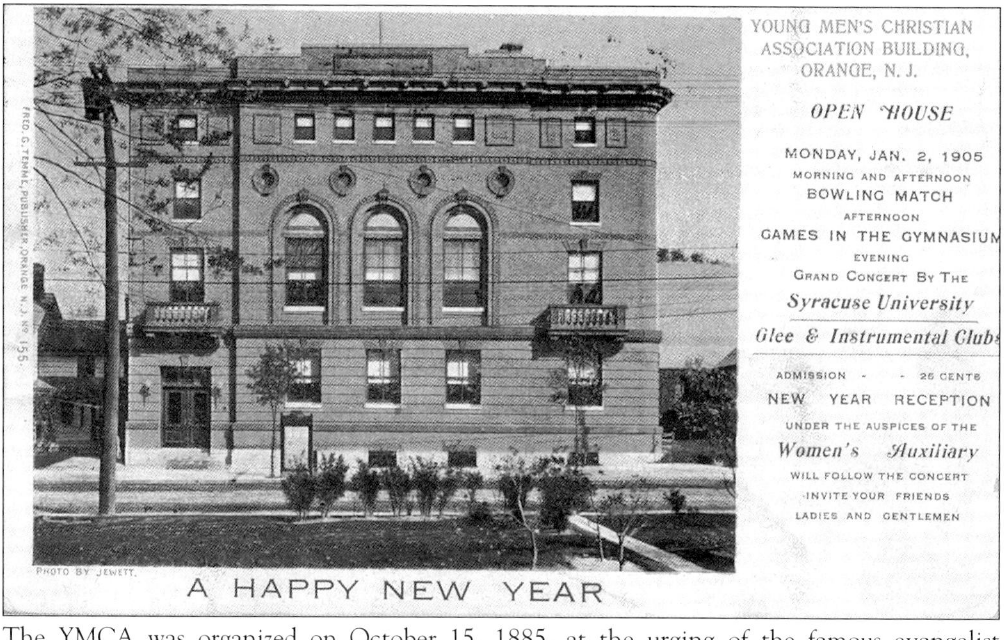

The YMCA was organized on October 15, 1885, at the urging of the famous evangelist Rev. Dwight L. Moody. Moody preached at the Park Roller Skating Rink on September 20, and by December 12 the Association was operating out of a two-story dwelling adjoining the North Orange Baptist Church. Twenty-five thousand dollars was pledged for the construction of this handsome brick structure, which formally opened on the north side of Main Street on January 11, 1887.

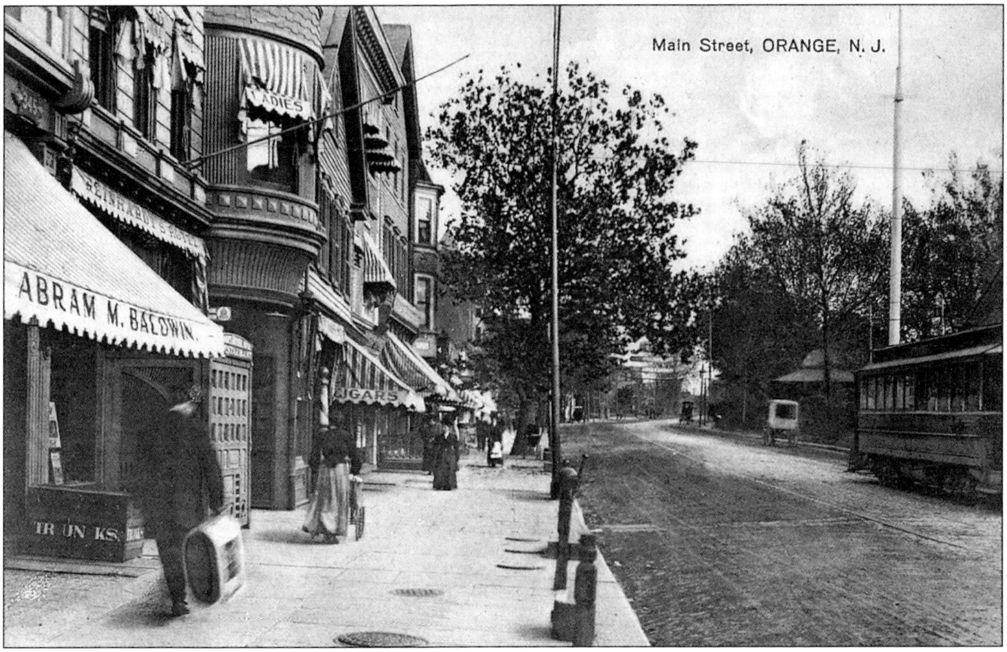

The more you look, the more you see in this cluttered vignette of the north side of east Main Street. Included are Baldwin's Store, hitching posts, the eastbound trolley, the barber pole, the Bell Telephone sign, the cigar store, the woman pushing the baby carriage, the horses and wagons, and the bandstand.

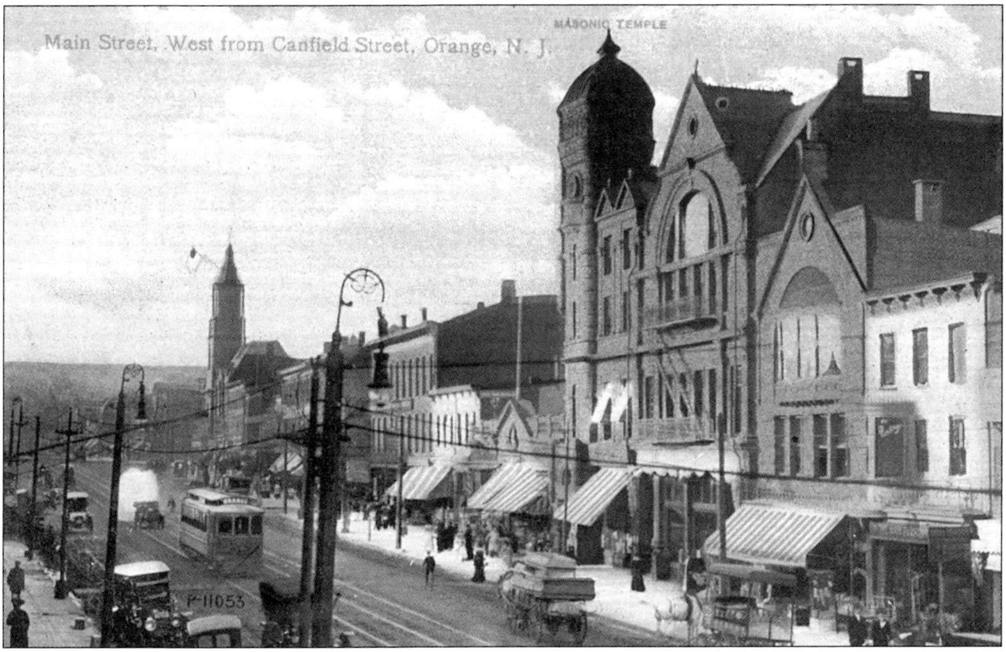

Dominant in this scene looking west from Canfield Street is the second Temple of Union Lodge No. 11, Free & Accepted Masons. Built of red brick, the structure was dedicated on November 16, 1887. For many years after, the Orange Post Office occupied the first floor. The automobile following the trolley appears about ready to explode.

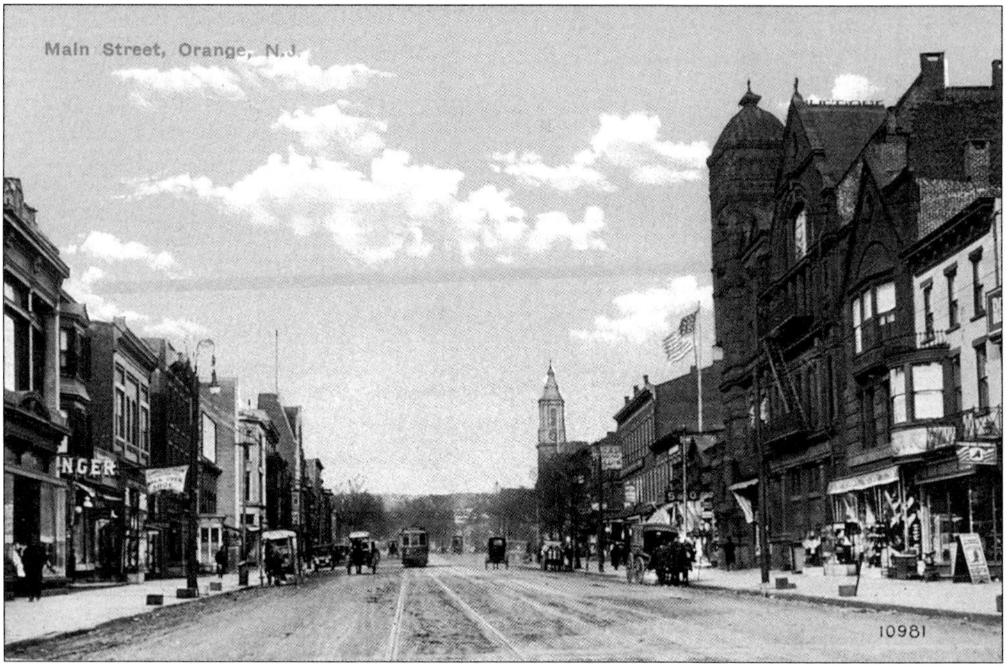

A similar view from street level looking west toward Center Street almost makes the viewer feel a part of the scene.

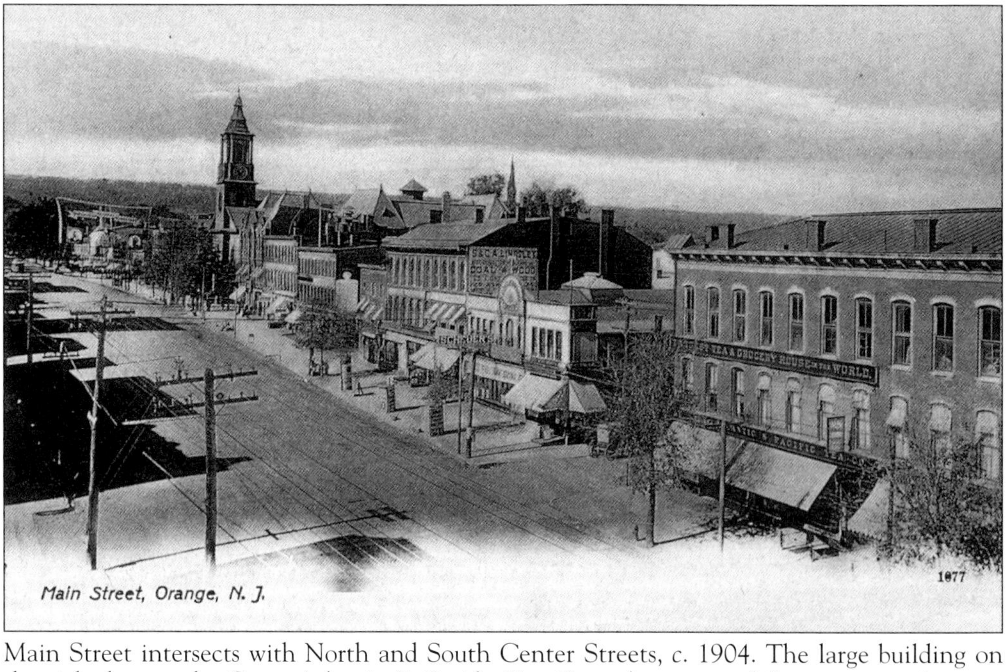

Main Street intersects with North and South Center Streets, c. 1904. The large building on the right houses the Great Atlantic & Pacific Tea Co., whose second-floor sign proclaims it the "Largest Tea & Grocery House in the World." In the distance, a banner hangs across the road with what appears to be the words, "Republican National Nomination," and pictures of Theodore Roosevelt and his running mate, Charles W. Fairbanks.

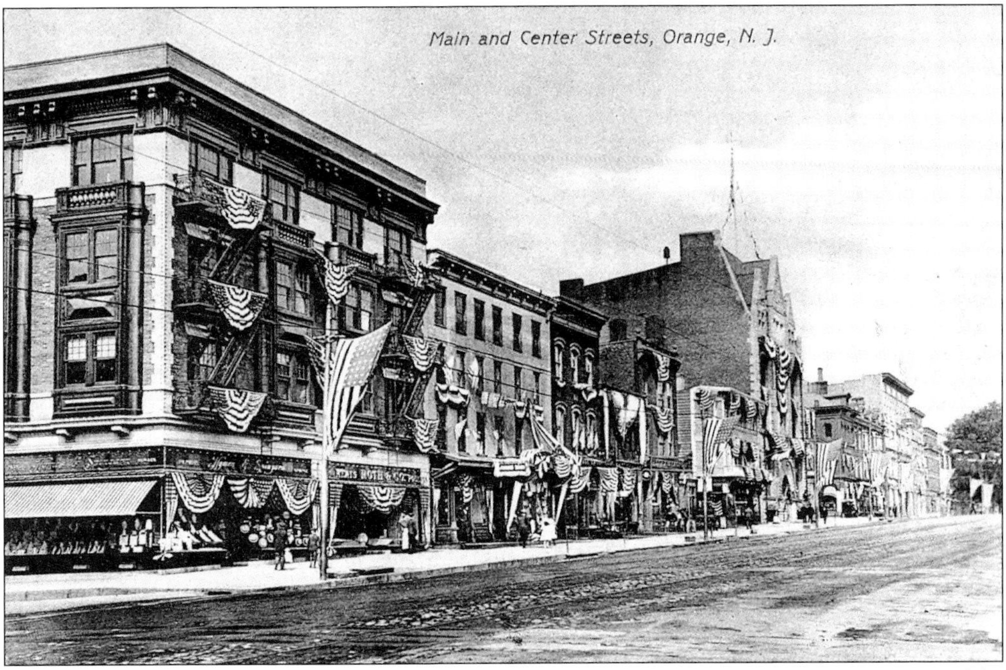

The impressive building on the southwest corner of Main and Center Streets was occupied by the odd combination of Hymes and Spingarn Men's Clothiers, and Roth & Company Meats and Poultry. The buildings appear to be decked out in full regalia for the Centennial Celebration of 1907.

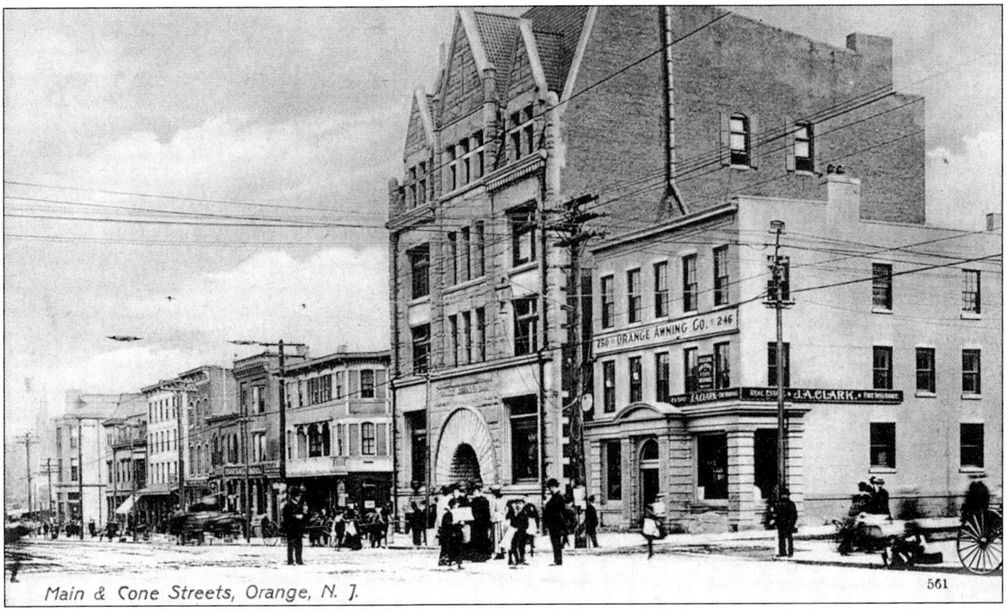

At least three paperboys are hawking the news on the corner of Main and Cone, so this could signal a big event, like the election of Teddy Roosevelt. The corner building with signs advertising the Orange Awning Company and J.A. Clark, Real Estate and Fire Insurance, actually houses the Orange Savings Bank on the ground floor. Next door is the impressive fortress-like Orange National Bank, completed in 1892.

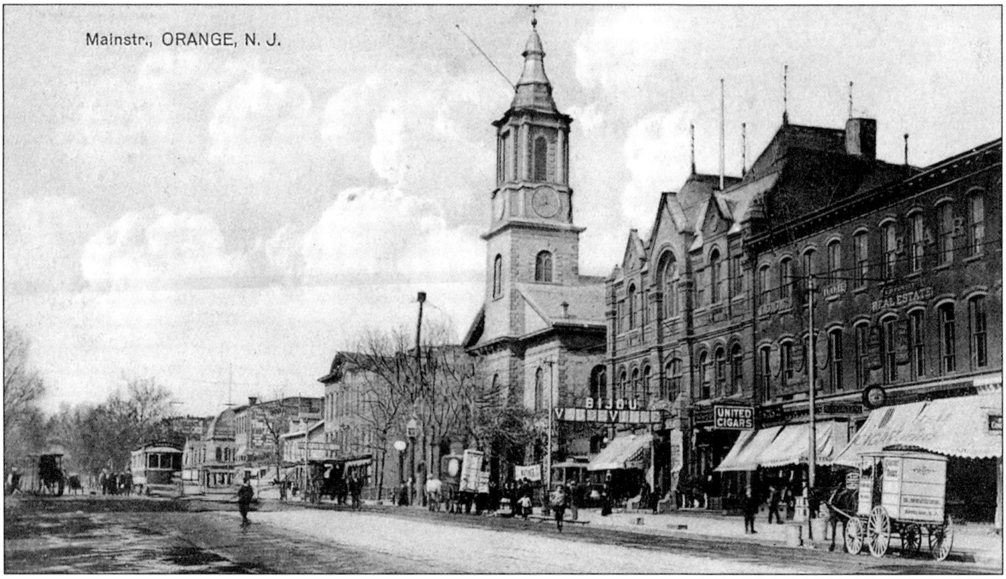

This view of the north side of Main Street looking west provides a time capsule of a simpler era. Henry Becker's white milk wagon, a standard sight in 1905, is parked at the curb in the right foreground. The street bustles with the usual cadre of carriages, drays, and trolley cars. Automobiles have yet to usurp the right of way, and Vaudeville is alive and well at the Bijou.

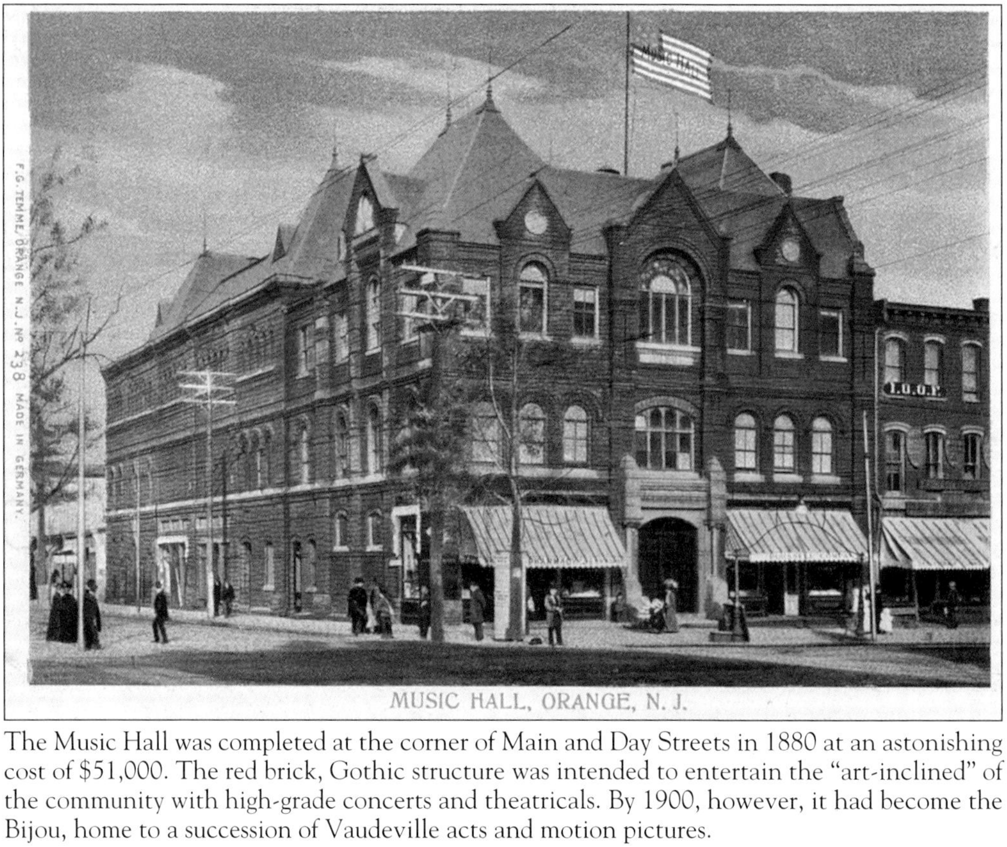

The Music Hall was completed at the corner of Main and Day Streets in 1880 at an astonishing cost of $51,000. The red brick, Gothic structure was intended to entertain the "art-inclined" of the community with high-grade concerts and theatricals. By 1900, however, it had become the Bijou, home to a succession of Vaudeville acts and motion pictures.

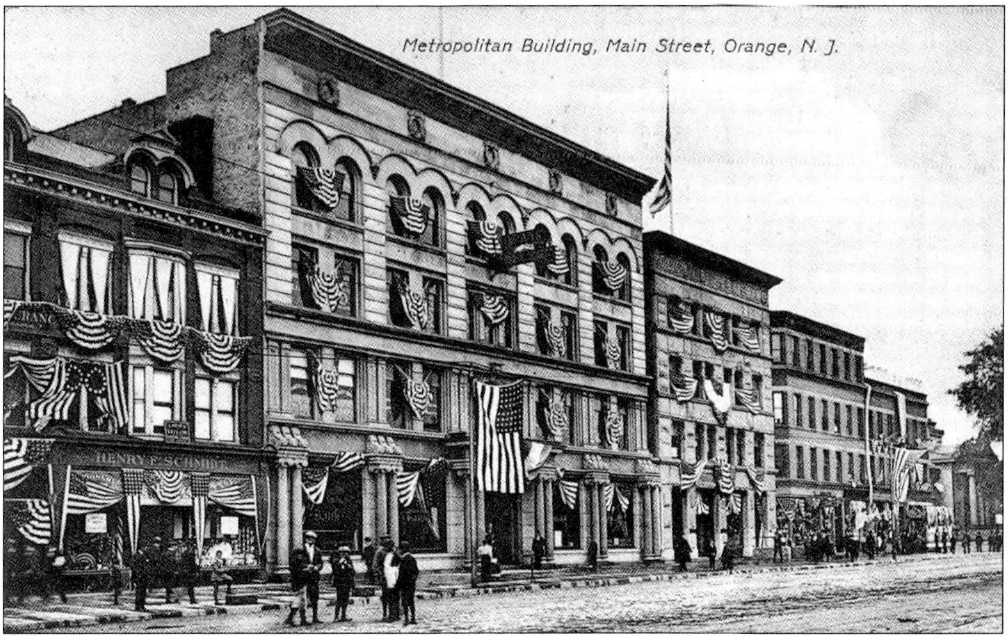

The Metropolitan Building is only four years old in this 1907 view of the south side of the block between Cone Street and Essex Avenue. The left half of the first floor is occupied by the Second National Bank. Henry F. Schmidt, the well-known local stationer, occupies the building to the left, and the smaller Decker Building is to the right. Flags and bunting signal the celebration of the Centennial of the Oranges.

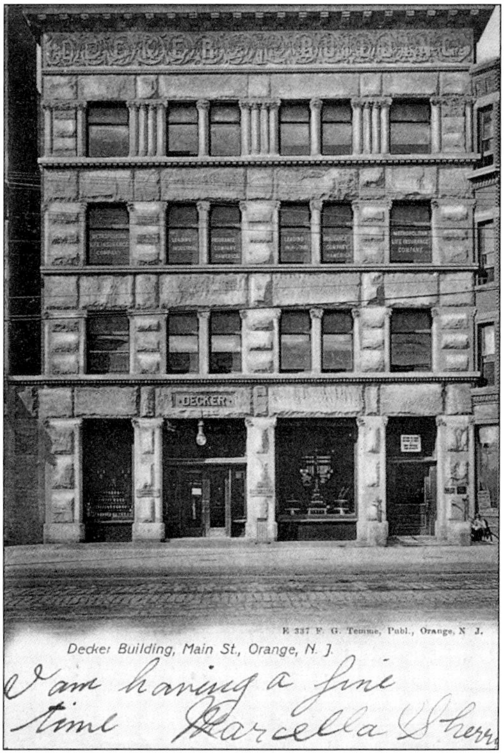

A close-up of Decker's reveals the curious fact that the primary tenant on the third floor is none other than the Metropolitan Life Insurance Company. The sign over the right door warns, "Store is NOT this Building," and another placard advertises Nelson's Neapolitan Ice Cream Bricks.

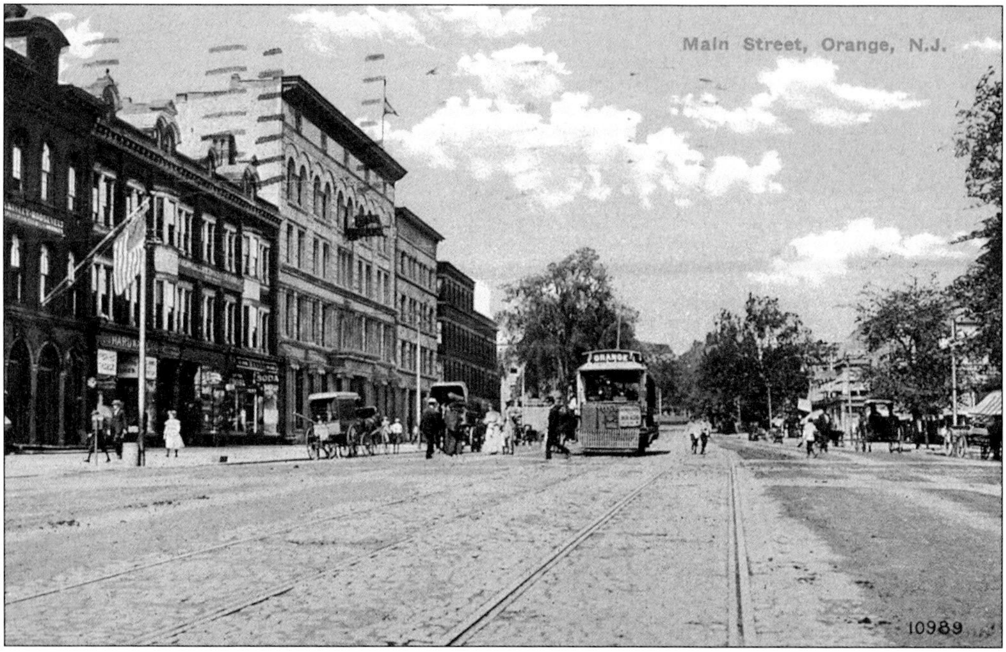

The Newark-bound trolley car has stopped just short of the Crosstown Line diamonds at Day Street to exchange passengers in this 1900 view, looking west. The banner above the flag to the left promotes "McKinley-Roosevelt" and is sponsored by the Republican Club of the Oranges. The broadside on the nose of the trolley advertises the "Mikado."

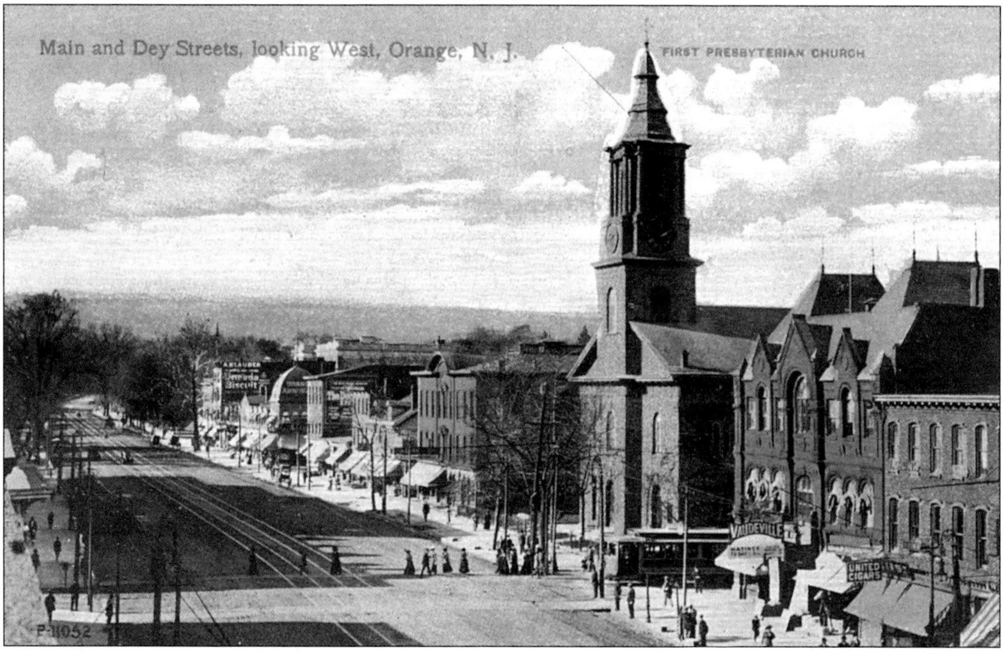

The steeple of the First Presbyterian Church dominates the north side of the block between Day Street and Essex Avenue. A Crosstown trolley peers out from behind the Music Hall, where the Vaudeville banner heralds the "Matinee Today at 3p.m."

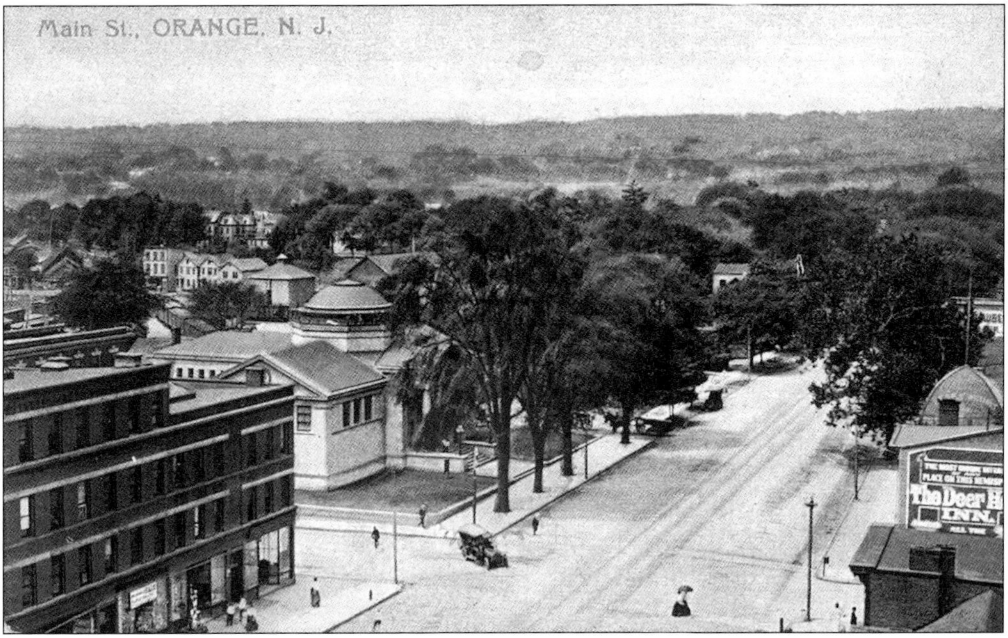

A panorama looking west from the steeple of the First Presbyterian Church, *c.* 1912, reveals the Stickler Memorial Library at the corner of Main Street and Essex Avenue. The painted advertisement for the "Deer Head Inn" proclaims it as "the Most Unique Interior of Any Place on This Hemisphere."

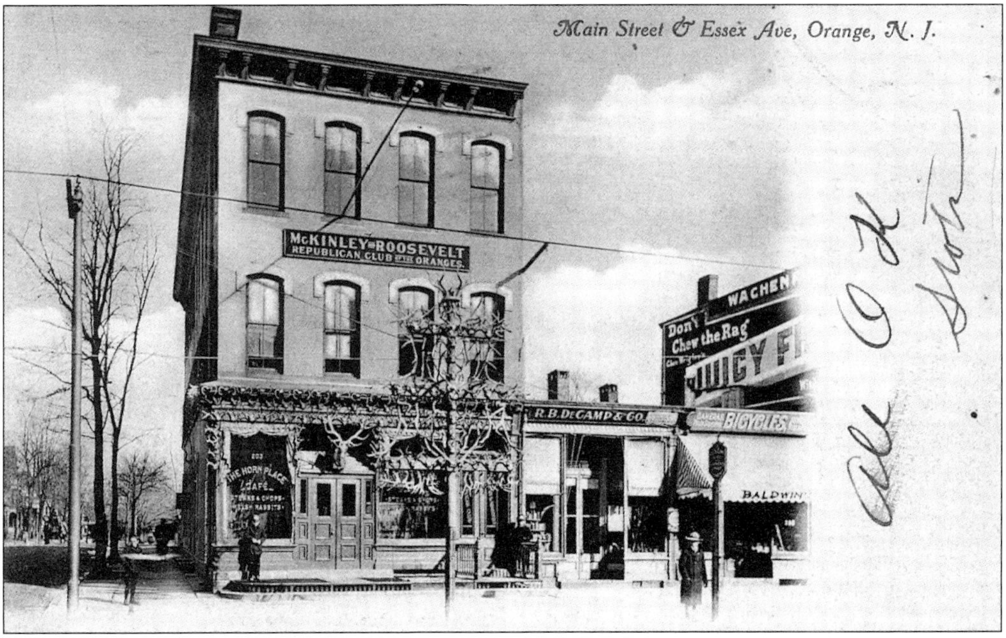

Before it was the Deer Head Inn, the unusual eatery on the corner of Main Street and Essex Avenue was known as The Horn Place Chop House. It is not hard to understand why, given the animal antlers that adorned its frieze, as well as the "horn tree" which stood outside. Teddy Roosevelt, running for Vice President under William McKinley, would have certainly enjoyed dining here!

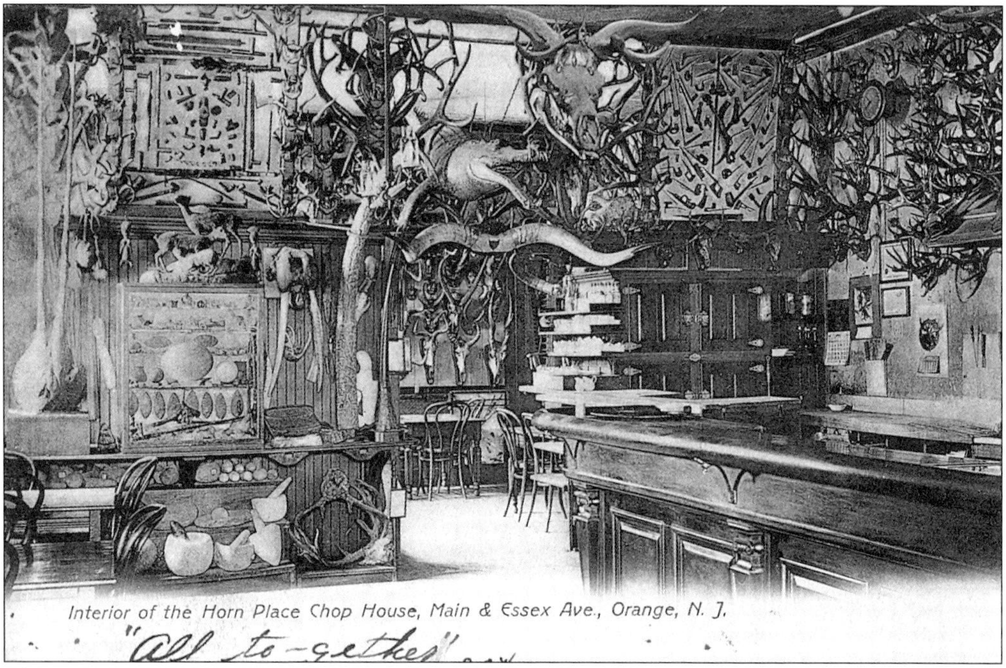

The interior of The Horn Place Chop House was even more bizarre than the outside, with virtually every square inch covered by animal parts, primitive tools and Native American artifacts. A close look reveals mounted walrus and crocodile heads.

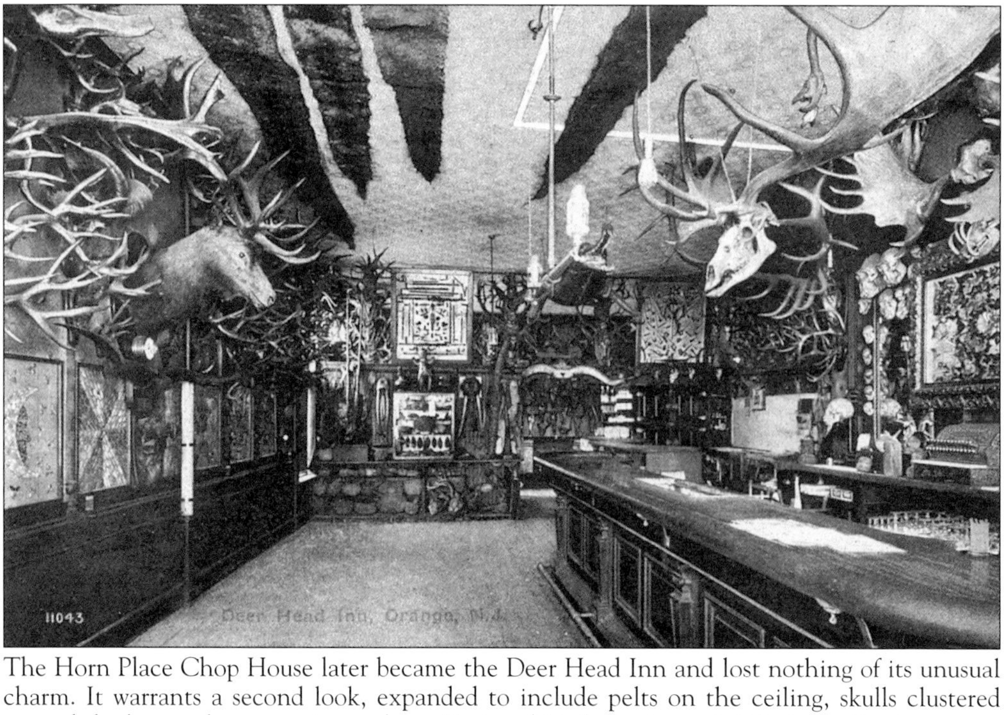

The Horn Place Chop House later became the Deer Head Inn and lost nothing of its unusual charm. It warrants a second look, expanded to include pelts on the ceiling, skulls clustered around the bar, and a great vintage brass National Cash Register. A "No Ladies" rule was not even necessary!

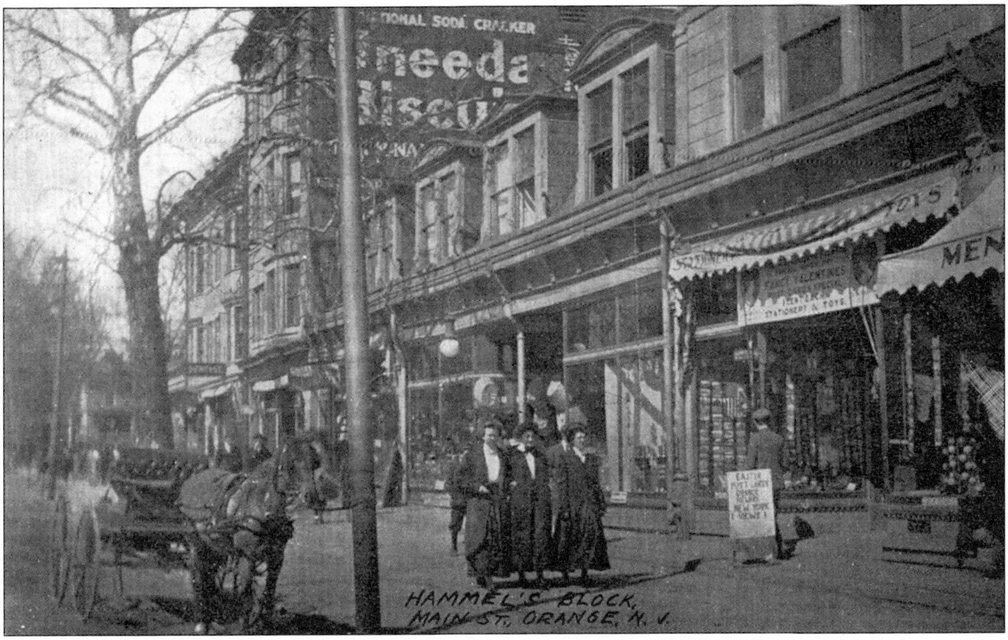

The north side of Main between Essex Avenue and Cleveland Street was once known as Hammel's Block, presumably named after one of the merchants there. The signboard in front of the stationery store advertises "Easter Postcards - Orange - Newark - New York Views," inviting passers-by to walk in and inspect the inventory.

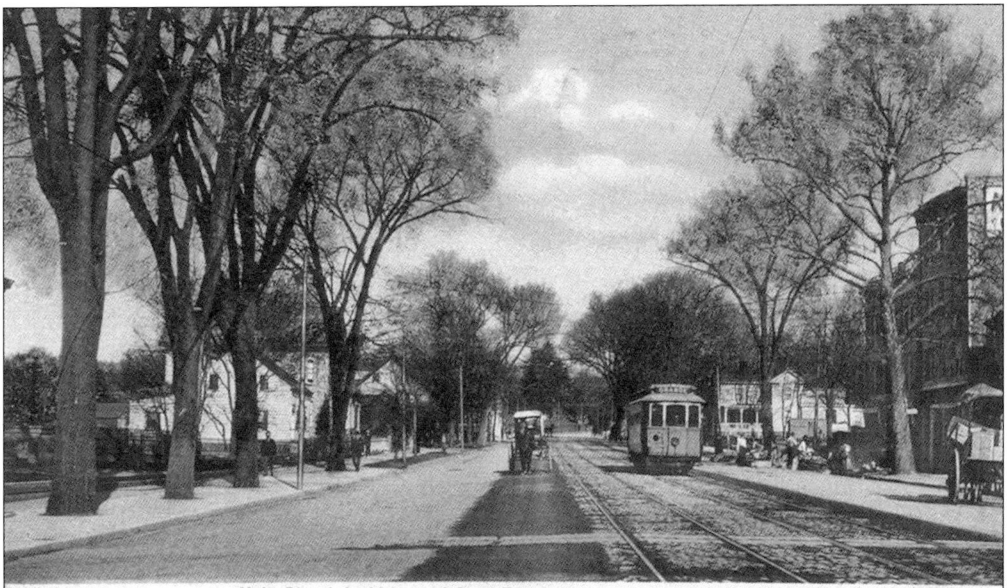

A solitary carriage passes a Main Street trolley that is headed westbound toward the Erie Loop at the West Orange border. The placard on the car reads, "Base-ball Today," at Wiedemayer Field. This scene unfolds in front of the Stickler Library. Today, stores and offices line the shaded street where spacious residences once abounded.

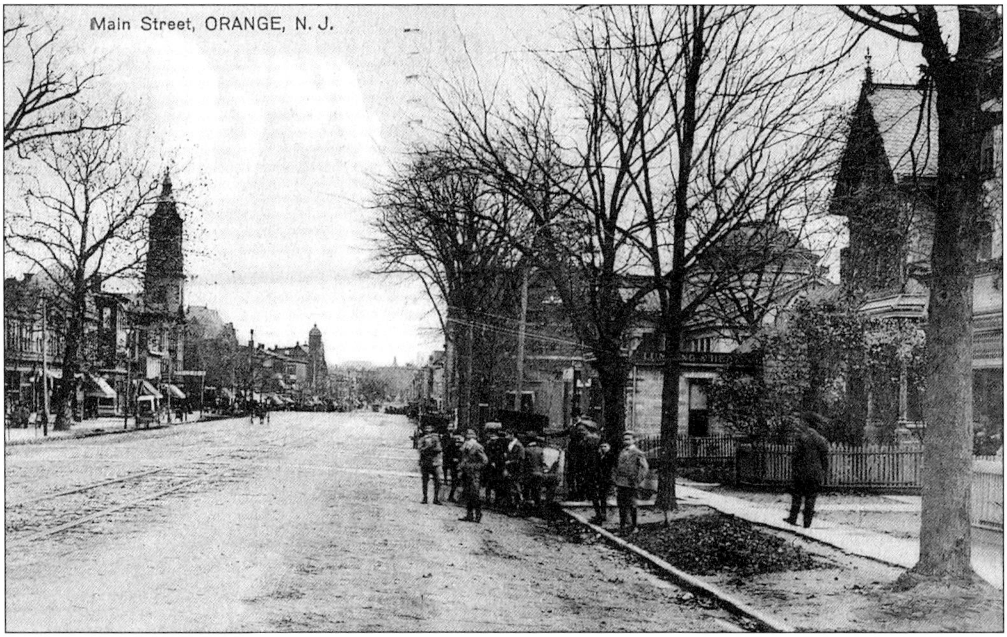

A gaggle of boys in their Sunday best find the photographer more interesting than anything that might be happening on Main Street in this view from about 1912. The trees are bare, so it cannot be the Fourth of July, but perhaps another notable day, such as Election Day or Thanksgiving. You can see an old trolley car any day, but a man with a Kodak is quite rare!

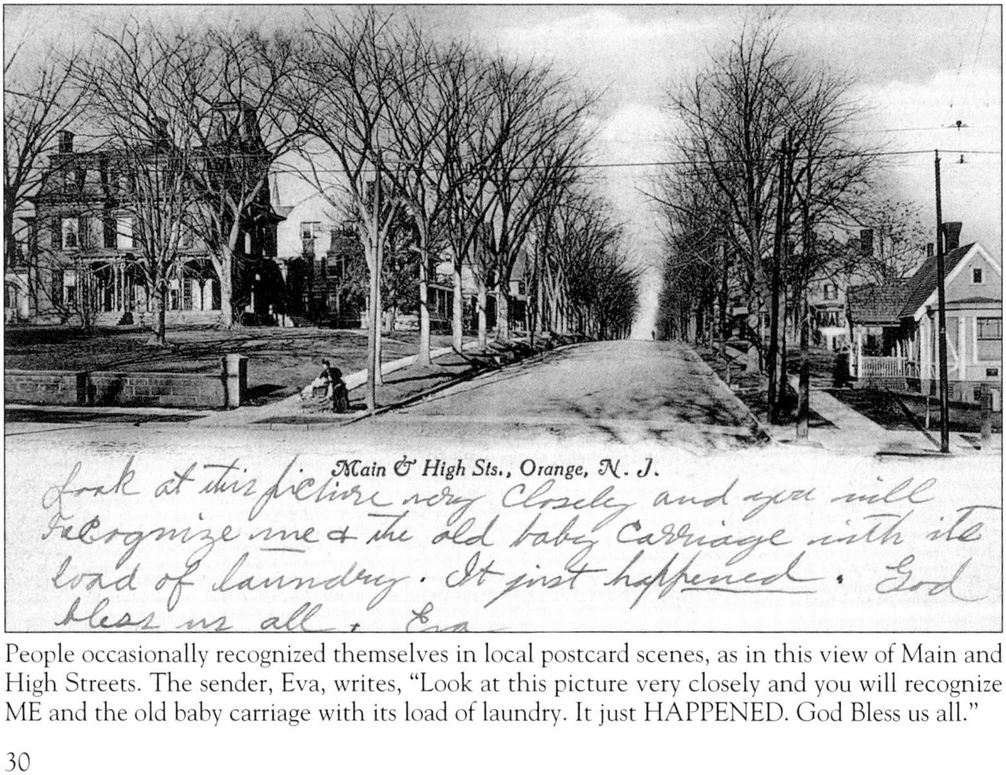

People occasionally recognized themselves in local postcard scenes, as in this view of Main and High Streets. The sender, Eva, writes, "Look at this picture very closely and you will recognize ME and the old baby carriage with its load of laundry. It just HAPPENED. God Bless us all."

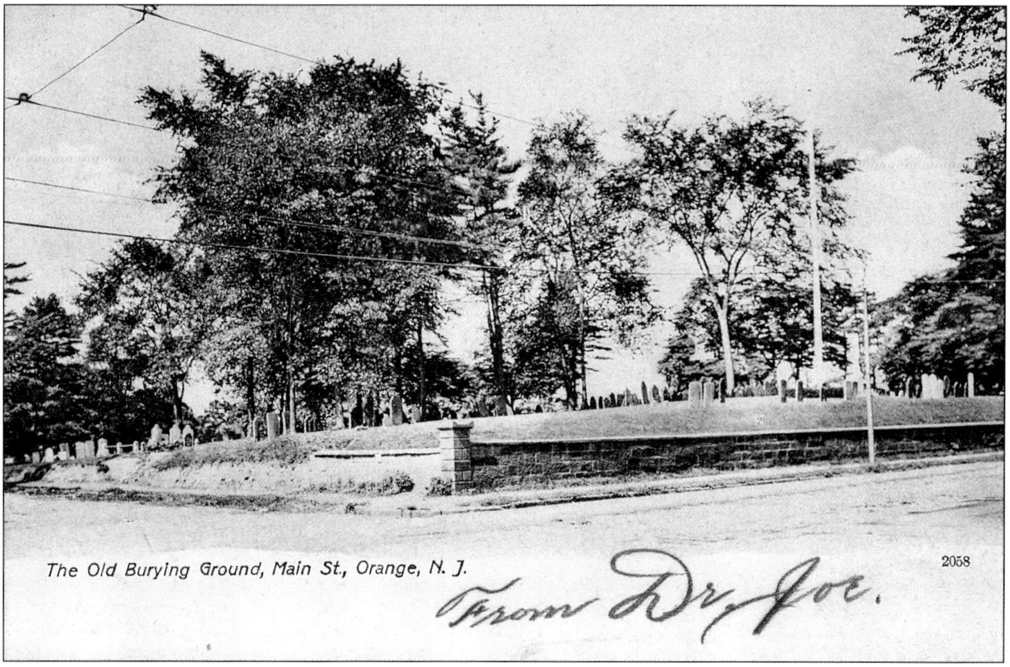

One hundred and eighty degrees from Eva and her carriage full of laundry was this view of the Old Burying Ground at the corner of Scotland Street. The scene predates the Centennial Celebration of the Oranges in 1907, as the Dispatch Rider statue has not yet been dedicated, and the wall along Scotland has yet to be improved.

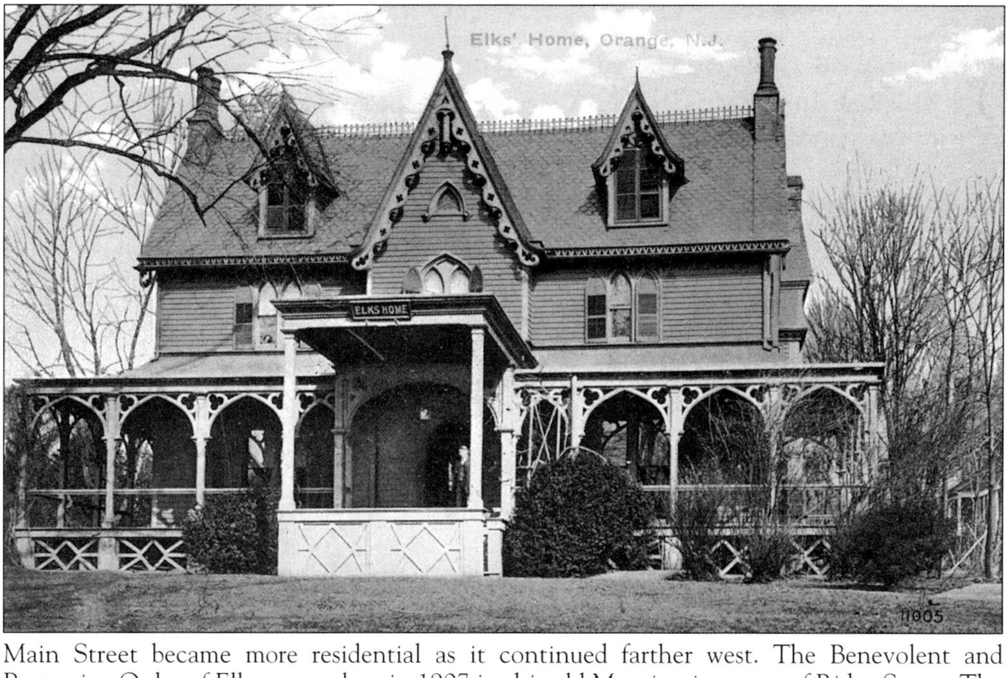

Main Street became more residential as it continued farther west. The Benevolent and Protective Order of Elks set up shop in 1907 in this old Mansion just west of Ridge Street. The porte-cochere would later be glassed in and display the famous life-sized elk that was familiar to generations of Orangeites.

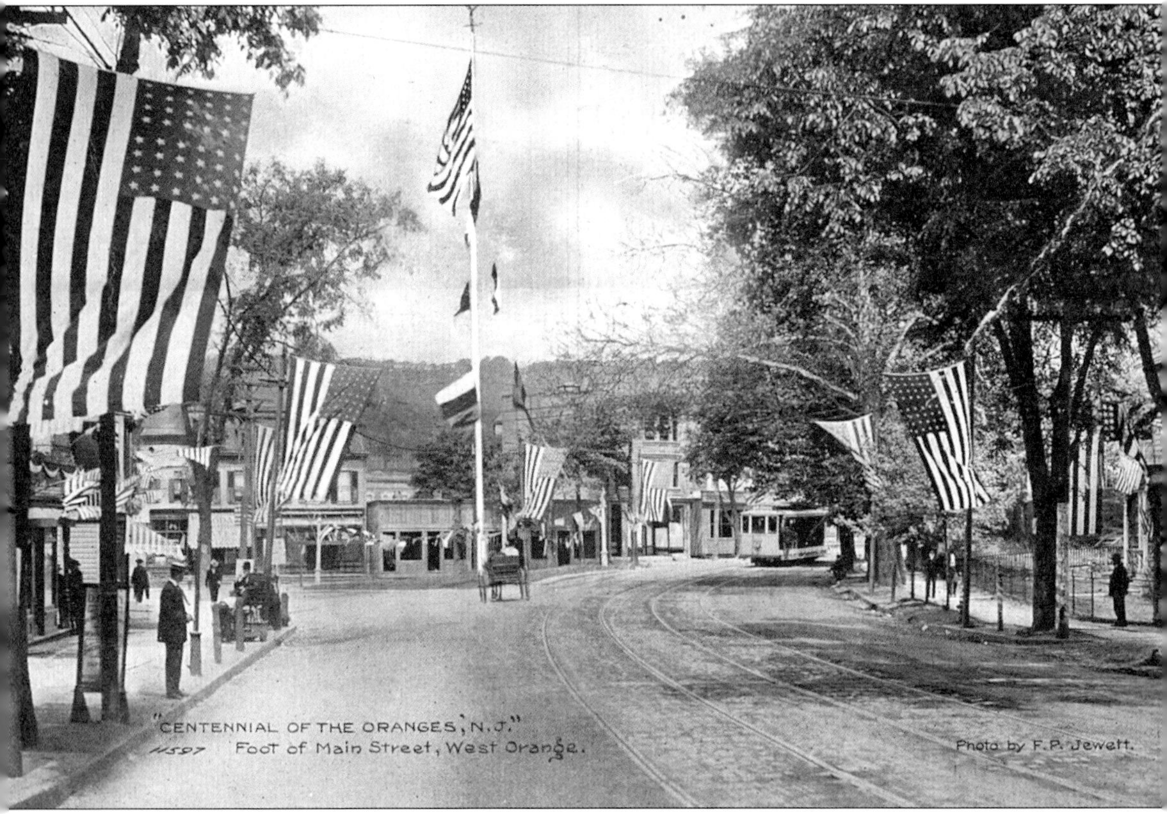

Main Street, Orange, ended at the West Orange border by the Erie Railroad station (out of sight to the right). Here, a westbound trolley proceeds around the bend. It will travel several more miles, passing Thomas Edison's sprawling factories and laboratory, before ending its journey at the foot of Eagle Rock Avenue at the Mississippi Avenue turning loop.

Three

CHURCHES AND SCHOOLS

The North Orange Baptist Church was organized on August 3, 1857, and recognized by the Council of Baptist Churches on November 5. Rev. J.B. Morse was the first pastor. Early services were held in Waverly Hall, which stood on the north side of Main Street near the intersection of North Center. When fire destroyed Waverly Hall in December 1860, plans were immediately underway for erection of a new church. The new structure would be built on a piece of property at the east end of Main Street by the Military Commons. At the time this photograph was taken, *c.* 1905, Dr. William M. Lawrence was pastor.

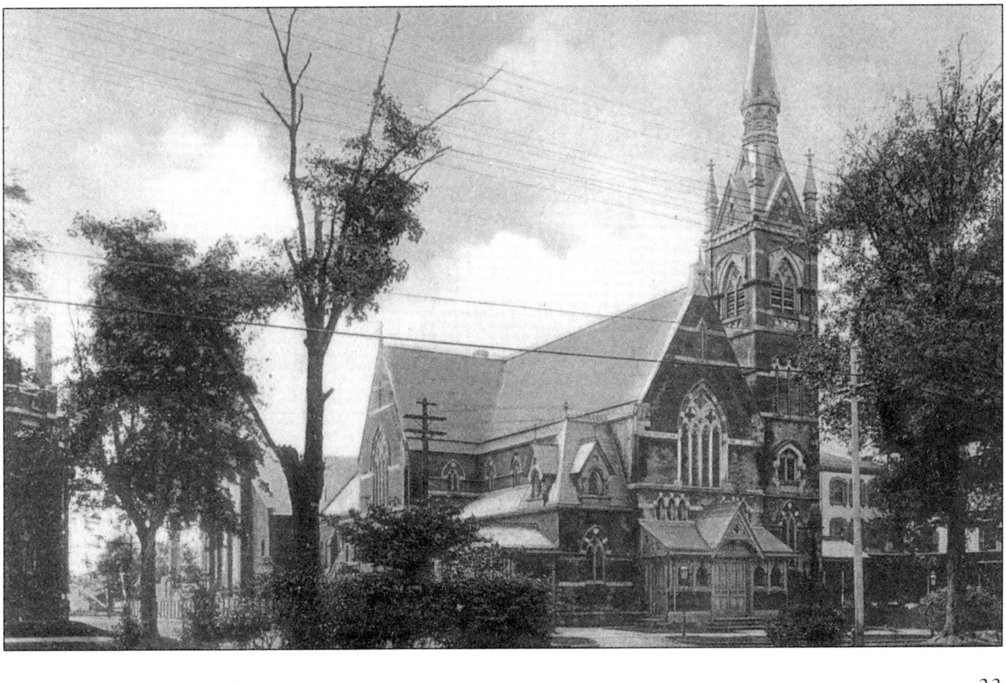

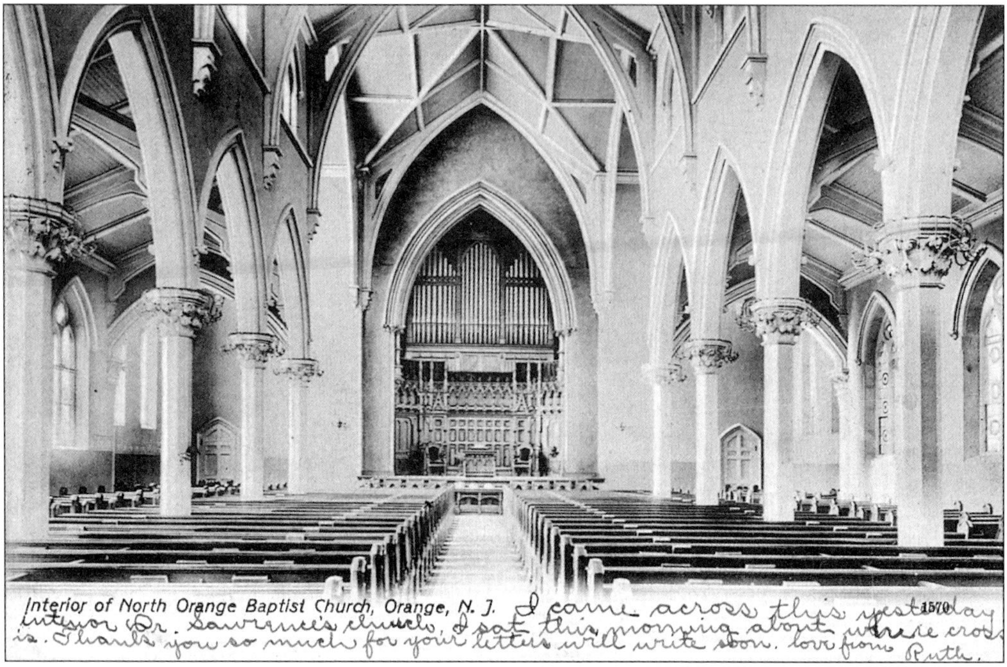

The North Orange Baptist Church was completed in a little over a year and formally dedicated on December 5, 1861. Here, an interior view shows off this splendid example of Gothic Revival architecture. The sender, Ruth ?, says ". . . Interior Dr. Lawrence's church. I sat this morning about where the cross is . . ." The date is June 22, 1903. The building is no longer standing.

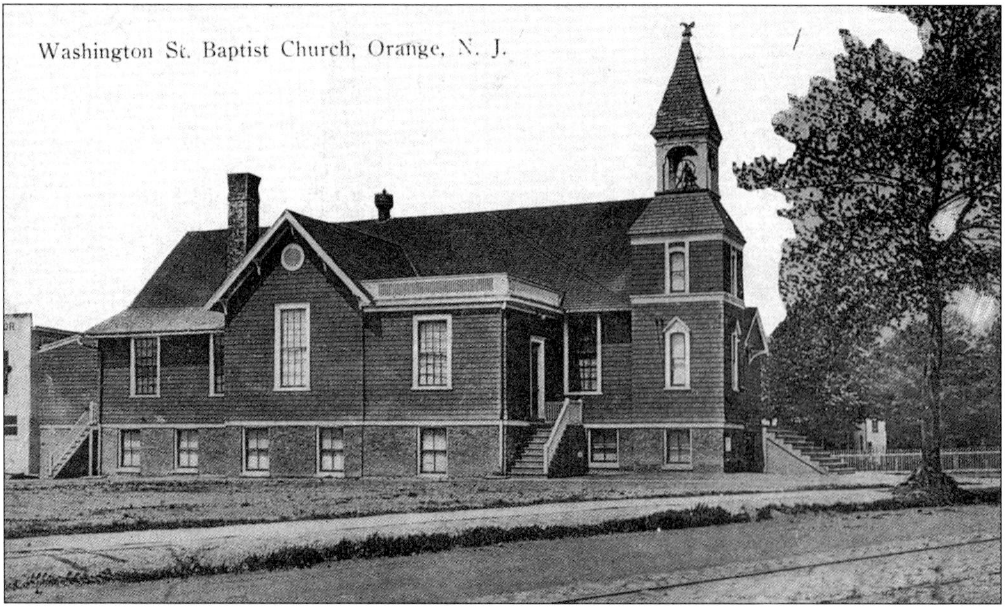

A cottage prayer meeting in 1873 at the home of Zenas Williams led to the formation of the Union Chapel, which was organized into the Washington Street Baptist Church in 1877. Rev. James L. Davis was the first pastor. By 1922, the parishioners numbered about 250, and the church was feeling the acute need to expand its facilities.

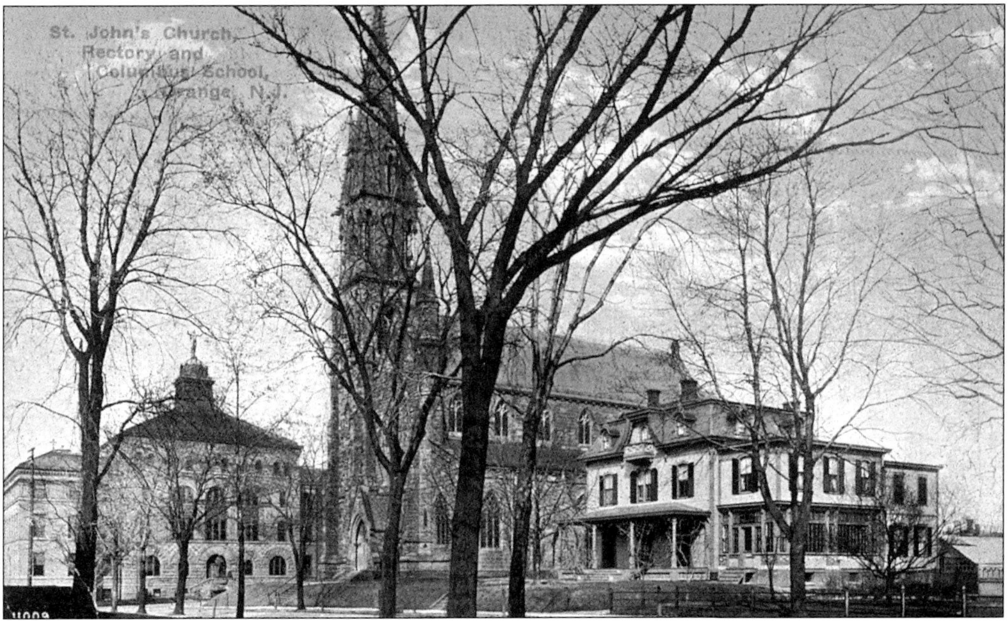

In this 1913 view, St. John's Roman Catholic Church dominates the corner of Ridge and White Streets. The Rectory is to its right and the Columbus School to its left. A parish cemetery, hidden behind the church building, extends from the intersection of White and High Streets all the way to Park Avenue. The parish was established in 1851, and that October, a small frame chapel was erected on the corner of White and Chapel Streets at a cost of $3,000. Rev. Louis Senez was the first pastor.

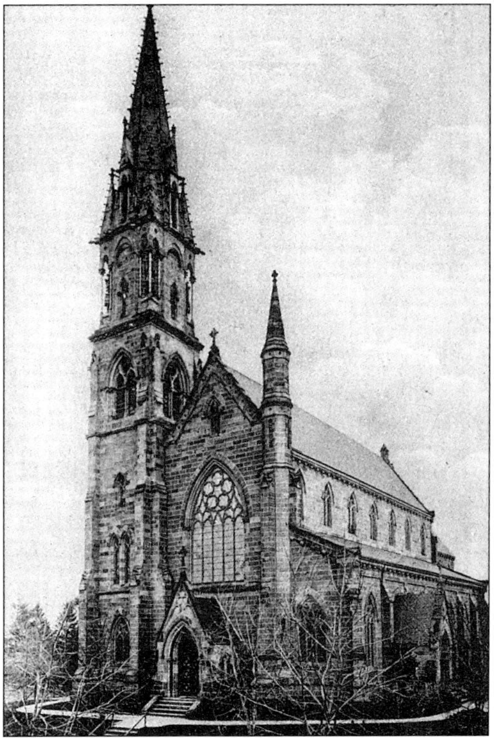

By 1865, the growth of the hat-making industry had greatly increased Orange's Roman Catholic population. The new Pastor, Rev. E. M. Hickey, raised $10,000 to purchase a lot on the corner of Ridge and White Streets. Construction of St. John's Church began in June 1866, seen here in 1909. Stone was donated by philanthropist Llewellyn S. Haskell, and much of the labor was volunteer. (Haskell was probably better known as the designer of West Orange's Llwellyn Park.)

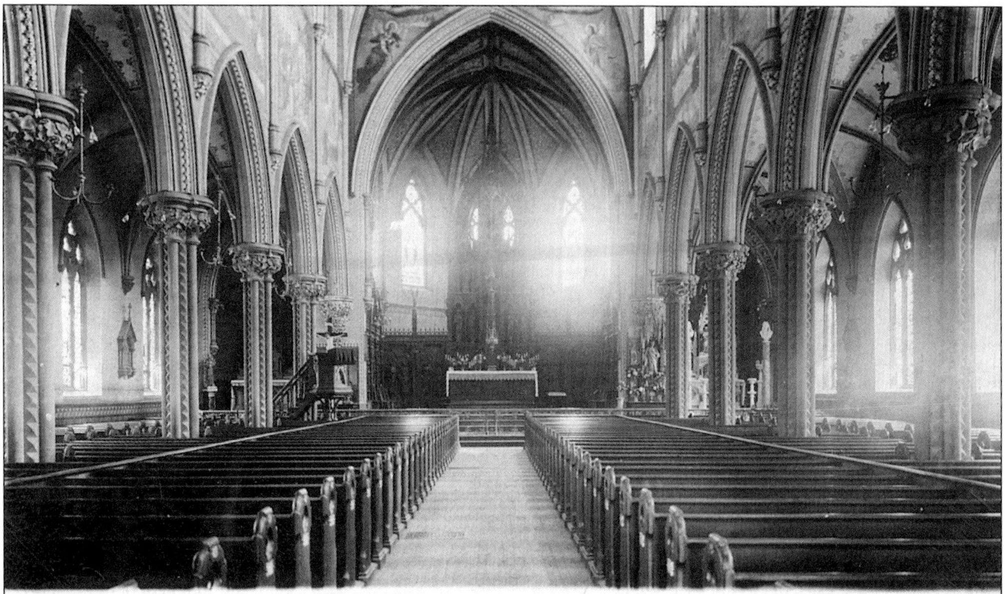

P2389 St. John's R. C. Church, Orange, N. J.

With meager funding, and relying heavily upon volunteer labor, it took over three years for the church, shown here in 1910, to be completed. The building was finally consecrated on October 10, 1869, but still lacked a tower and spire, which were added in the 1870s. The main altar, dedicated in 1892, was hand-crafted in Belgium and donated by Father Francis C. O'Reilly. The statuary is magnificently carved from oak.

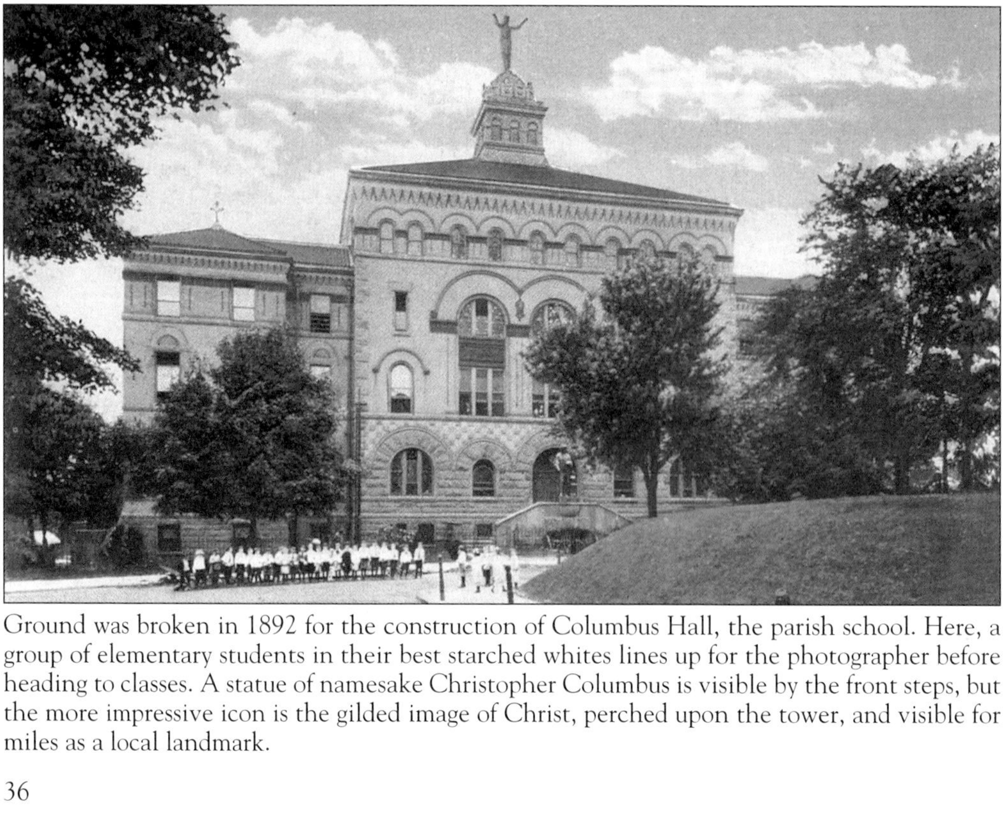

Ground was broken in 1892 for the construction of Columbus Hall, the parish school. Here, a group of elementary students in their best starched whites lines up for the photographer before heading to classes. A statue of namesake Christopher Columbus is visible by the front steps, but the more impressive icon is the gilded image of Christ, perched upon the tower, and visible for miles as a local landmark.

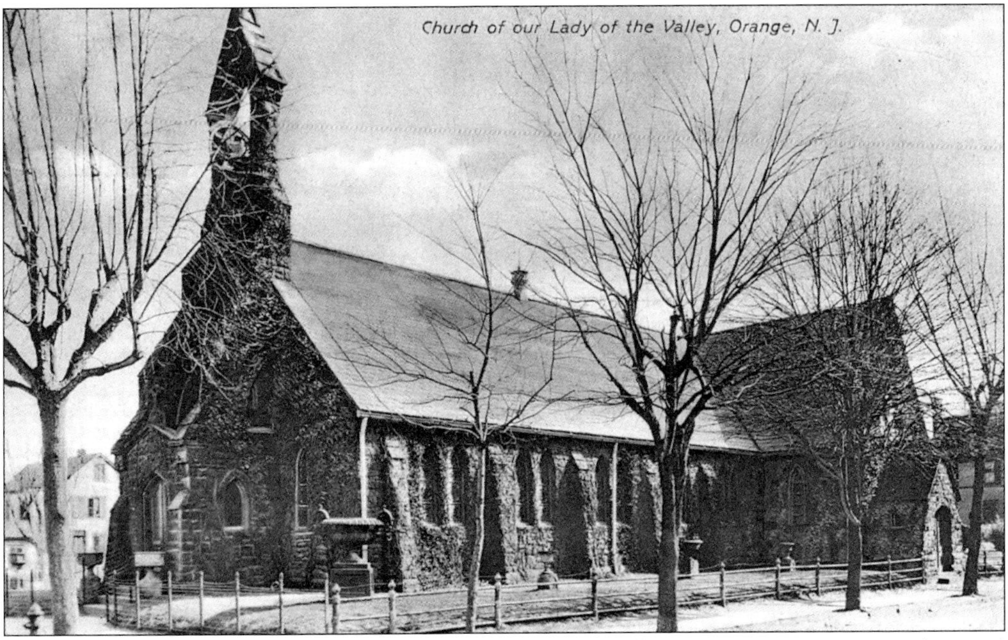

Catholics in Freemantown, later known as Orange Valley, were growing in such rapid numbers that they demanded a parish of their own. Our Lady of the Valley was organized as a mission to St. John's on September 8, 1873. The trustees purchased the vacant Orange Valley Congregational Church building on the corner of Valley and Nassau Streets. The Reverend G.A. Vassaldo was its first rector. This building was demolished in 1909 to make way for the present structure.

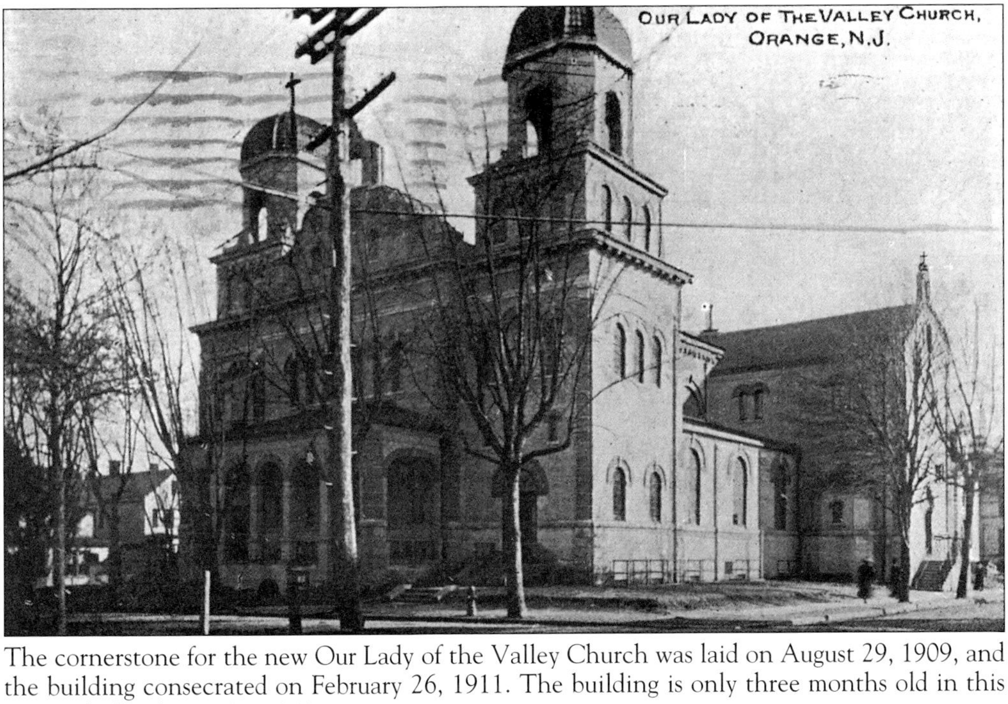

The cornerstone for the new Our Lady of the Valley Church was laid on August 29, 1909, and the building consecrated on February 26, 1911. The building is only three months old in this postcard, dated May 28, 1911.

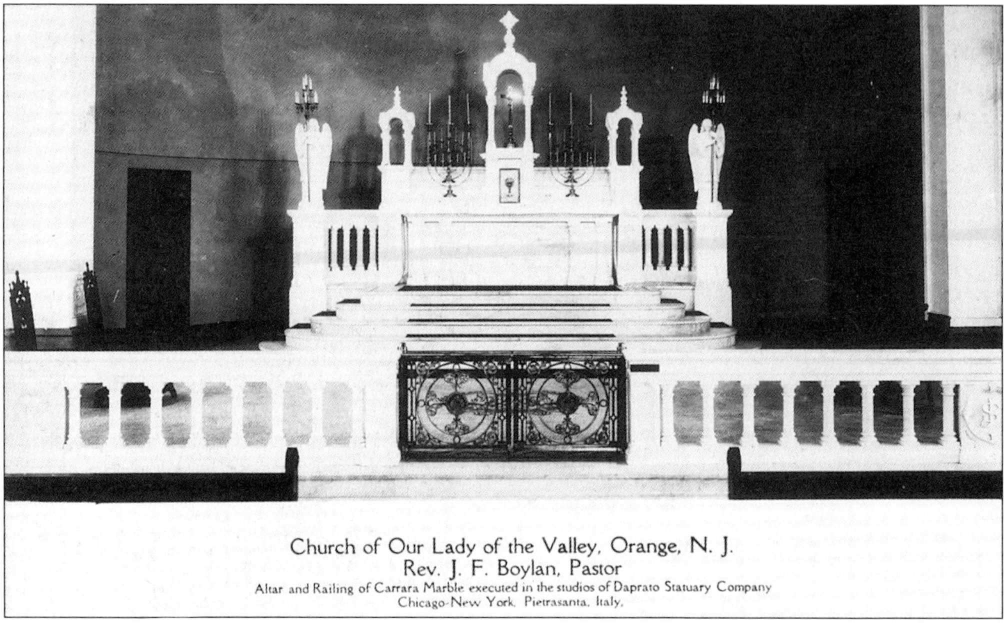

The fund-raising of $100,000 and construction work was overseen by Pastor Rev. John F. Boylan, who had previously been in charge of the construction of the church at Franklin Furnace, New Jersey. The well-known frescoes have not yet been added at the time of this interior view of the new altar in Our Lady of the Valley Church. The altar and railing were made of Carrara Marble, executed in the studios of the Daprato Statuary Company, Pietrasanta, Italy.

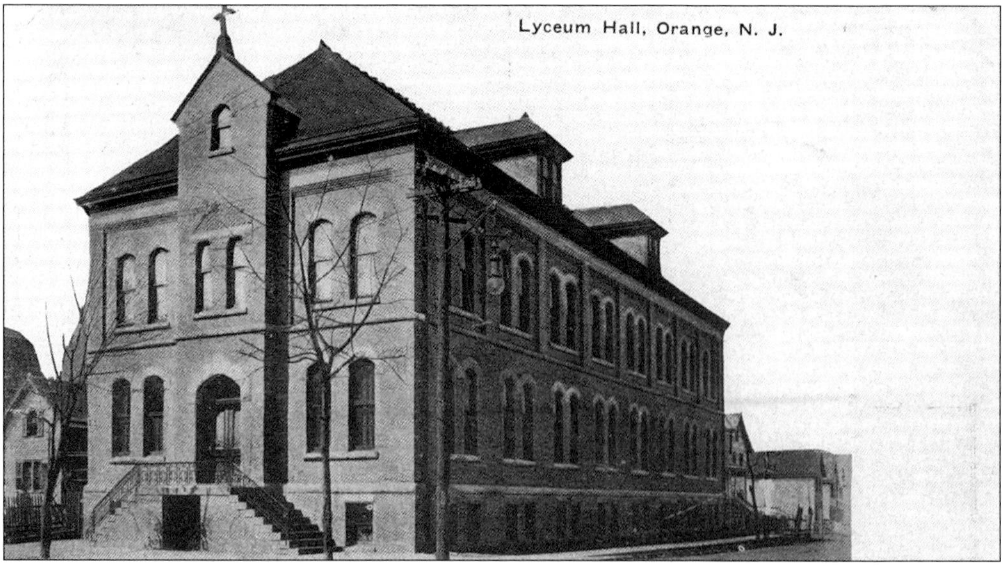

Under the direction of Pastor W.R. Callan, a resolution was passed December 11, 1891, to construct and equip a Lyceum Building for the leisure time activities of the young men of the Valley parish. The building, however, was not completed until around 1901. It was renovated in 1938, adding a gymnasium and basketball court for the use of the parish high school, which had been established in 1924. By 1960, much of this space had been converted into classrooms, and the entire grammar school had moved in.

Diocesan priests founded Our Lady of Mount Carmel parish in 1896. The first church was built in 1902 at South Center and Reock Streets. In 1926, the parish was entrusted to the Capuchin Friars. Designed to serve the Italian Catholics of Orange, it moved to this new edifice, located almost directly across the street, on December 8, 1933. The photographer is standing directly in front of the old church to take this photograph. The parish school was dedicated on September 12, 1940.

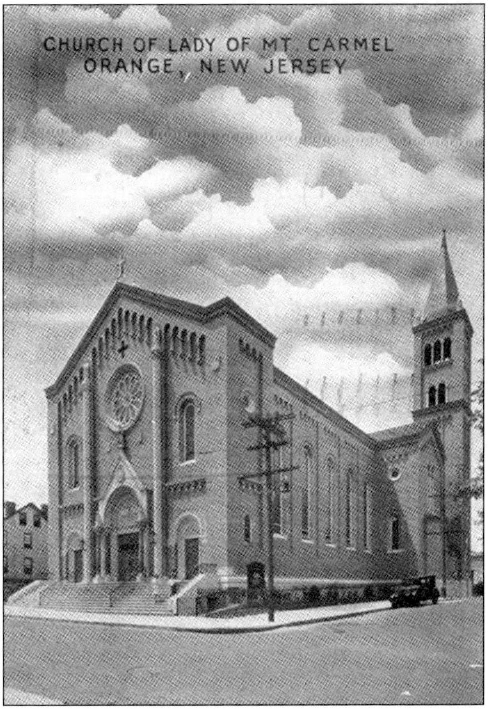

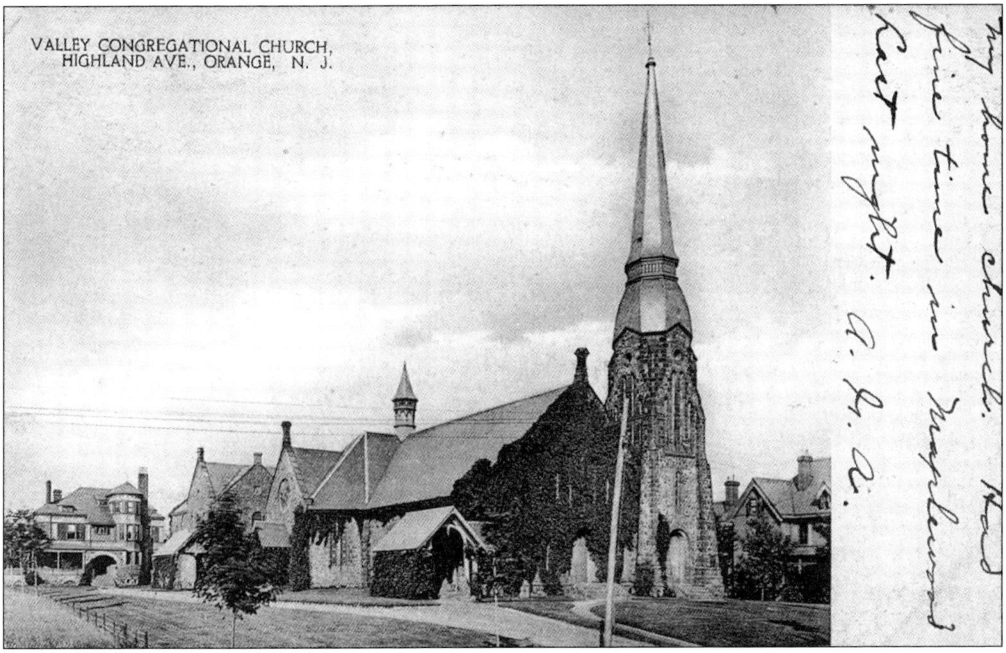

The first pastor of the Orange Valley Congregational Church, Rev. Dr. George Blagdon Bacon, was installed March 21, 1861. The original church building at the corner of Valley and Nassau Streets became surplus when this handsome edifice was completed in 1868 on Highland Avenue. The old building was sold to the new Our Lady of the Valley Parish. A chapel was added in 1880 and a parsonage in 1886. In 1916 the parish was renamed the Highland Avenue Congregational Church.

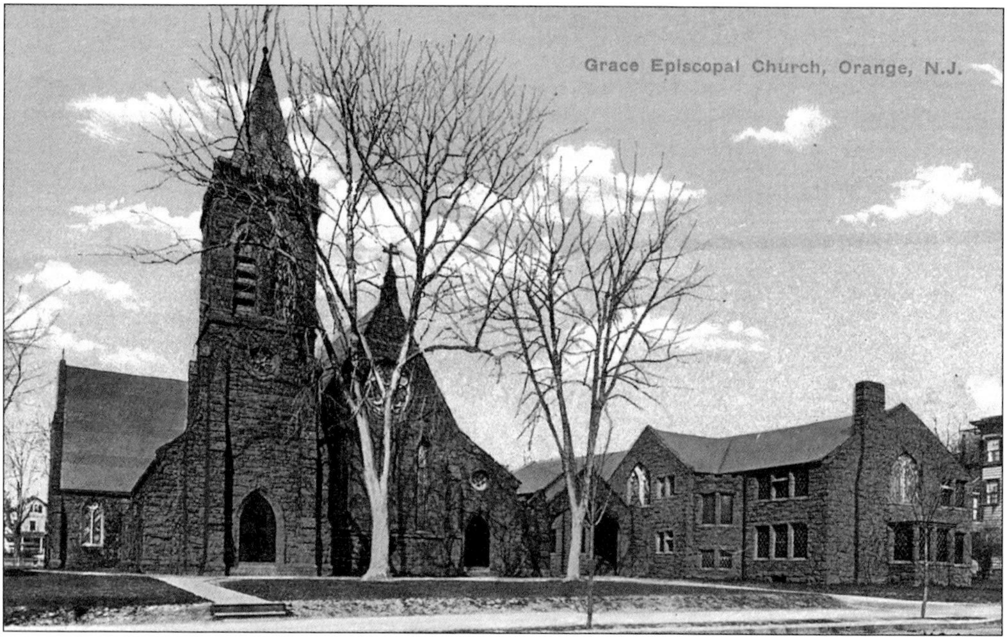

Grace Episcopal had been a mission of St. Mark's Church of West Orange and was formally organized on March 5, 1854. First services were held in Bodwell's Hall at the corner of William and Park Streets. Rev. James Bush was the first rector. The property on Main Street where the permanent church was built was purchased from the First Presbyterian.

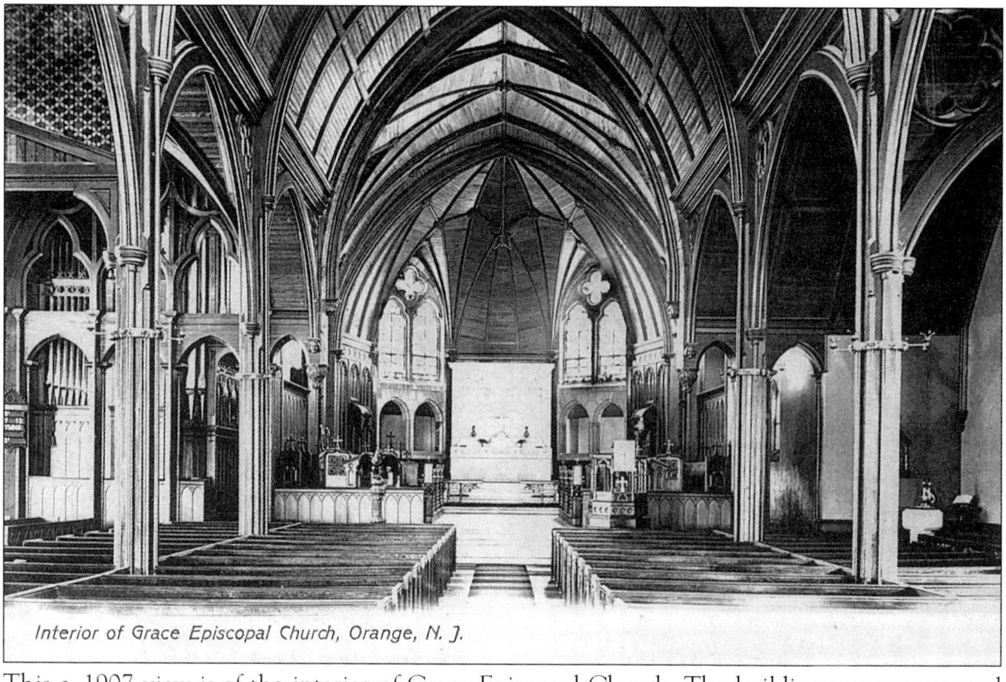

This *c.* 1907 view is of the interior of Grace Episcopal Church. The building was consecrated on July 16, 1857. A rectory fronting on William Street was added in 1868, and the transept and chancel in 1872. A Sunday school building was constructed in 1877, and a parish house, gift of Mr. and Mrs. Jonathan J. Broome, added about 1905.

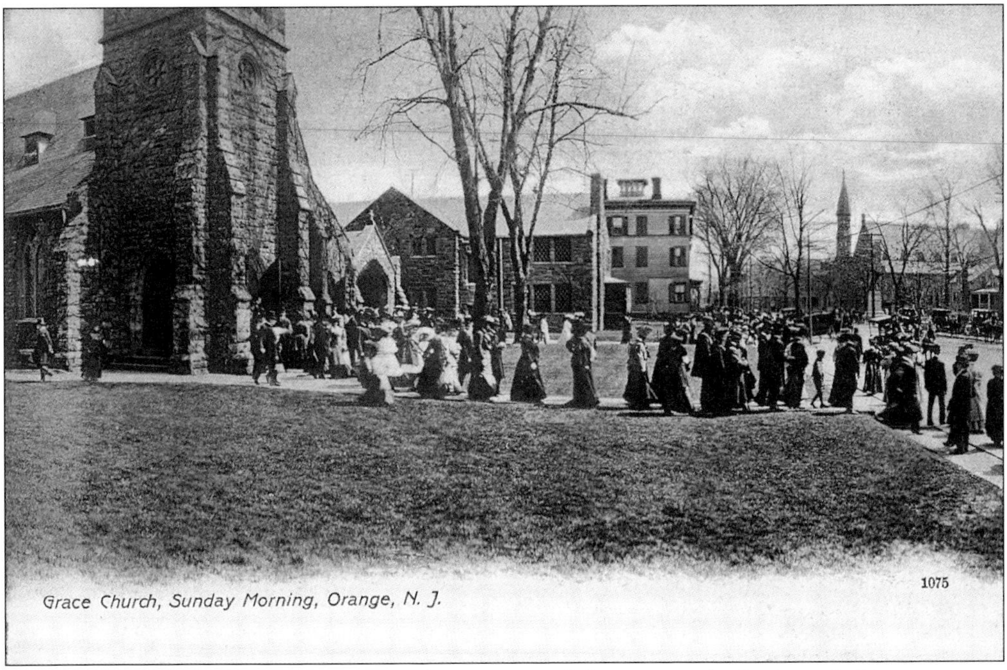

"Grace Church, Sunday Morning," is the caption of this postcard which probably captures a special occasion, such as Easter. Finery is evident as the parishioners stream out, and leaves have yet to appear on the barren trees.

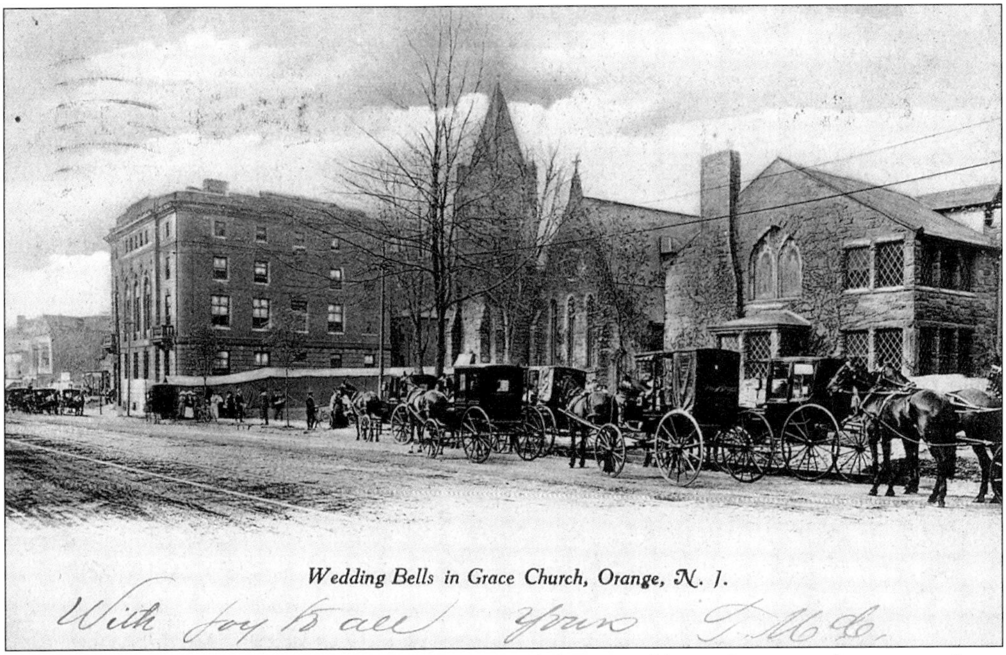

An entourage of carriages awaits a wedding party while a sprinkling of interested spectators lines the sidewalk. No automobiles are evident in this 1905 view, and the YMCA in the background has yet to have its second wing added.

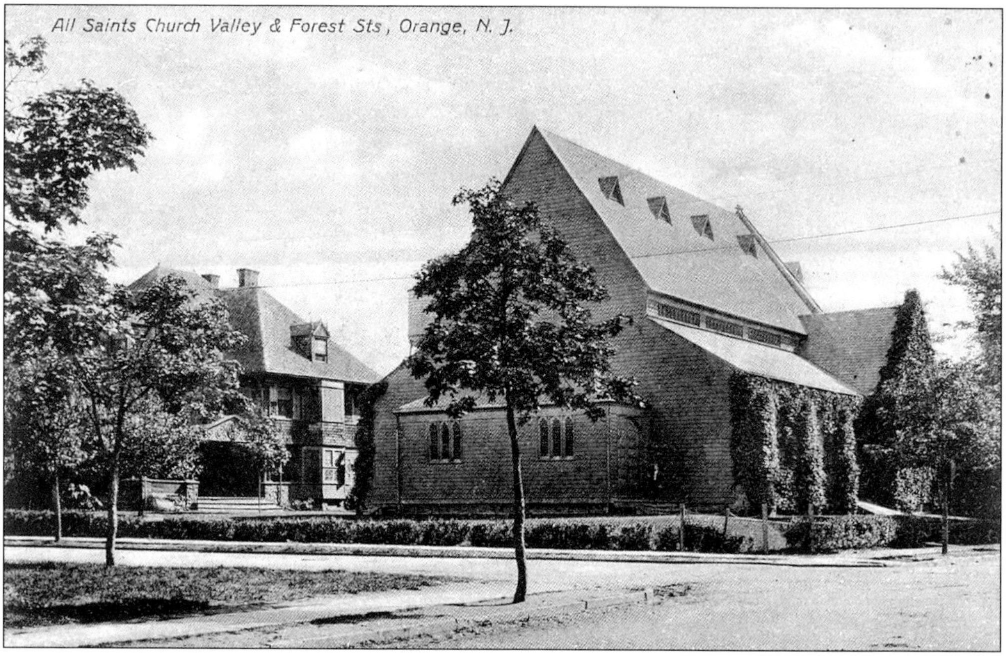

In 1876, a mission of St. Mark's Church was started in an old schoolhouse at the corner of Valley Road and Forest Street. Rev. William Richmond headed the mission, which was also called St. Mark's. On September 14, 1879, a chapel opened at the corner of Forest and Tompkins Streets and 85 parishioners took communion. The name was changed to All Saints on April 13, 1885. As the parish grew, it purchased land for a new building on the corner of Valley and Forest Streets. This handsome church was erected and dedicated April 24, 1887.

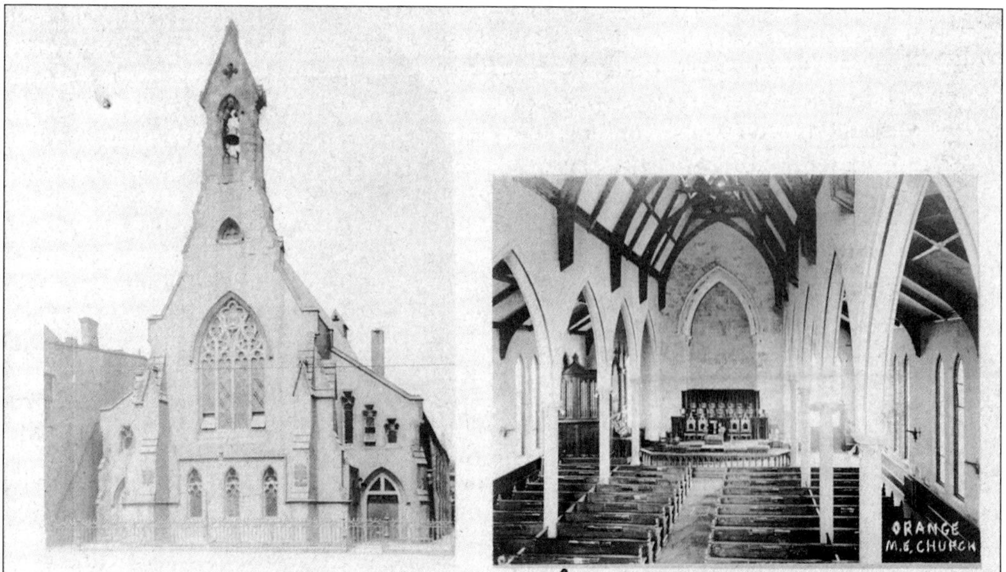

In 1831, the First Methodist Episcopal Church erected a frame building on the Main Street property adjoining the western side of the present Masonic Temple. Membership grew quickly, and in 1858, this new gothic structure of brick was completed. Dedication ceremonies were held on July 23.

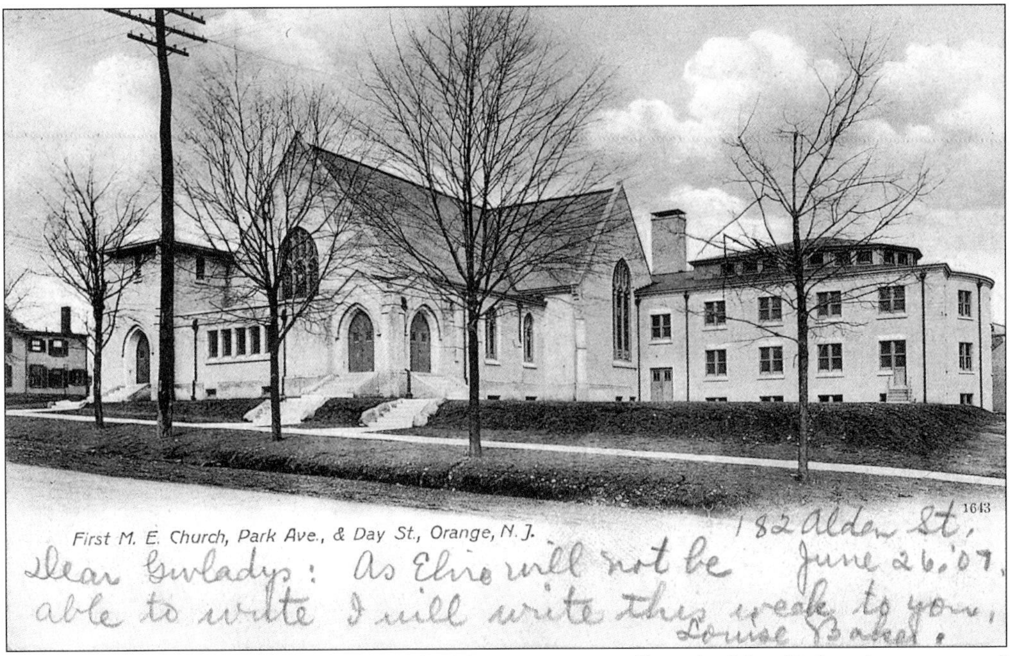

By the new century, the 1858 building had become too small, and a "third" church was erected on the corner of Park Avenue and Day Street at a cost of $30,000. Ground was broken in July 1904, the cornerstone laid on October 1, 1904, and the completed building dedicated on November 12, 1905.

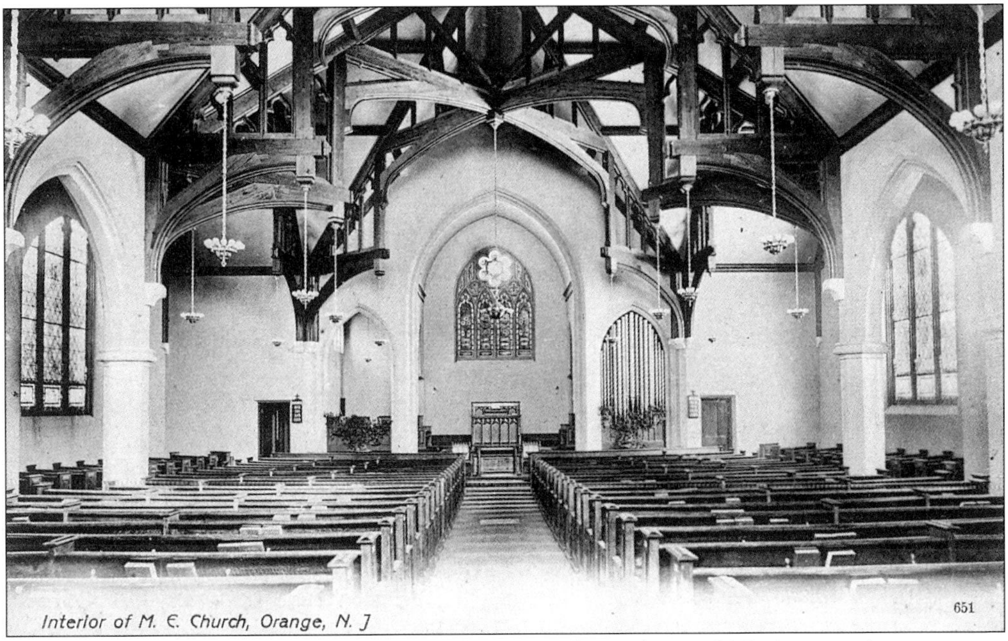

The interior of the new First M.E. Church is seen here about 1907. Among the numerous articles placed in the cornerstone of the new building were an autographed photo of the great inventor, Thomas Edison, a phonograph record, and a plate from an Edison Storage Battery.

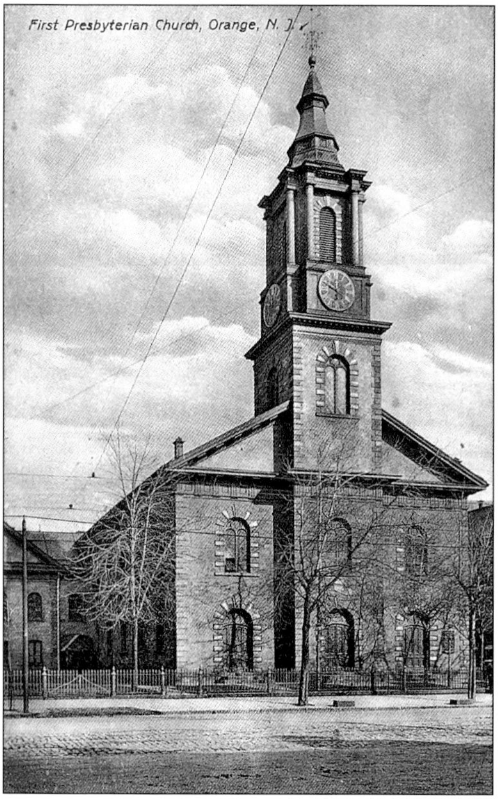

Oldest of all the churches in the Oranges was the First Presbyterian, designed in 1812 by Moses Dodd. It stood on the corner of Main and Day Streets for nearly 120 years until fire consumed it on April 5, 1927. The structure was rebuilt in the Old Buying Ground at the corner of Main and Scotland Streets. To accomplish the reconstruction, the parish had to obtain total ownership of the property, and relocate a number of late parishioners who rested in the path of the foundations.

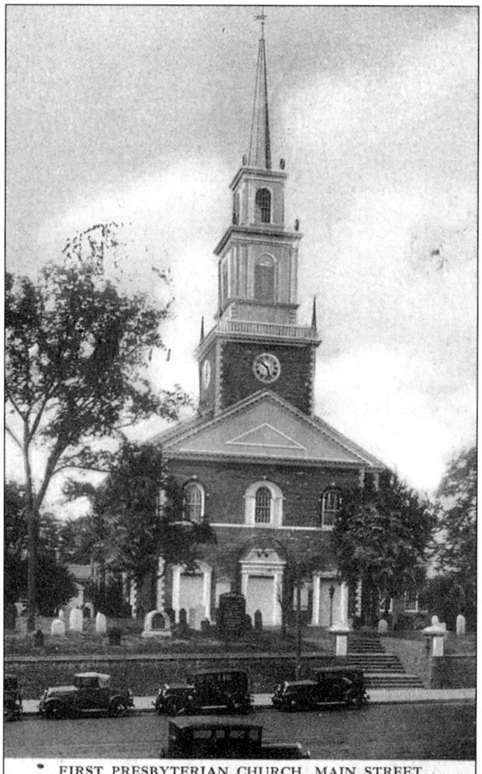

FIRST PRESBYTERIAN CHURCH, MAIN STREET AND SCOTLAND ROAD, ORANGE, N. J.

The "new" First Presbyterian Church looked antique almost immediately, and most visitors who see it are surprised to find that it was completed as recently as 1928. The restoration of the town clock to a place of prominence was a significant part of the steeple plan.

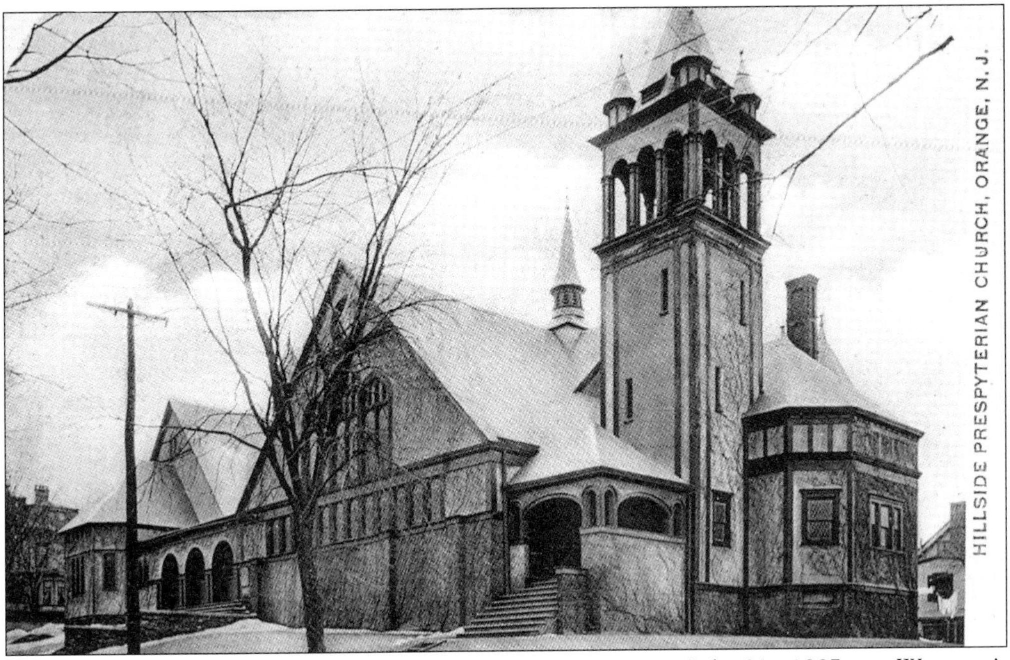

The Hillside Presbyterian Church held its first services on July 31, 1887, in Westcott's Gymnasium on Highland Avenue. The church was formally organized on November 21, though the first unit of construction was not completed until 1888, and the church proper not until 1891. A parish house, memorial chapel, and pastor's study were subsequently added. Rev. Dr. Stanley White was the first pastor.

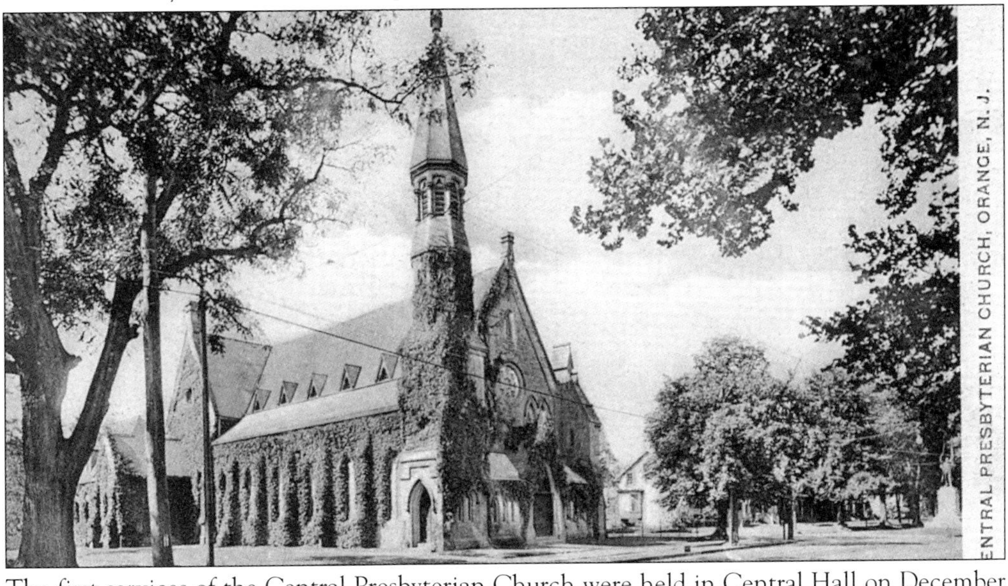

The first services of the Central Presbyterian Church were held in Central Hall on December 15, 1866. Its congregation had split from the First Presbyterian, and created so much agitation for the First's pastor, Rev. James Hoyt, that he suffered a stroke and died that very night. The parish ultimately purchased land on Main Street extending from Prince Street to Oakwood Avenue from Nathan Pierson at a cost of $22,000, and opened their chapel for worship on December 19, 1869.

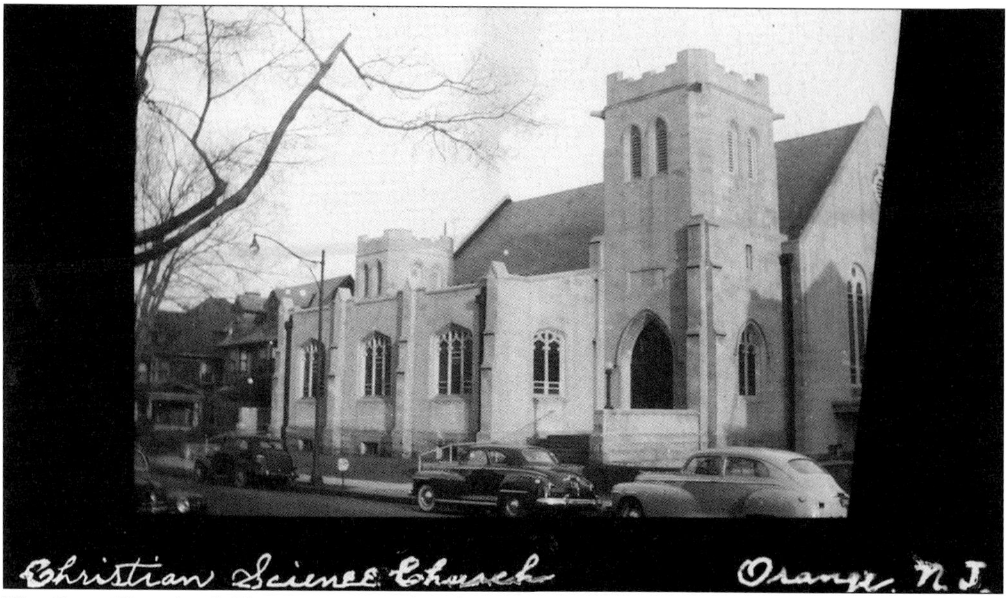

The First Church of Christ, Scientist first held services in December of 1895. The parish was incorporated in 1898, and secured a building lot on Cleveland Street the following year. The church, constructed of Indiana Limestone at a cost of $65,000, was completed in 1911 and services first held in the new building on Thanksgiving Day.

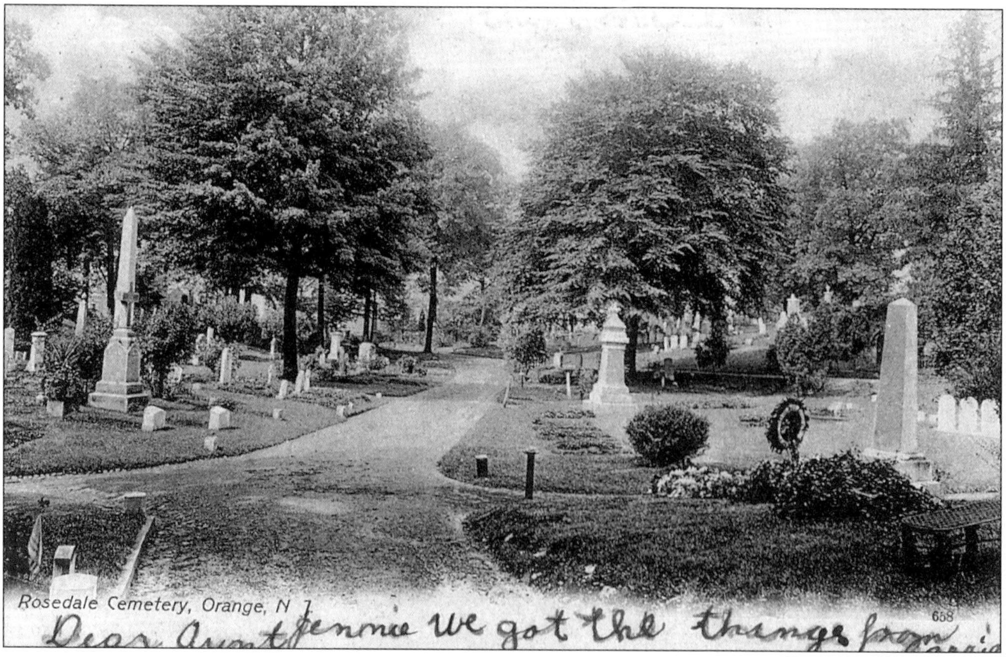

Rosedale Cemetery dates from 1840, when 10 acres of land were purchased at the border of Doddtown and the cemetery incorporated. The Old Burying Ground at Main and Scotland Streets was nearing exhaustion and additional space was required for the repose of the souls of Orangeites. A second purchase doubled its size, and several additional random parcels were added later. The portion east of the bridge opened first; plots west of the bridge were not used until 1872.

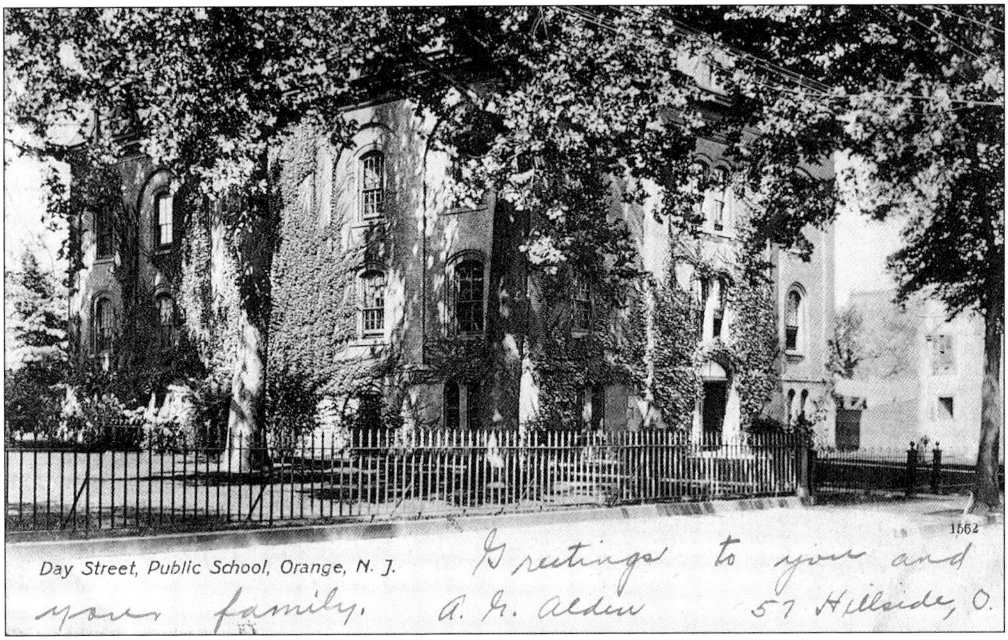

The first "permanent" school building in Orange was constructed in 1869 on Day Street property adjoining the First Presbyterian Church. The total cost of land, building, and furniture only reached $50,000. Eight classrooms served the high school (enrollment: 37), the intermediate school (enrollment: 70), and the grammar school (enrollment: 218.) The primary school with its 211 pupils was housed in the basement. The third floor was used as an assembly hall. The building now houses the Orange Municipal Offices.

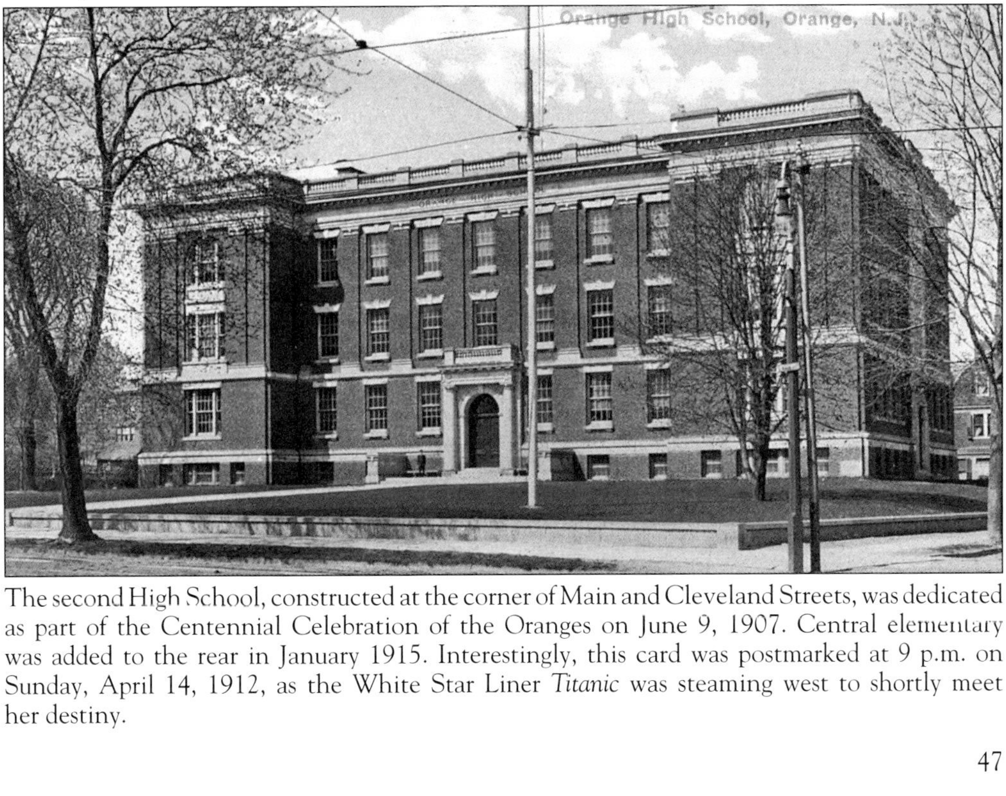

The second High School, constructed at the corner of Main and Cleveland Streets, was dedicated as part of the Centennial Celebration of the Oranges on June 9, 1907. Central elementary was added to the rear in January 1915. Interestingly, this card was postmarked at 9 p.m. on Sunday, April 14, 1912, as the White Star Liner *Titanic* was steaming west to shortly meet her destiny.

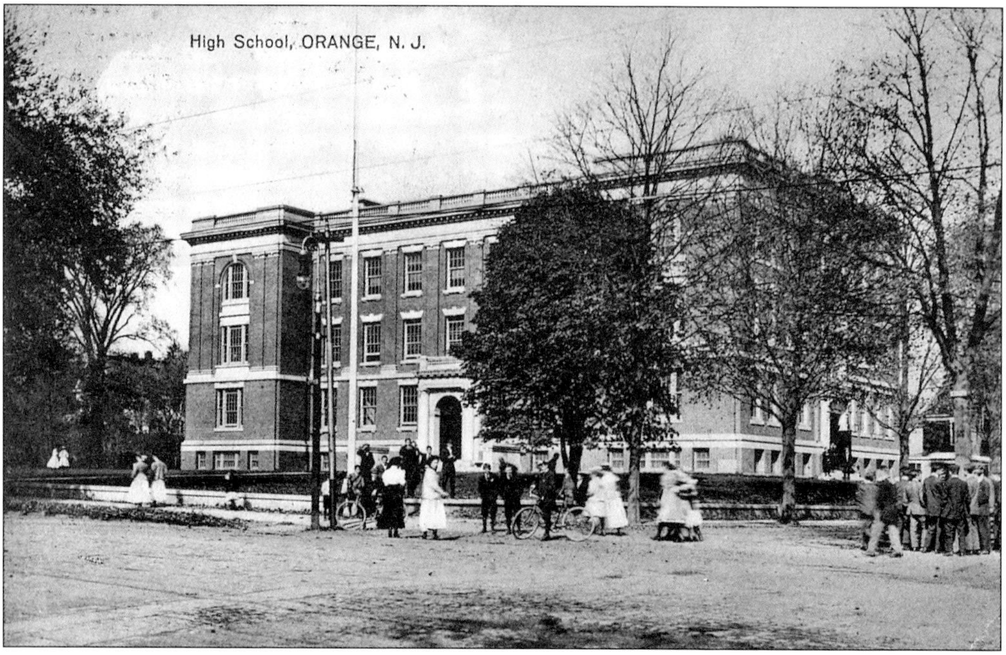

The fancy dresses and long suits may signal graduation day in this view of the new Orange High School in 1910. The property was originally purchased by the common council in 1901 from Daniel Minahan at a cost of $40,000, and was intended for the construction of a town hall. By 1906, however, the council had decided not to build there. The property was exchanged with the board of education for their Day Street building, which then, with $50,000 worth of modifications, became the town hall.

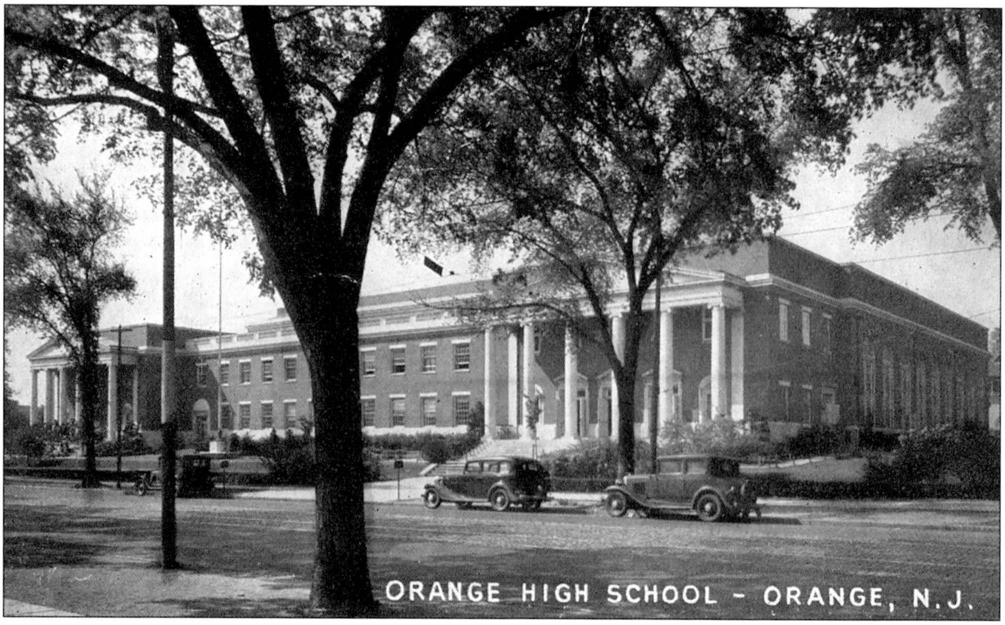

By 1925, the Main Street building was obsolete and a "third" high school was constructed on property at the corner of Central and Lincoln Avenues. The wing to the right with the Greek revival façade houses the auditorium.

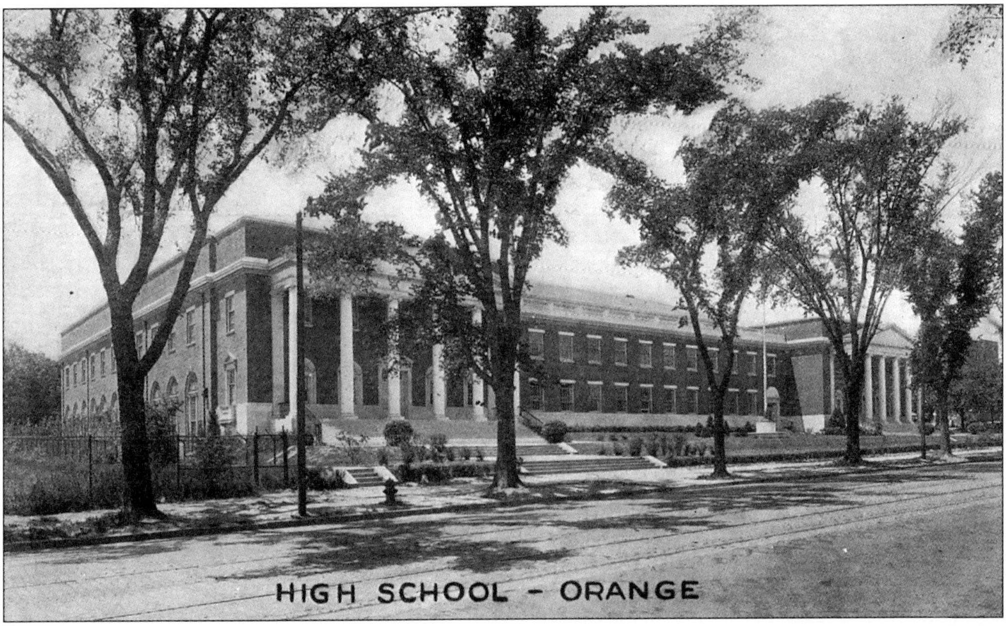

Another view of the high school building shows the left or east wing, which housed the gymnasium. By the 1960s, the building had become woefully inadequate for the growing school population. Facing the loss of the school's accreditation, the board of education constructed a "fourth" high school at a cost of $5 million on Lincoln Avenue property immediately behind this building. When the new facility opened on September 5, 1970, the old building became the Orange Middle School.

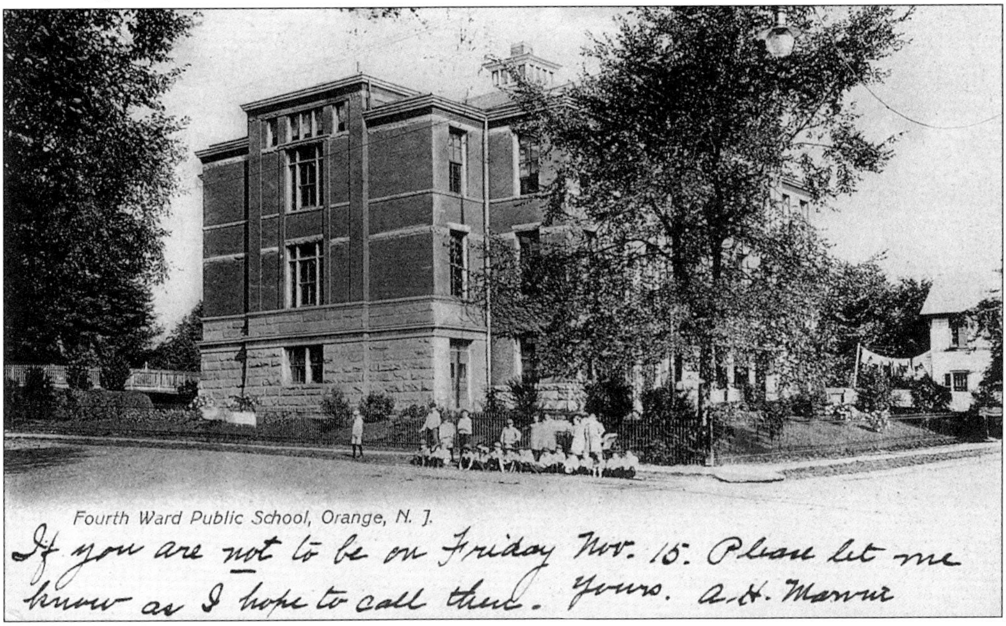

The "Fourth Ward" School is really the Forest Street School, located on the corner of Valley Road. The brick building was completed in 1889 at a cost of $43,750.51 and had a capacity of 300. By 1920, Andrew Scarlet was principal, presiding over a student body of 742 crammed into 12 classrooms. The assessed value of the property at that time was $99,000.

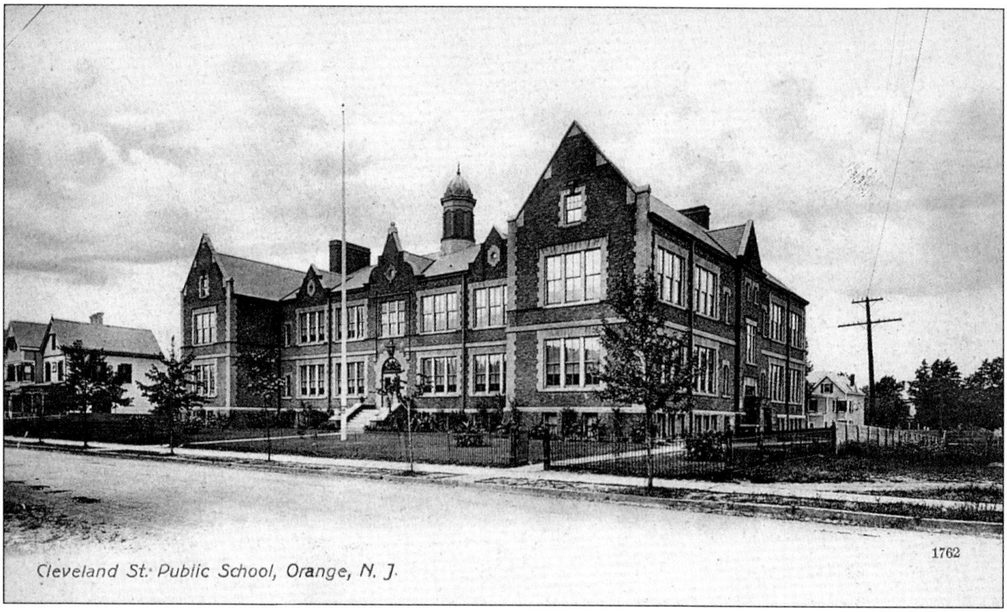

The Cleveland Street School opened on October 16, 1899. Frank L. Yost, who eventually became superintendent of schools, was principal in 1920. At that time the building boasted 847 students in 18 classrooms, and had an assessed value of $184,000.

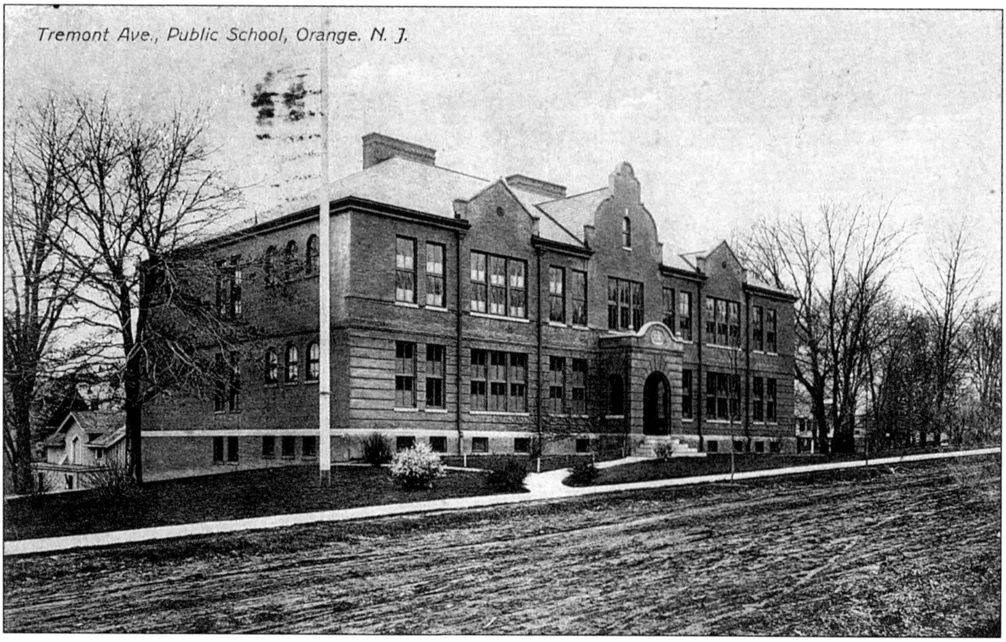

The street is still dirt in this 1910 view of the Tremont Avenue School. The card's authors, Brent and Anna bragged, "This is where we go this year and like it so much." By 1920, 409 students occupied its ten classrooms, under the tutelage of Principal Florence J. Lacey. The school was eventually closed and converted into Orange Police Headquarters.

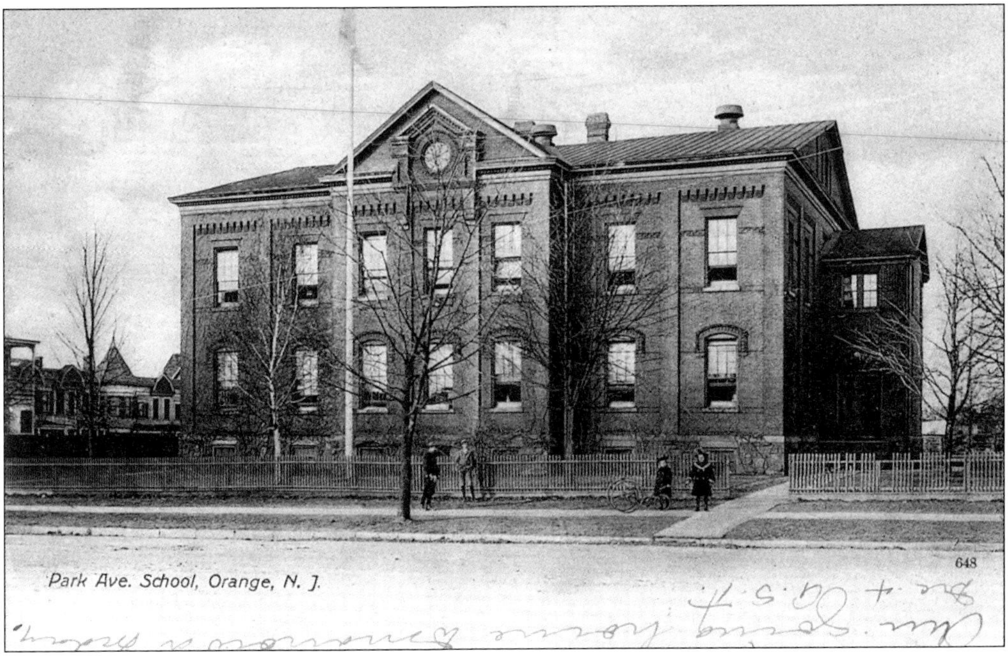

The Park Avenue School was opened in September 1883. The 100-by-150-foot property was purchased at a cost of $3,900, and the building erected for only $18,997.22. It had 13 classrooms, and a capacity of 614 pupils taught by a staff of 14. By 1920, the student body had grown to 765, and five classrooms had been added. George B. Schulte was principal.

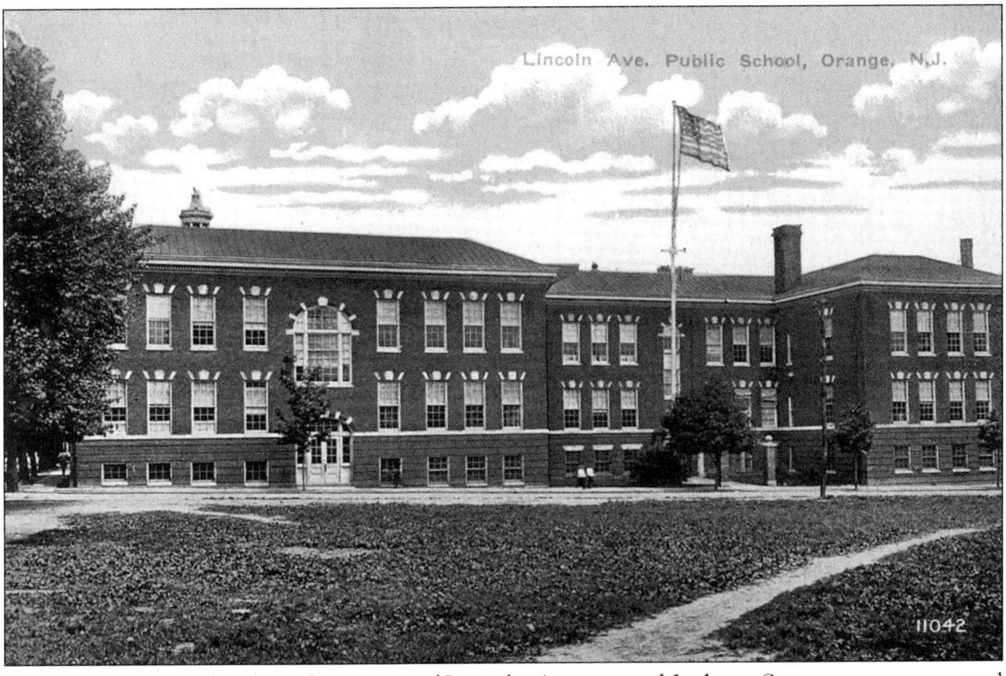

Lincoln Avenue School, at the corner of Lincoln Avenue and Jackson Street, was constructed in 1899 of red brick. In 1920, when Howard J. McNaughton was principal, the building sported 26 classrooms and an enrollment of 1,467. At that time, the plant was valued at $527,000.

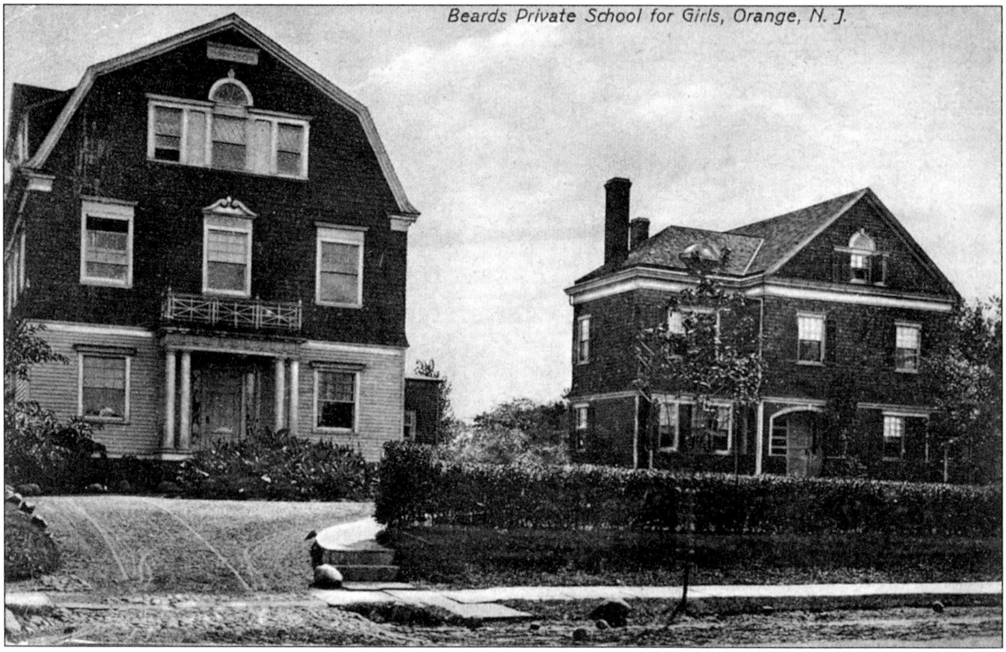

Orange boasted several private educational institutions as well. Lucy and Lizzie Beard and their sister, Mrs. Hiram Foster, established The Beard School for Girls in a private home on Clarendon Place. It began as a kindergarten in 1891, but each year the school "grew a grade." In 1899, the "Recitation Building" was constructed on Berkley Avenue between Tremont Avenue and Elmwynd Drive.

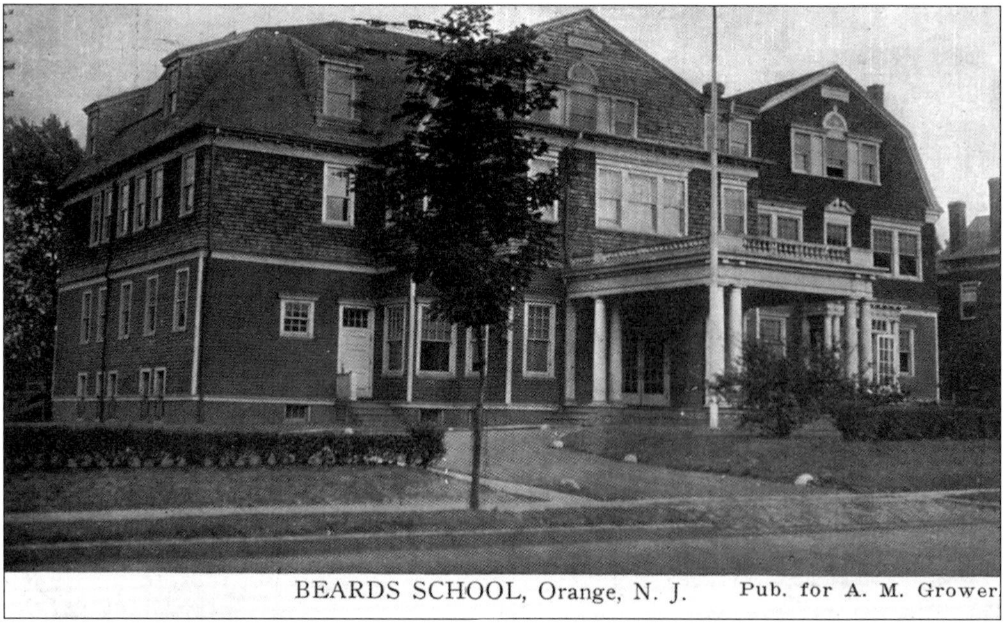

The Recitation House was expanded in 1902 and a corner house was occupied that year as a dormitory. The school motto, "We Rise Through Effort" was sorely tested on November 25, 1953, when several of the buildings of the school were destroyed by fire. Plans were developed immediately for the construction of a new facility at a cost of $600,000.

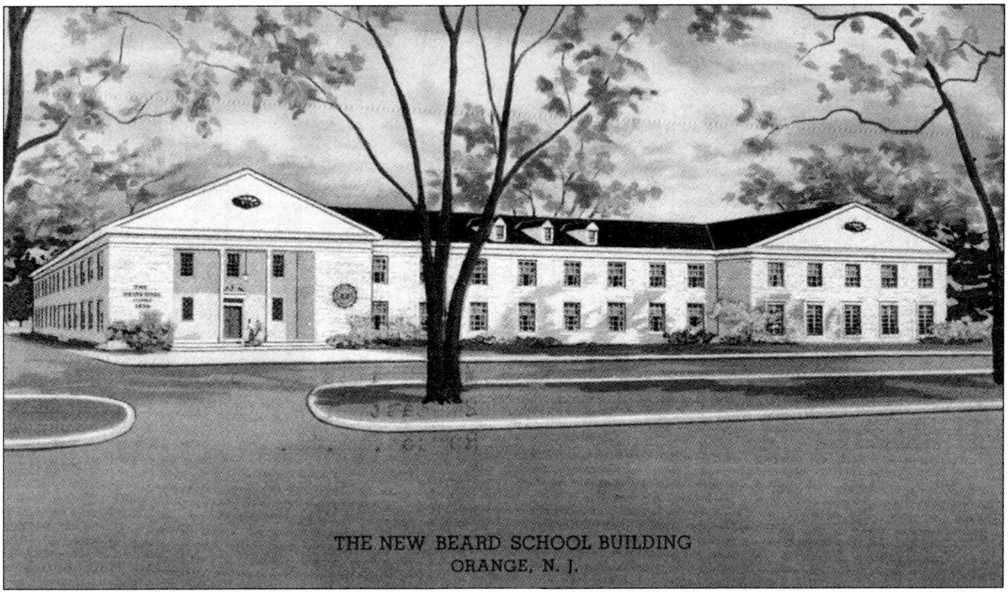

The new Beard School building appears in an architect's rendering dated March 15, 1954. The whitewashed fireproof brick structure was occupied April 29, 1955, and contained classrooms, administrative offices, and an auditorium-gymnasium. Declining enrollment in the 1970s eventually forced the school to abandon its Orange roots and merge with Morristown School at their campus, forming Morristown-Beard in 1972. The Orange building became the White House Nursing Home.

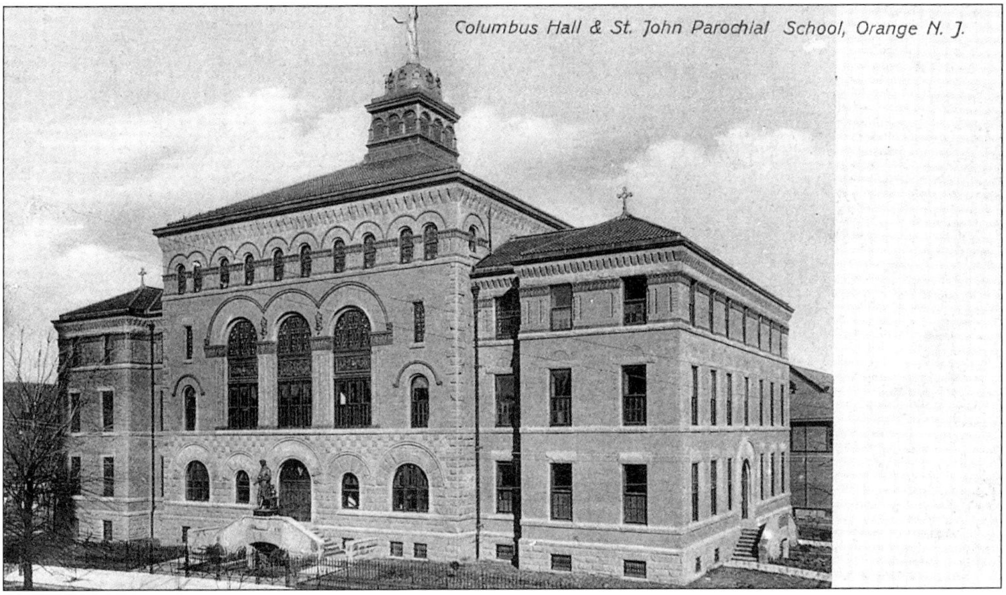

Catholic education was handled by parish schools such as St. John's, Our Lady of Mount Carmel, St. Venantius, and Our Lady of the Valley. Our Lady of the Valley also operated the city's lone Catholic high school. St. John's and Mt. Carmel survive as parish elementary schools, but the other schools no longer exist. The Valley High School closed in 1981, and the grammar school shut its doors in 1997 after an unsuccessful merger with St. Venantius' new owner, the Korean parish of St. Andrew Kim.

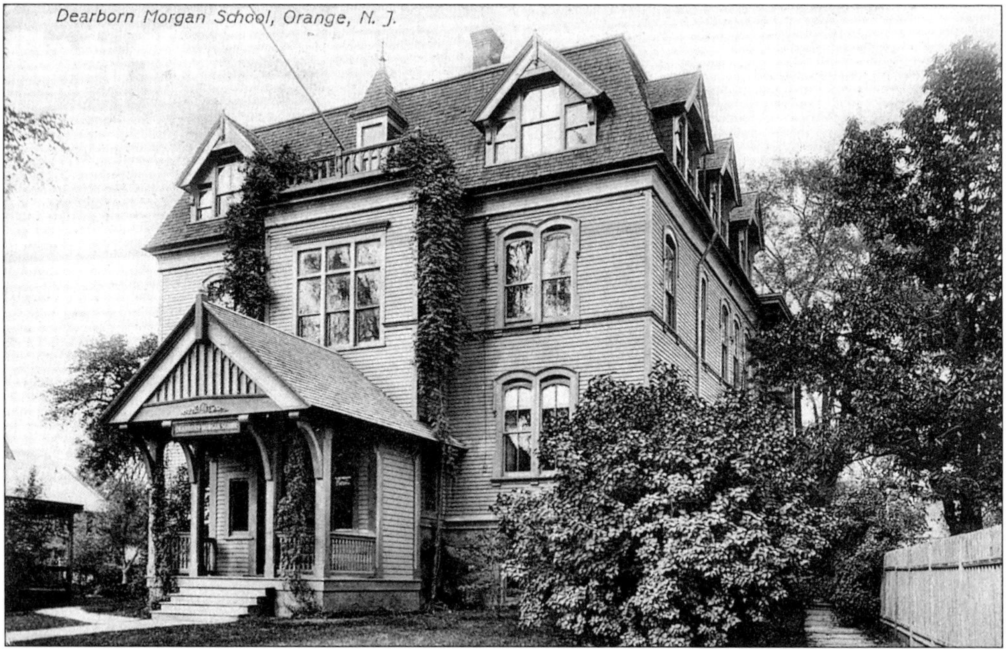

The Dearborn-Morgan School was founded in 1876 after a merger of three private co-educational institutions operated by Jane Dearborn, Abby Morgan, and Charles H. Mann. Located on Main Street by the Military Commons, it was sold in 1911 to George Shelly. Shelly operated it until it closed in 1937, and the building was demolished three years later.

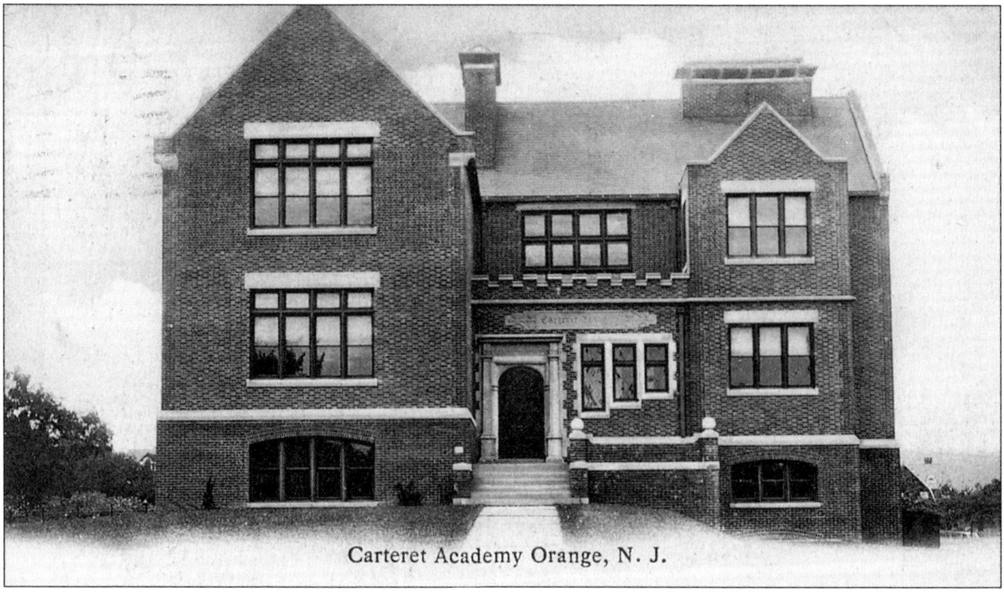

In response to public requests for an all-male academy, Carteret Academy opened September 25, 1901, on three acres at the corner of Central and Essex Avenues. It was founded by two former staff members of the Dearborn-Morgan School, Dr. David Kennedy and Charles Mead. Lack of expansion room prompted Carteret to move to West Orange in January of 1940.

Four

ORANGE PARK

The Essex County Park System was established in 1895 largely through the efforts of Orange resident Fredrick W. Kelsey. On December 6, 1893, Kelsey submitted a resolution to the Newark Board of Trade for legislation to provide "a system of parks and parkways" for the people of Essex County. A bill was introduced into the state legislature establishing a parks commission and providing for the appointment of five commissioners. Voters enthusiastically passed a subsequent bond issue for $1.5 million for the purchase and development of parkland in April 1895. Kelsey, of course, was one of the first five commissioners.

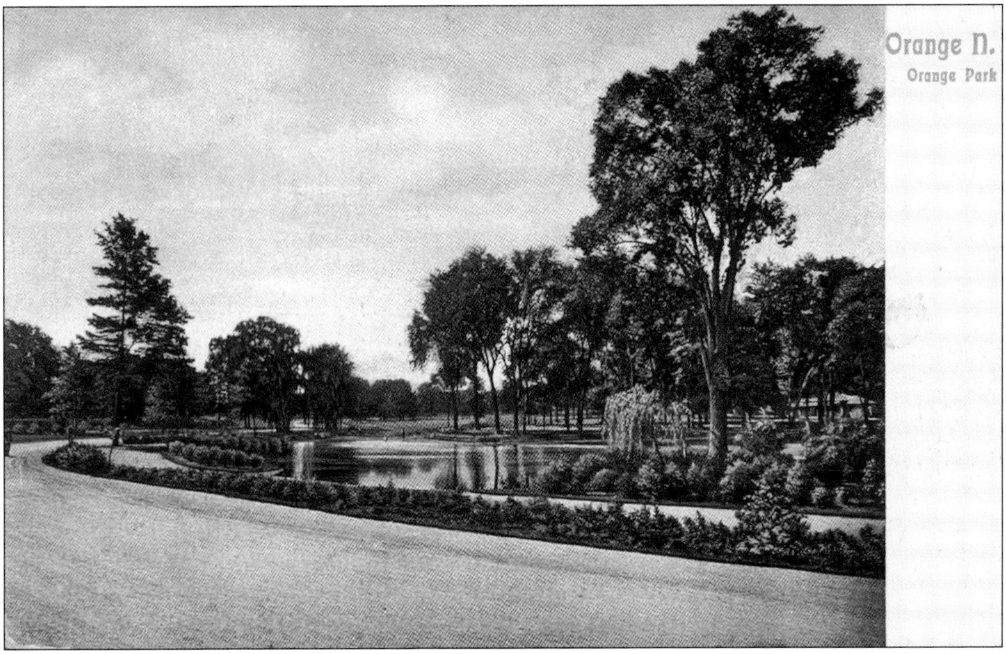

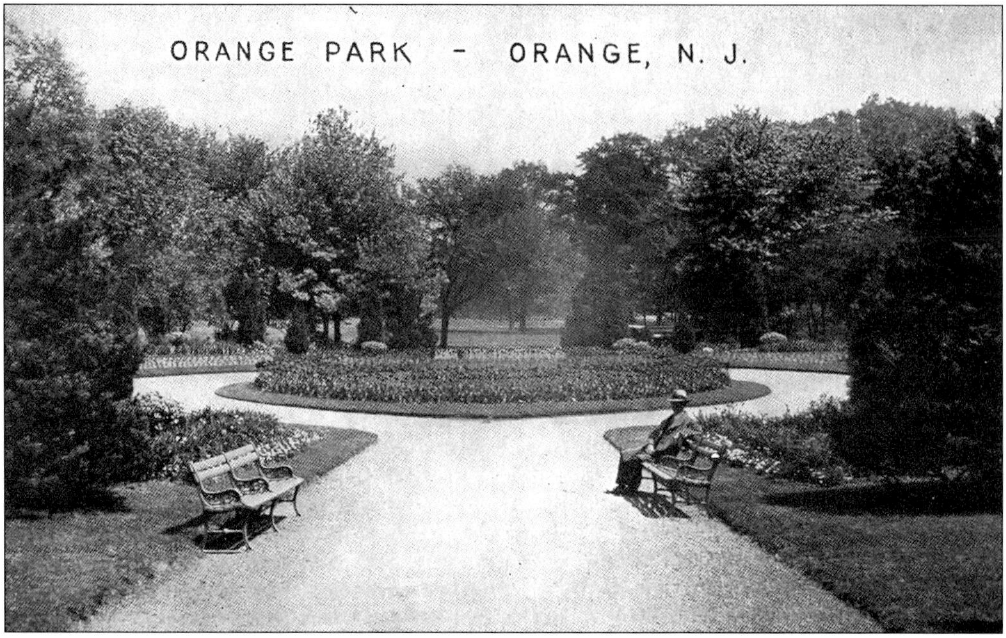

Carefully tended flowerbeds greeted visitors entering the south end of Orange Park from the intersection of South Center and South Harrison Streets. At different times over the years, the plantings varied from irises and tulips to a variety of other annuals with a smattering of evergreens.

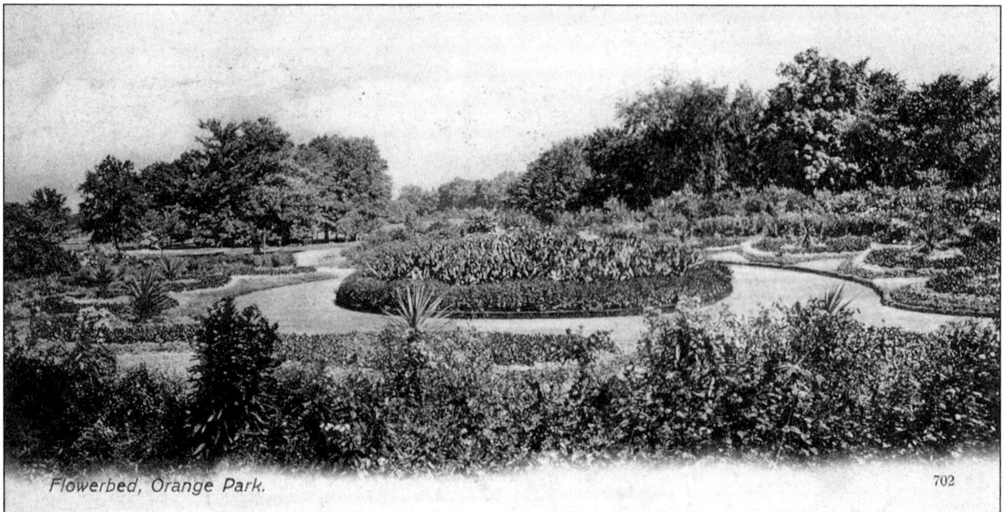

This is another view of the flowerbeds from the South Center Street vantage. The pathway in the previous view is to the right. During the 1950s and '60s, tulips were the primary planting, and the warmer months always found a cadre of wedding parties lined up here for group photos.

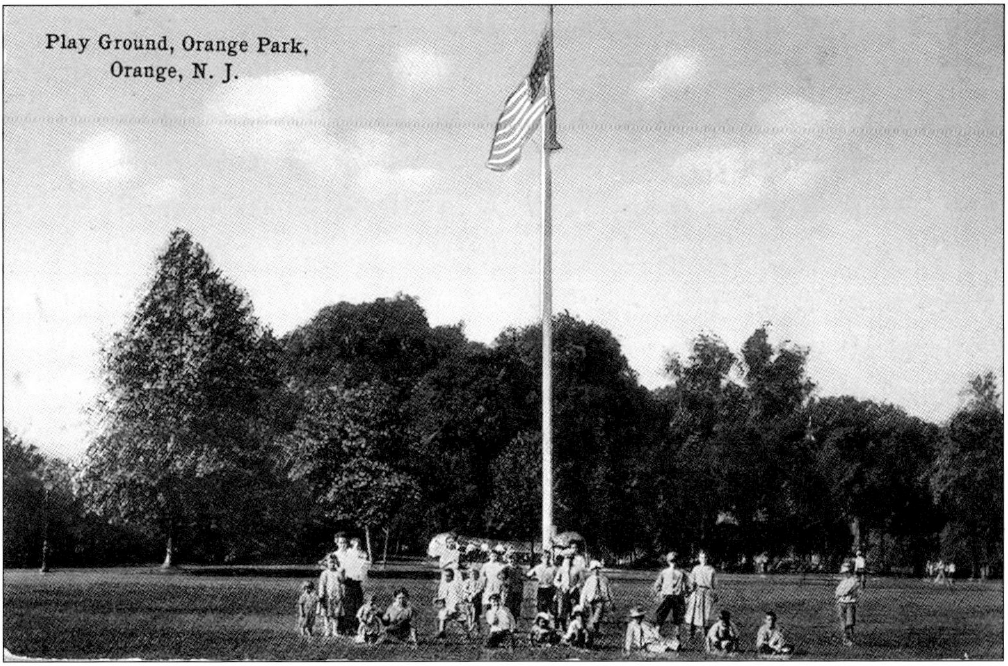

At its apex, the park included about 50 acres of land in a rough triangle bordered by South Center Street, Harrison Street, and Central Avenue, and divided approximately in the center by a one and a half acre lake. The flagpole was a notable landmark on the southern half as you approached the children's playground.

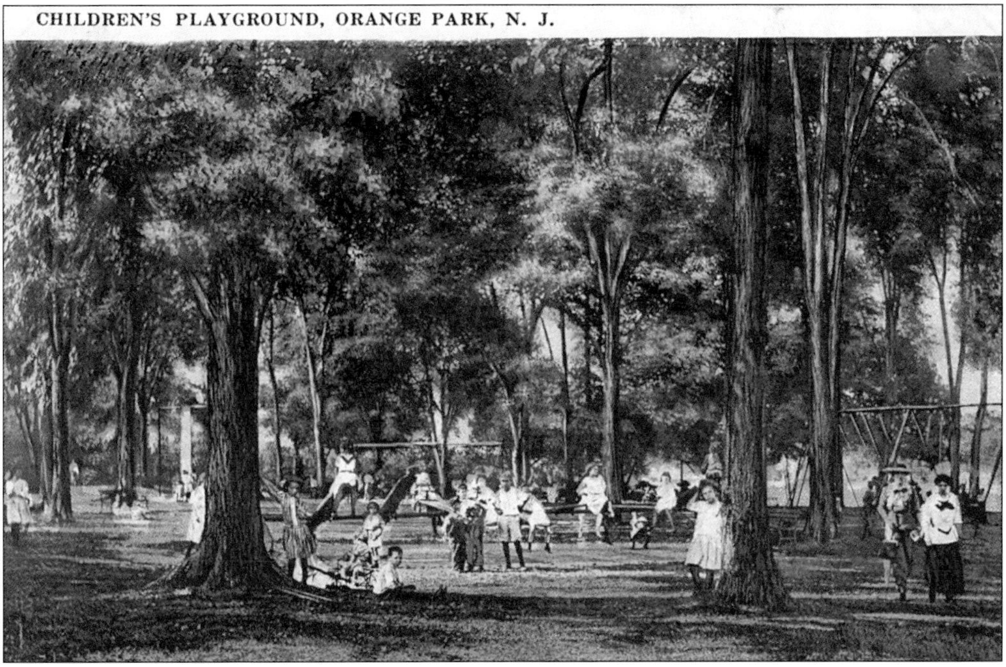

The children's playground was nestled in a grove of trees adjacent to the south shore of the lake and included swings, slides, merry-go-rounds, see-saws, an enormous sand box, and a wading beach.

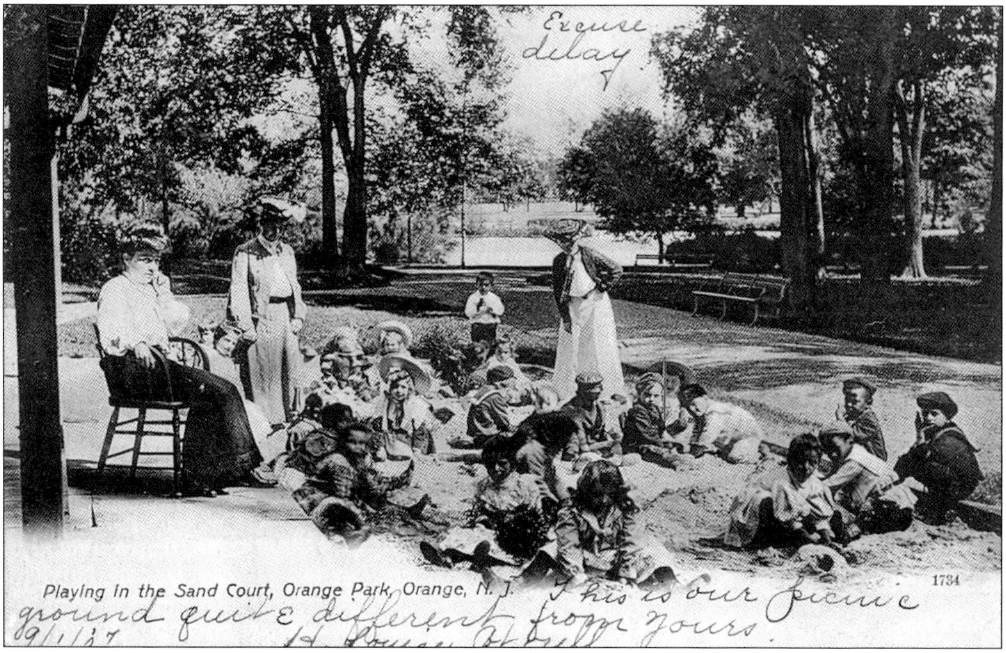

A mixture of diverse ethnicity is evident in this busy scene at the sand-box. It is likely that the well-dressed women are nannies, tending to the offspring from the adjacent south-end estates of the Colgates and Metcalfs. Their property would later form the nucleus of the extensive Seven Oaks Park residential development.

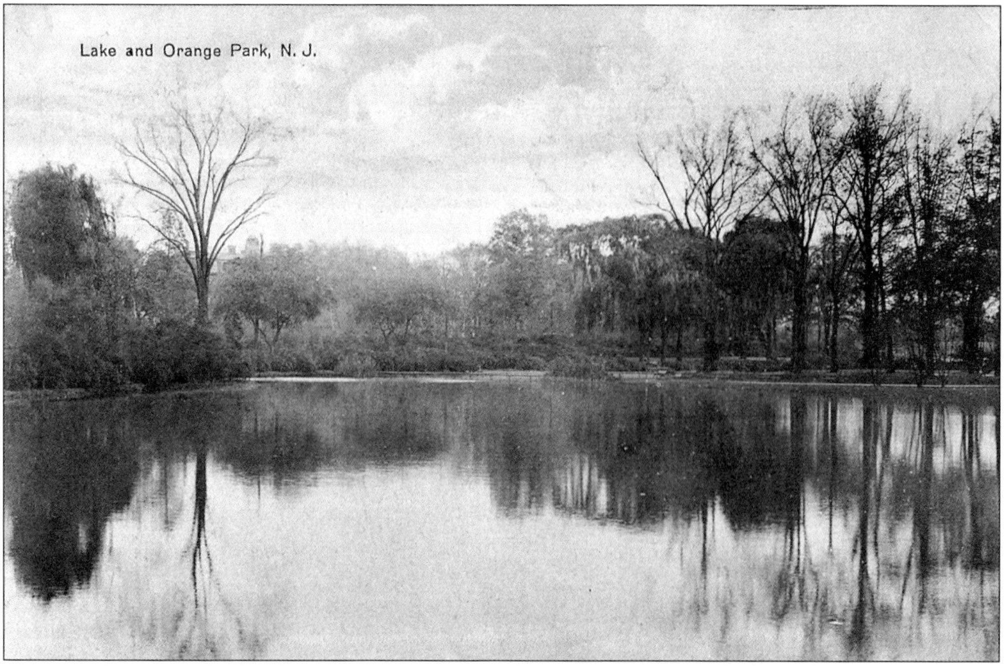

The lake formed the geographic center of Orange Park and provided a focal point for many activities. Spring-fed and contained by a small dam, it was notable in winter for the fine ice skating it provided.

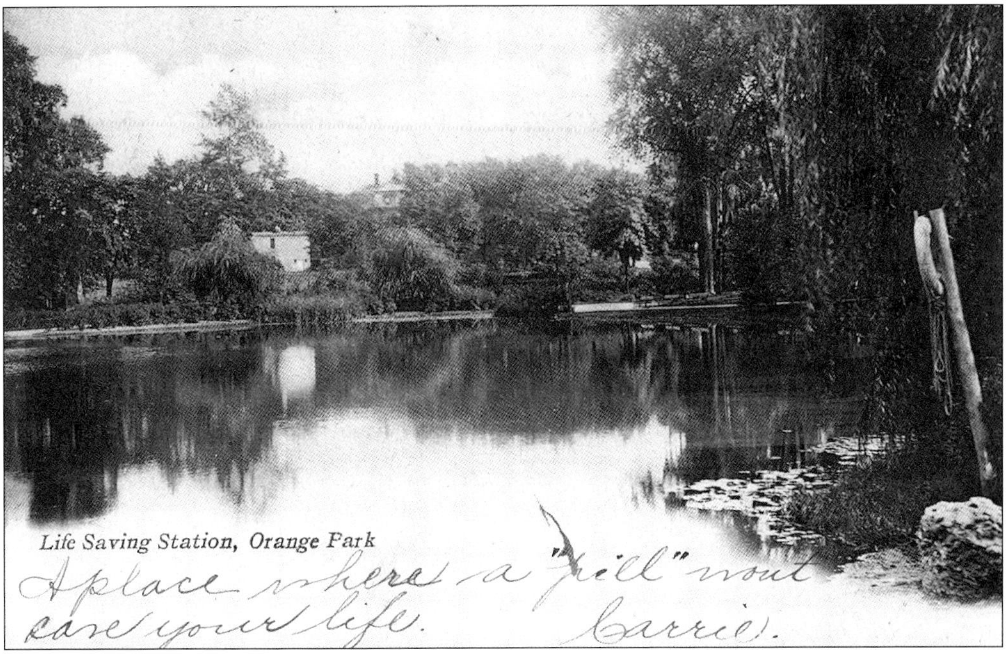

The "Life-Saving Station" was something of a misnomer, for it consisted only of a kapok life saver mounted on a post. The spring which fed the lake was located approximately in this area, and the moving water always created thin ice and a hole here in the winter.

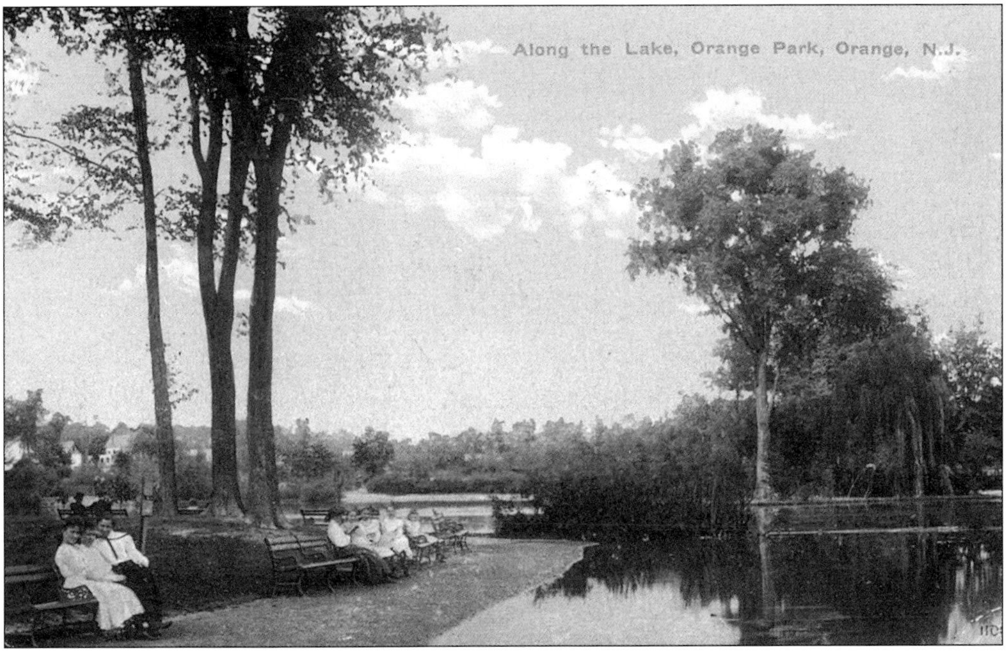

It was possible to enjoy a quiet moment in the "cove" at the south shore, which was used as a wading beach for children in the summer. The wading area was gone by the 1920s.

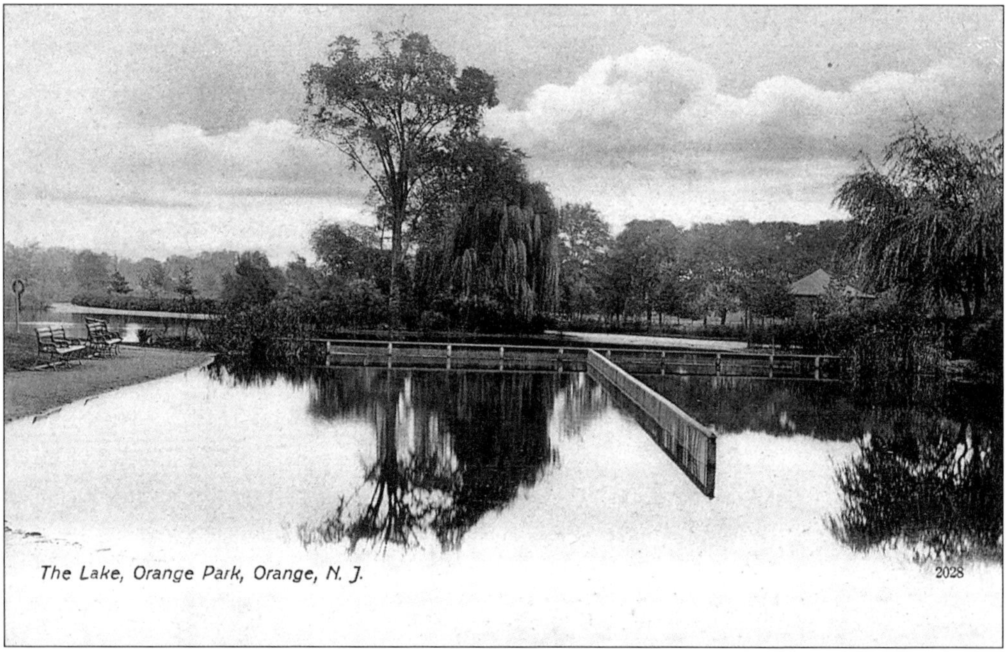

In a quieter moment, the shallow wading pond is clearly defined by the T-shaped fence that separated it from deeper water. The vertical line of the T may at first be baffling, but upon closer inspection, its purpose becomes crystal clear.

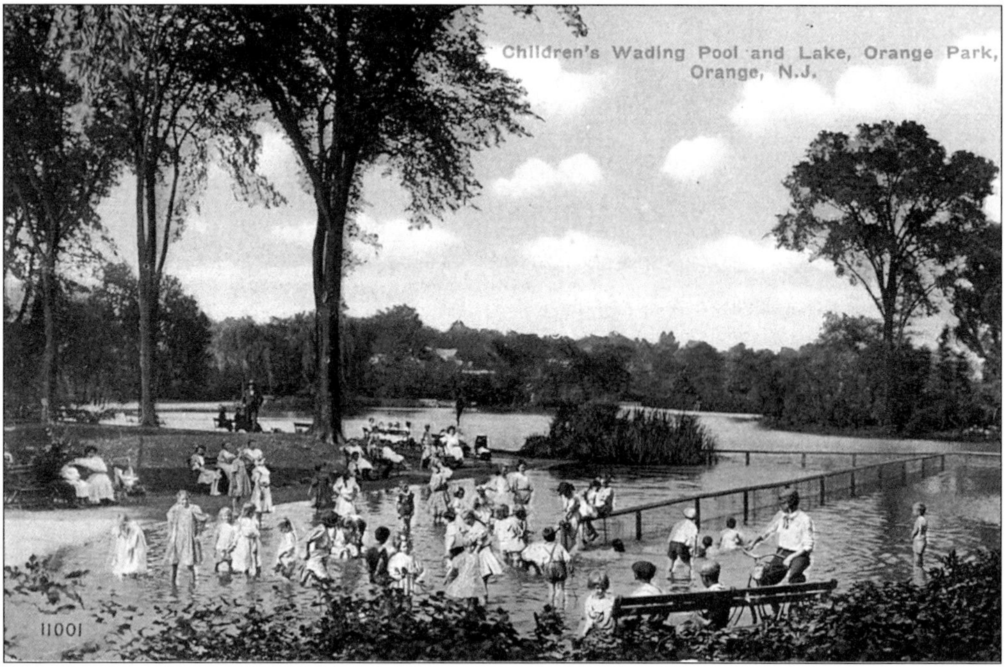

In a frenetic vignette of summer long gone by, the vertical element of the fence shows its true purpose. While we first thought it was simply for support, this view clearly demonstrates that it segregates the sexes! "Boys to the right, girls to the left, please!" Pants are rolled up, dresses are hiked, but there is not a bathing suit in sight.

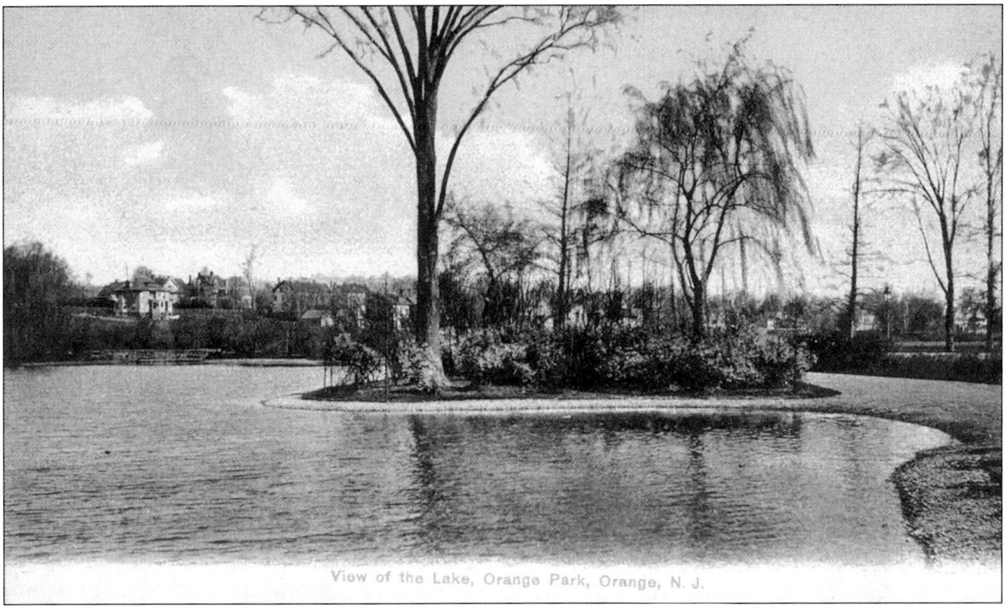

The north shore of the lake was easily identified by this little spit of land that protruded into the water, and its picturesque weeping willow. The dam that created the lake is visible in the background.

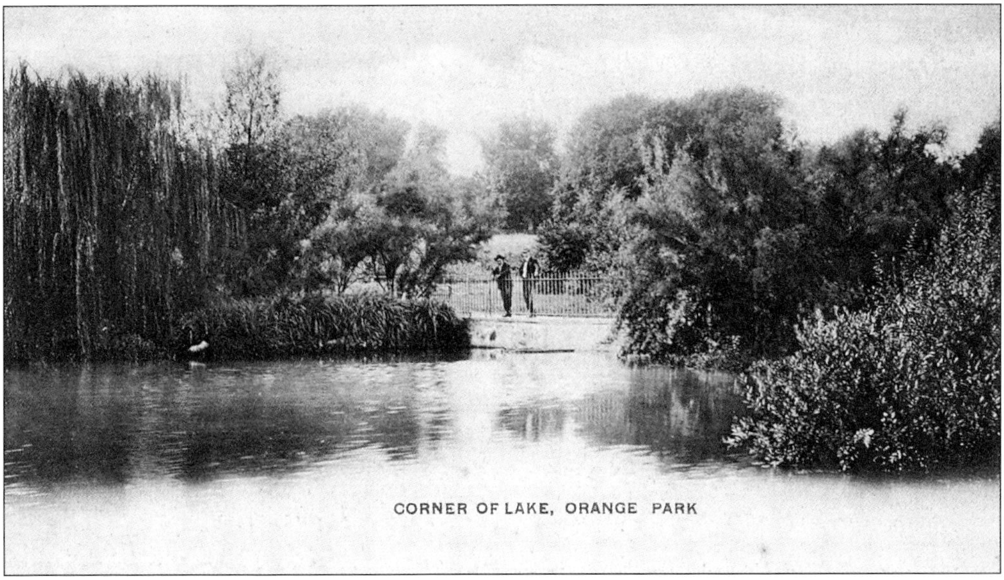

Here is a closer view of the dam and its "bridge." About 16 acres of the proposed park was swampland, but its owner, seeking a higher profit and knowing that Orange desperately wanted to run a much-needed storm sewer through the property, refused to sell. Frederick Kelsey was given the authority by the Commission to deal directly with the "scoundrel," and authorized a maximum of $20,000 expenditure. On December 7, 1896, Kelsey closed the deal on that parcel for $17,500.

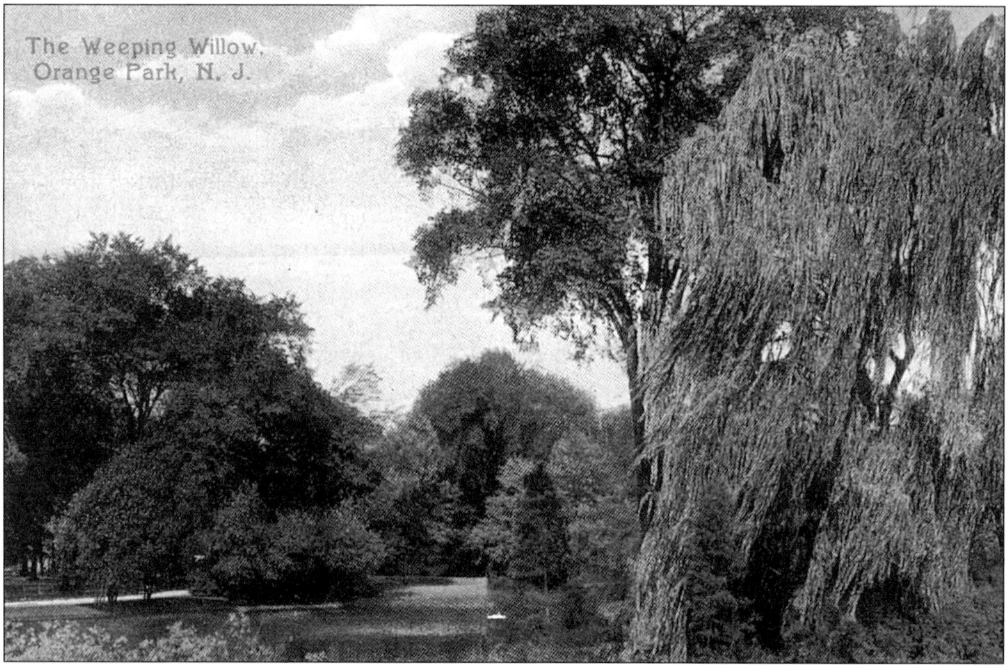

This is another view of the weeping willow in a more mature stage. The lush nature of the surrounding vegetation is also evident. As crime in the park increased during the 1960s, much of the surrounding vegetation was either cut back or removed to provide a safer environment for park-goers.

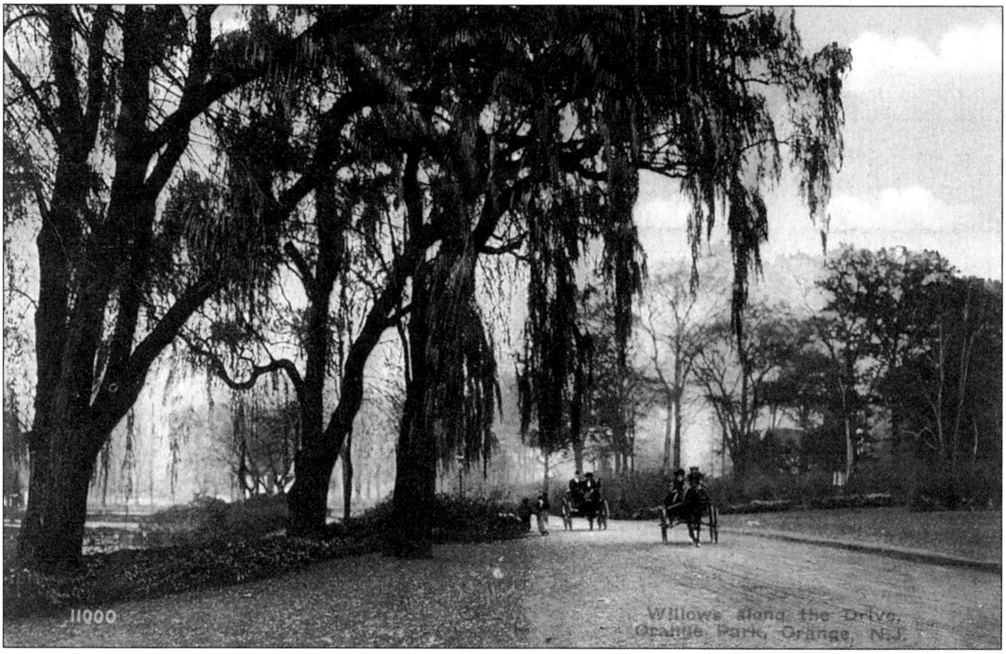

Horse and carriage is the only mode of transportation on this day in 1913, as two couples drive around the east side of the lake. The view looks toward Central Avenue. In 1999, all Park roads are closed to traffic, and one must walk to get to this location.

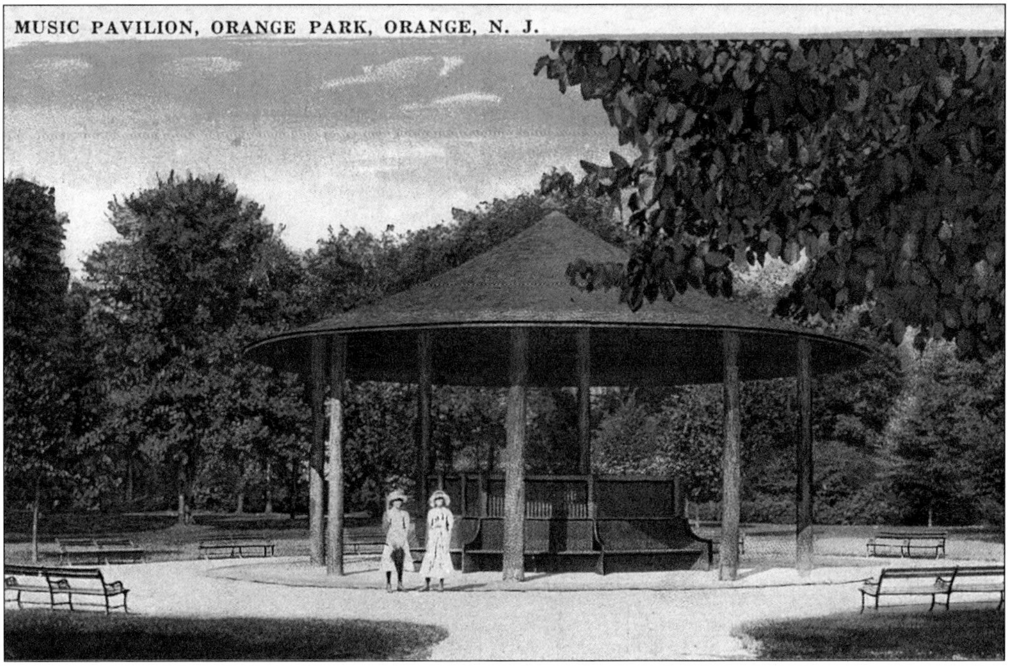

The Music Pavilion was located in the northern half of Orange Park. On the evening of August 25, 1900, after three years of construction, the park informally opened with a concert by Markwith's Brass Band. Total cost of land acquisition and construction was $157,366.17. Of this amount, local residents contributed $16,219.

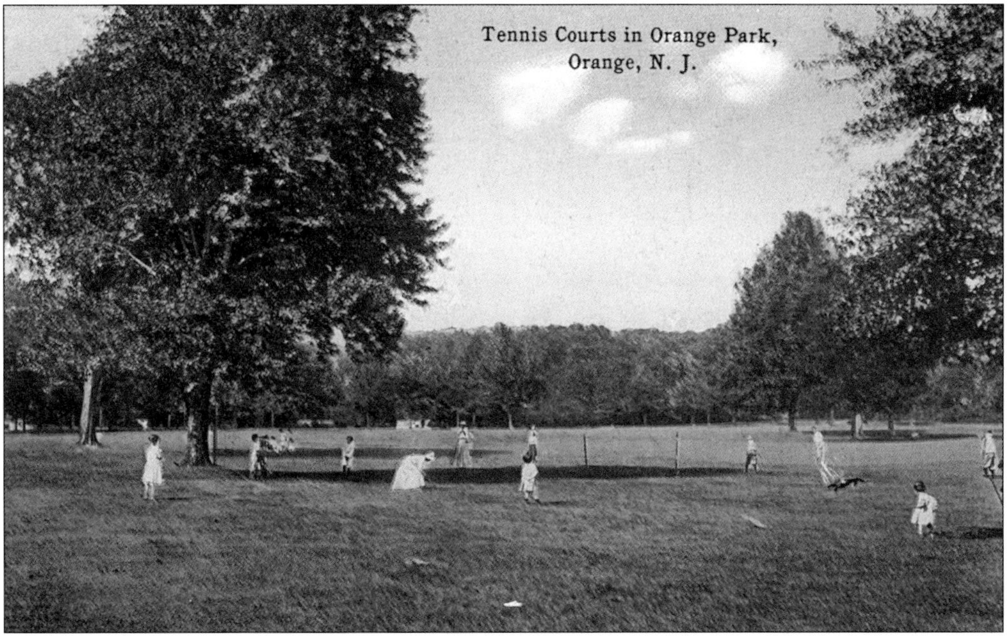

The caption of this card is somewhat misleading, as the participants are actually involved in a game of "lawn tennis" or badminton. The scene appears to be at the south lawn of the park between South Center and Harrison Streets.

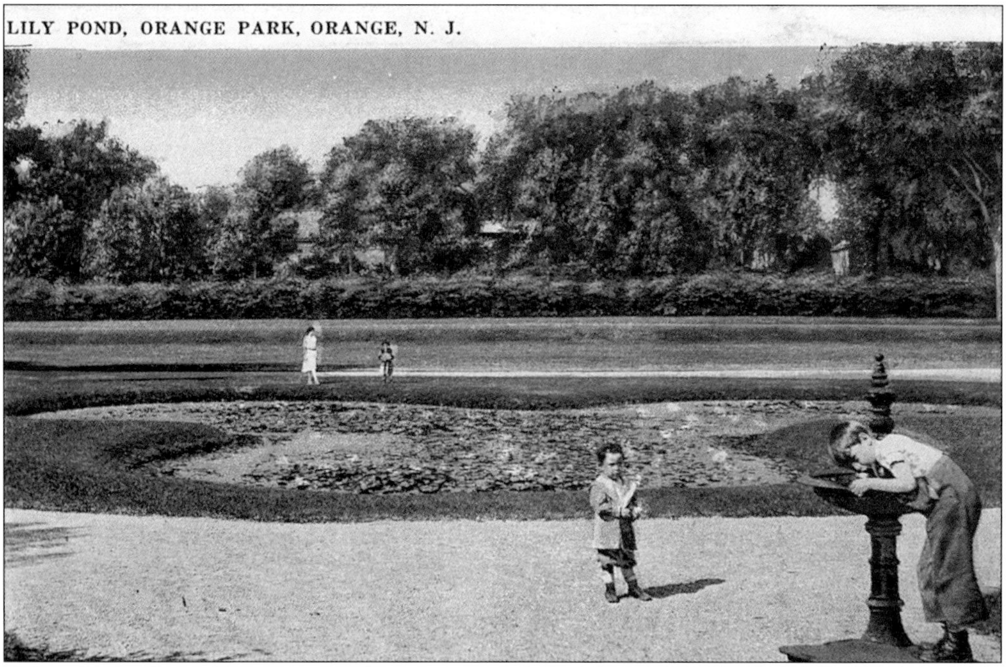

The lily pond was a feature of the north end of the park near Central Avenue, and was always intriguing because of its symmetrical "three leaf clover" design. Here, a youngster grabs a cool drink out of one of the many cast iron water fountains that dotted the park. Regrettably, the lily pond was filled in years ago.

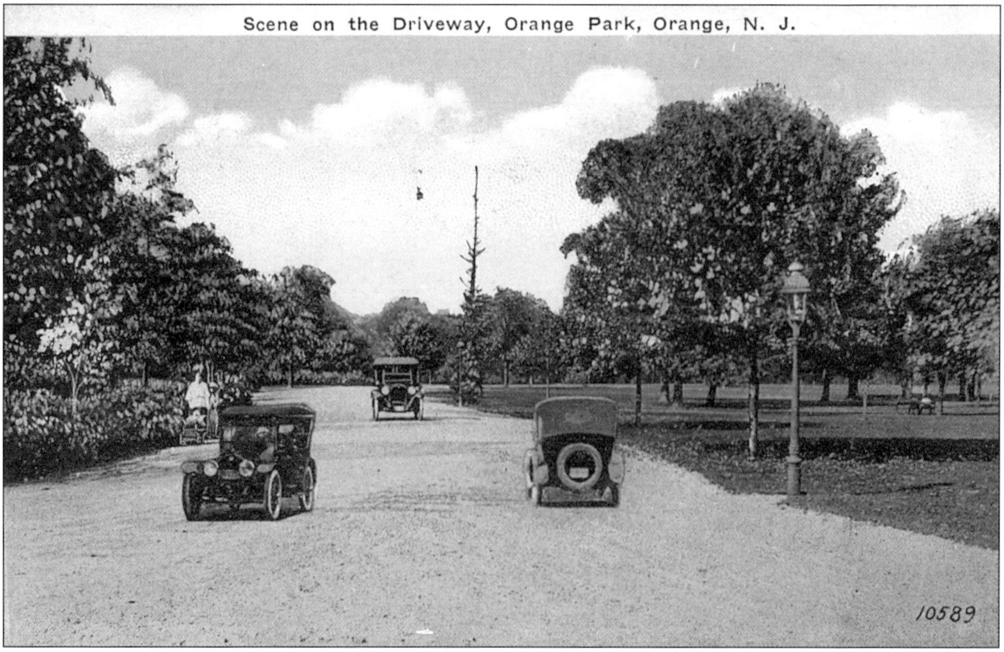

Automobiles have prevailed over horse and buggy in this 1922 image of the main driveway from Central Avenue. The mother-daughter combination with the baby carriage is keeping to the side of the road, well out of range of the chugging monsters.

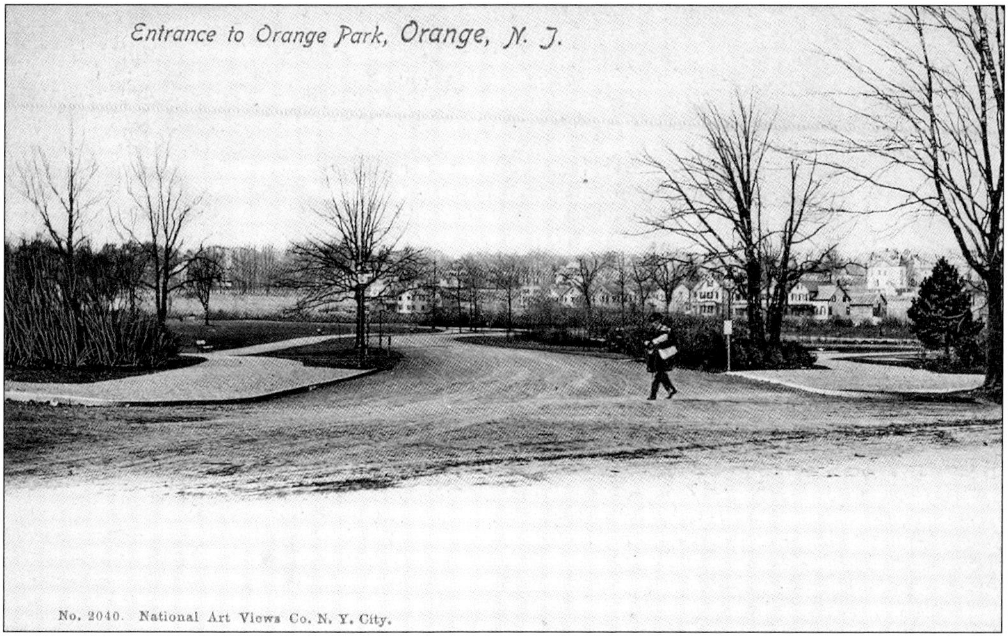

A solitary pedestrian with a large package ambles slowly across the deserted drive on a winter day, about 1905. Bare trees and empty benches attest to the loneliness of the scene, which would not have made this card a hot seller, and probably explains its unused condition.

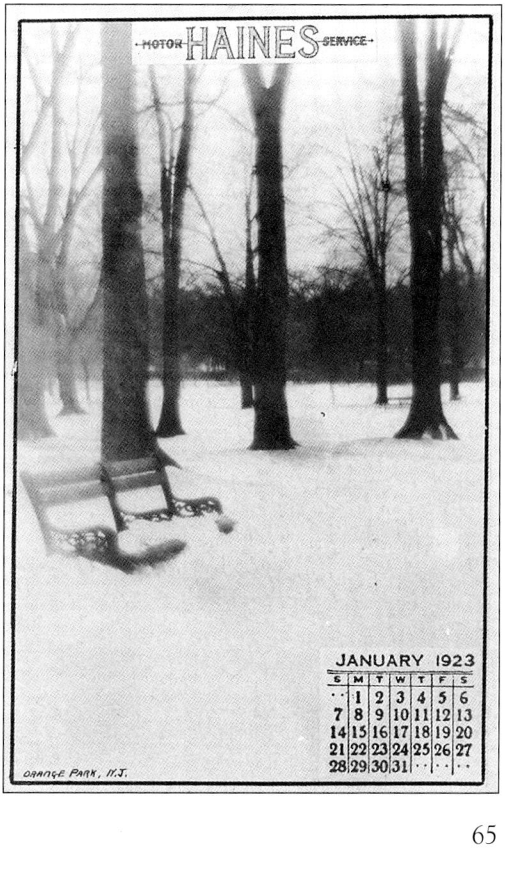

A winter view with snow provided a much more salable commodity, even if it was an advertisement for Haines Motor Service. The calendar dates the storm prior to January 1923, and the drifts are about two feet deep.

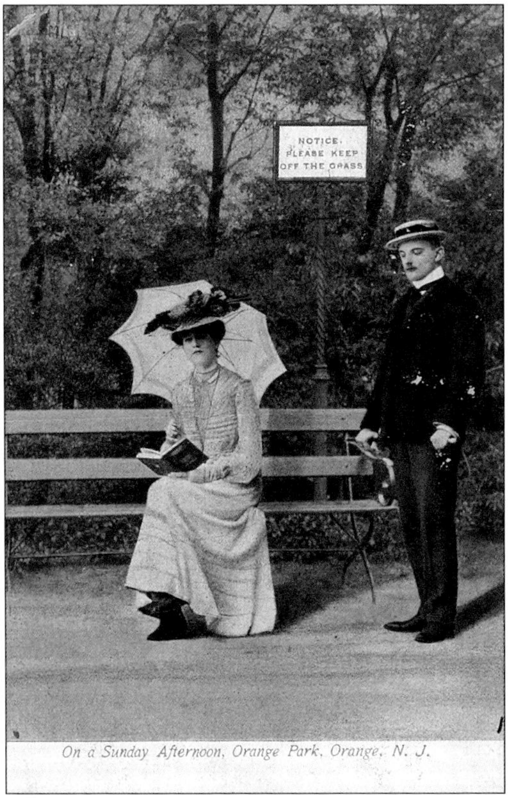

Novelty cards were all the rage in 1907, even if the scene was staged in a studio rather than in the park itself. This was the first in a rare series showing the travails of a demure maiden confronted by a brassy swain "On a Sunday Afternoon in Orange Park." Here, he contemplates his opening line while she plays hard-to-get. (First installment of five cards.)

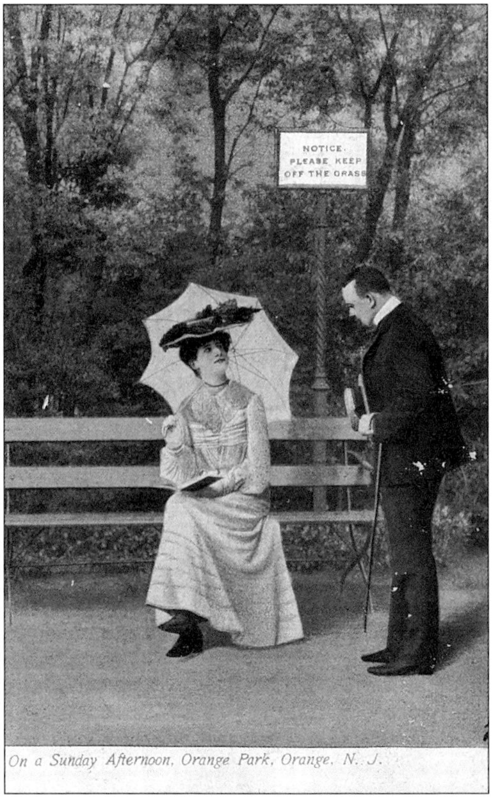

The proper way to send this series was a card a day for five consecutive days, thus creating an early version of the "serial." In view number two, he has the audacity to speak to her, and her disinterest is evident. "Pardon me, young lady, but is this seat taken?"

In installment #3, he gives her the "once-over" as she ignores him and returns to her reading. Never in a million years would she show any interest, even if she were dying to meet him. "My Mother told me not to talk to strangers."

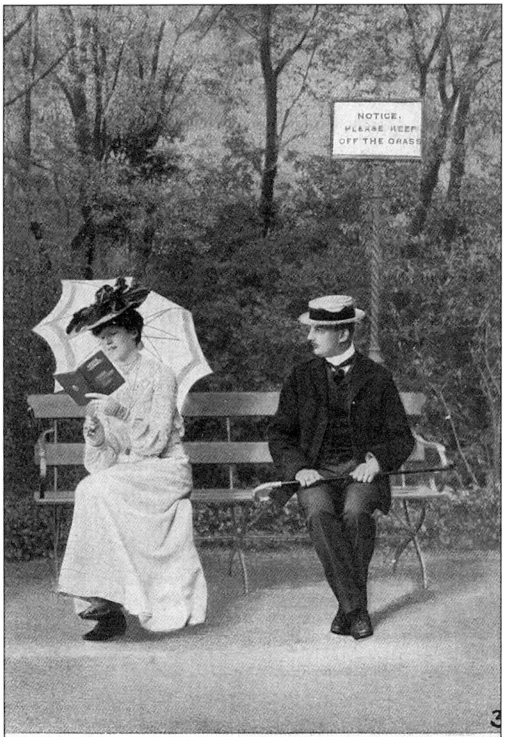

On a Sunday Afternoon, Orange Park, Orange, N. J.

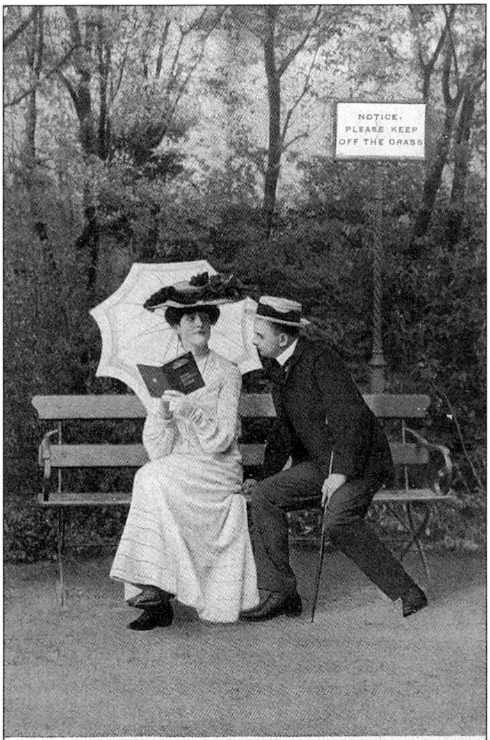

On a Sunday Afternoon, Orange Park, Orange, N. J.

Is that "Ivanhoe?" he says coolly. "I really enjoyed that one. Sir Walter Scott is absolutely wonderful. By the way, my name is Egbert LaCad. What's yours?"

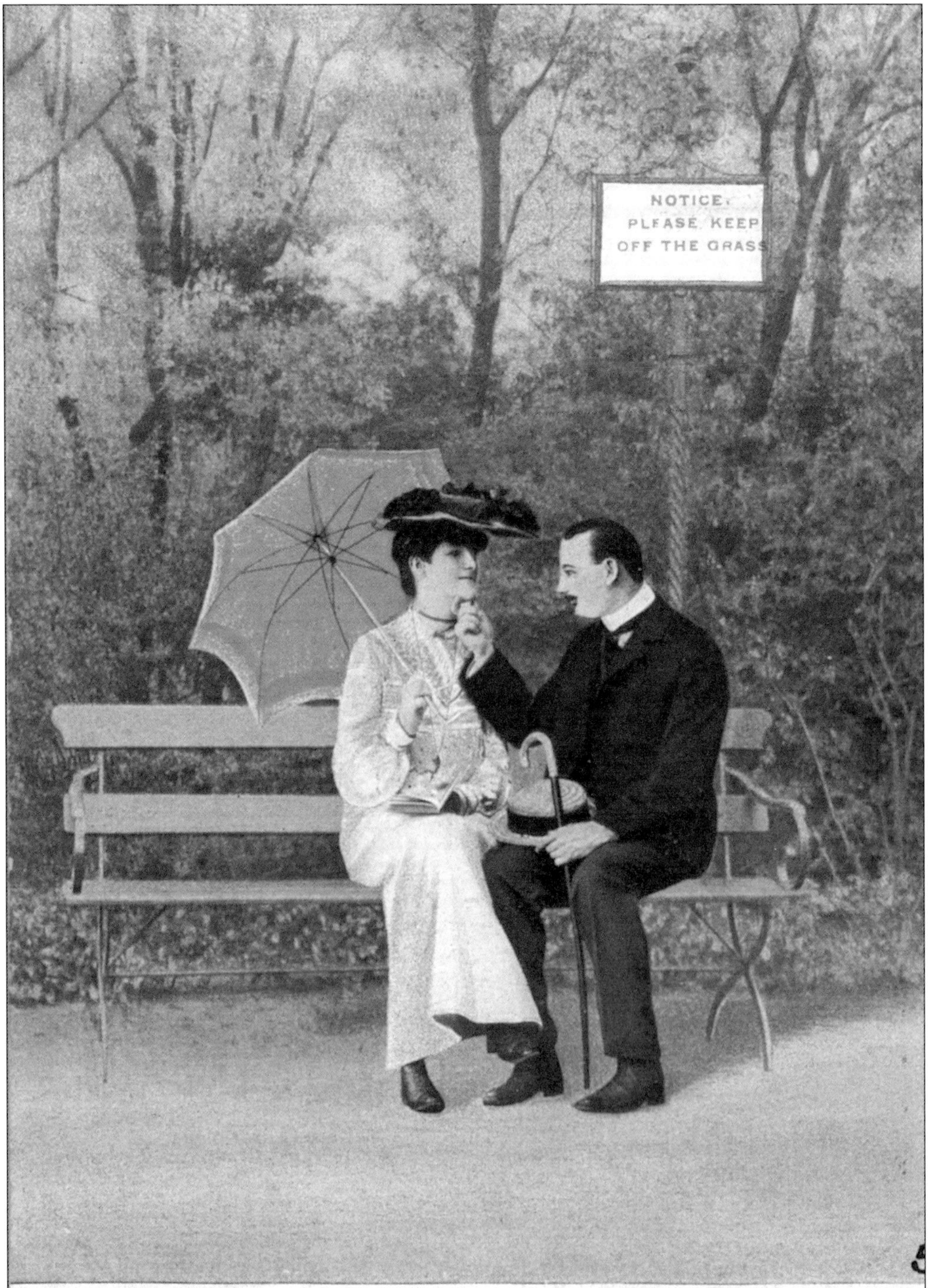

She surrenders at last to his charms. After all, any guy that loves Sir Walter Scott or the "Police Gazette" can't be all bad. Even the umbrella has changed from an off-white to a bright crimson. And, as we leave our happy couple, we leave our tour of Orange Park.

Five

Public Buildings, Institutions, and Businesses

Orange City Hall, shown here c. 1920, was originally constructed in 1869 as the Day Street School and was designed to house the first Primary-High School Institution in the city. By 1906, it was outmoded, and the board of education agreed to swap the property and structure for city-owned land at the corner of Main and Cleveland Streets, where a new high school would be built. With $50,000 worth of renovations, the old school became the city hall, and continues to serve in that capacity today.

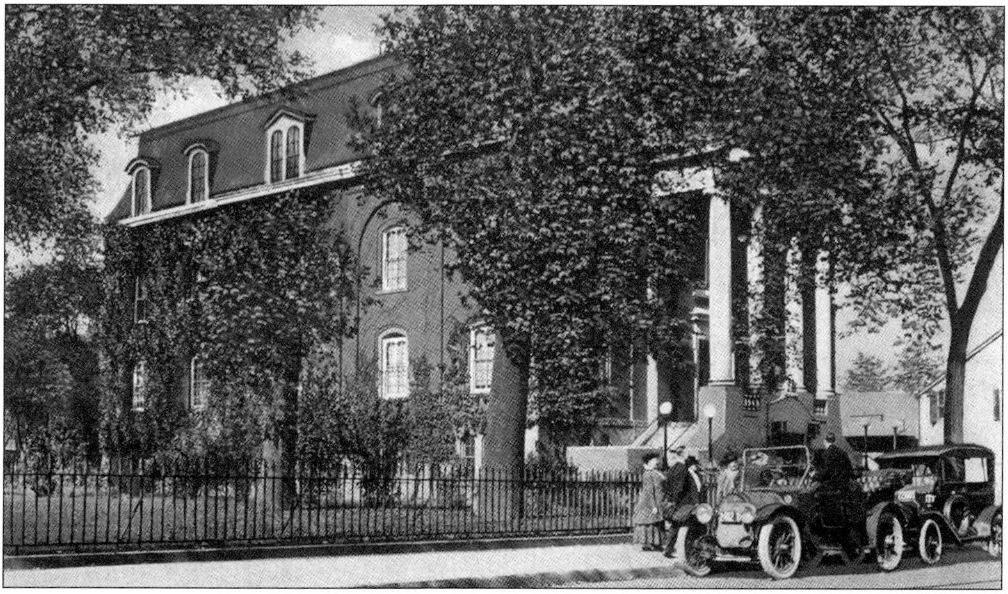

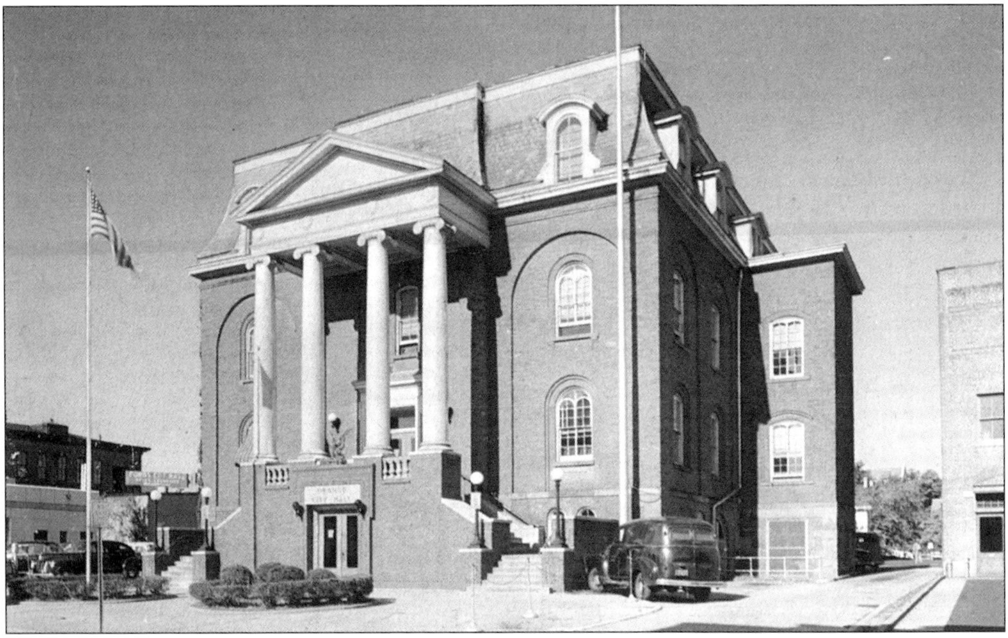

This view of the Orange City Hall in the 1950s shows the changes that have taken place since the building was first converted for the Municipal Offices and Police Department in 1907. Most notable is the loss of trees and shrubbery and the encroachment of concrete and surrounding buildings. The property to the left was formerly occupied by the First Presbyterian Church.

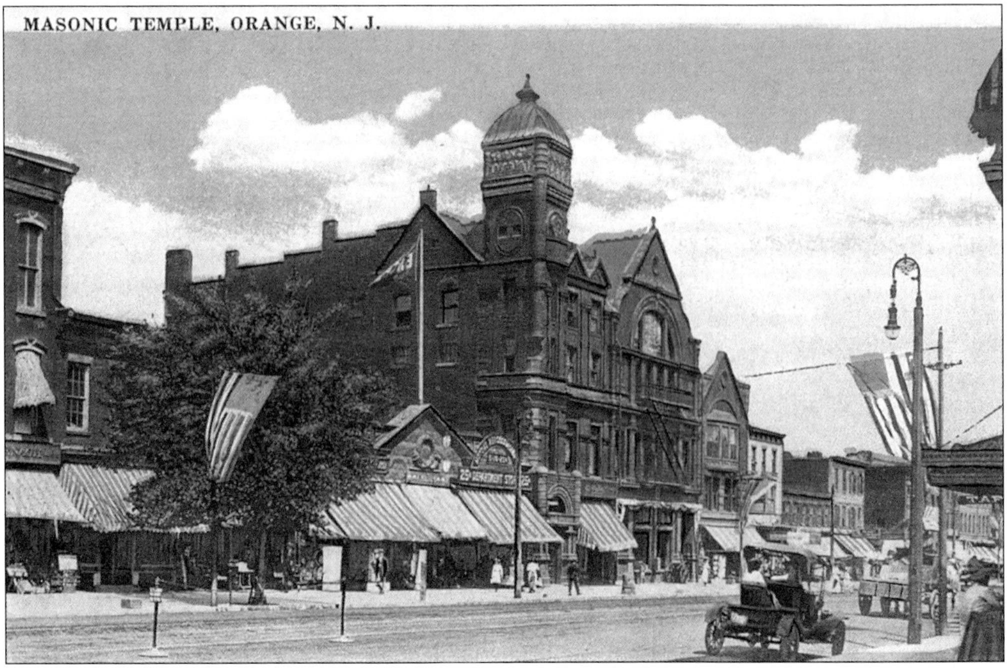

The Masonic Temple of Union Lodge No. 11, F&AM dominated the block between North Center and Canfield Streets. The building, four stories high and constructed of brick at a cost of $50,000, was dedicated on November 16, 1887. In 1888, the Orange Post Office moved into rental quarters on the first floor.

The Orange Post Office was created in September 1812 as an offshoot of the Newark Post Office. President James Madison appointed Henry P. Stryker as its first postmaster, and the original quarters were located at the east quadrant of Main and North Center Streets. Free delivery was inaugurated on September 1, 1887, with five carriers. With the completion of the new Masonic Temple in 1888, the post office abandoned its old corner site and became the ground-floor tenant.

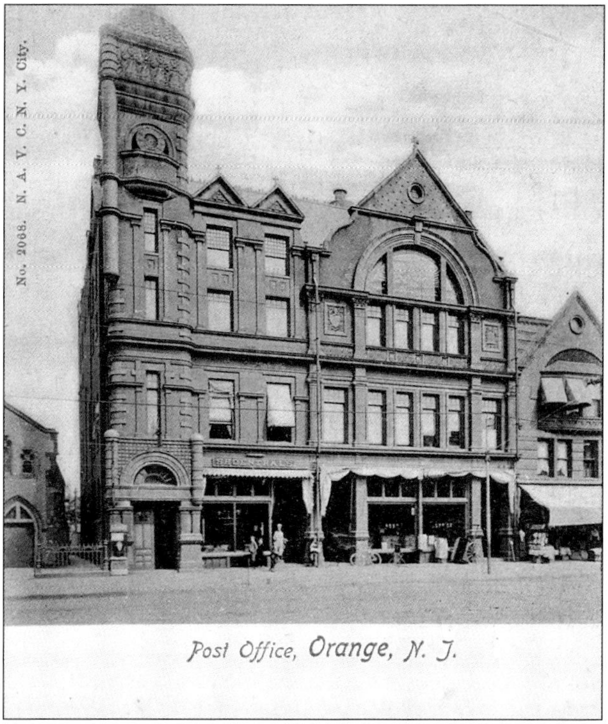

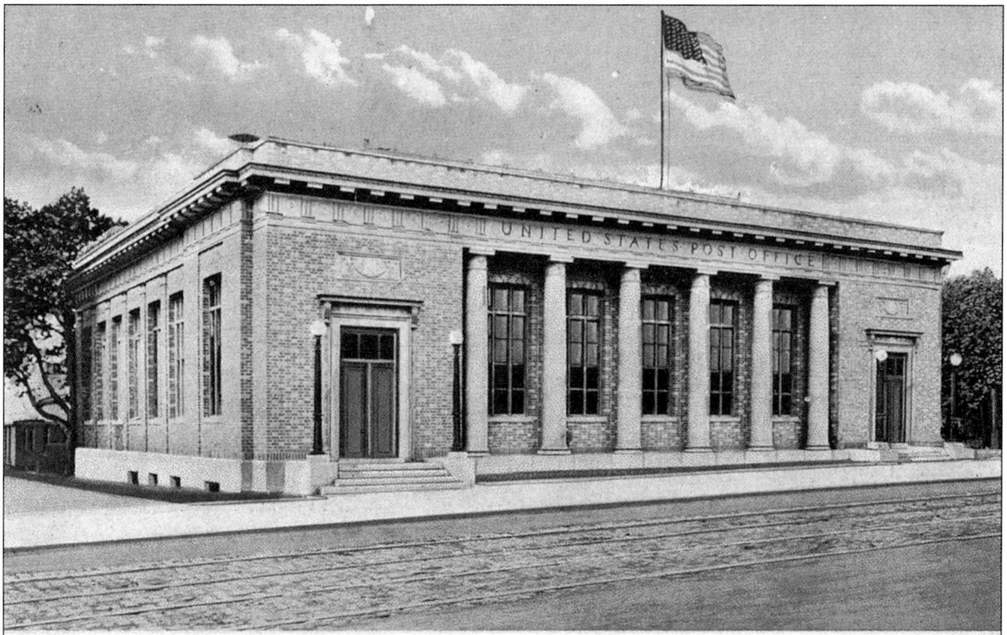

The present Orange Post Office is located at the corner of Main Street and Lincoln Avenue. The cornerstone for the first phase of construction was laid on October 31, 1914, and the building occupied on February 12, 1916. Built from pressed brick at a combined cost of $130,000 for building and land, the building was situated near the Lackawanna Railroad Station. Edward S. Perry was postmaster at the time.

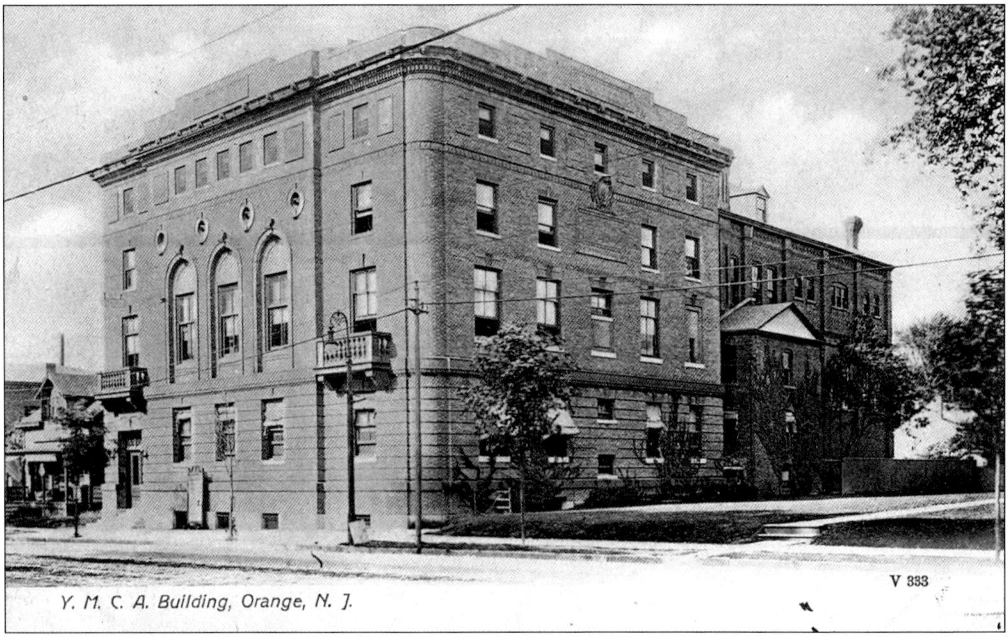

The Orange Young Men's Christian Association originated from an 1885 revival meeting when the noted evangelist Rev. Dwight L. Moody suggested the need for such an organization. On December 12, 1885, rooms were opened in a two-story frame house adjoining the North Orange Baptist Church. A total of $25,000 was subscribed for the erection of a permanent home on the north side of Main Street, and the building was dedicated on January 11, 1887.

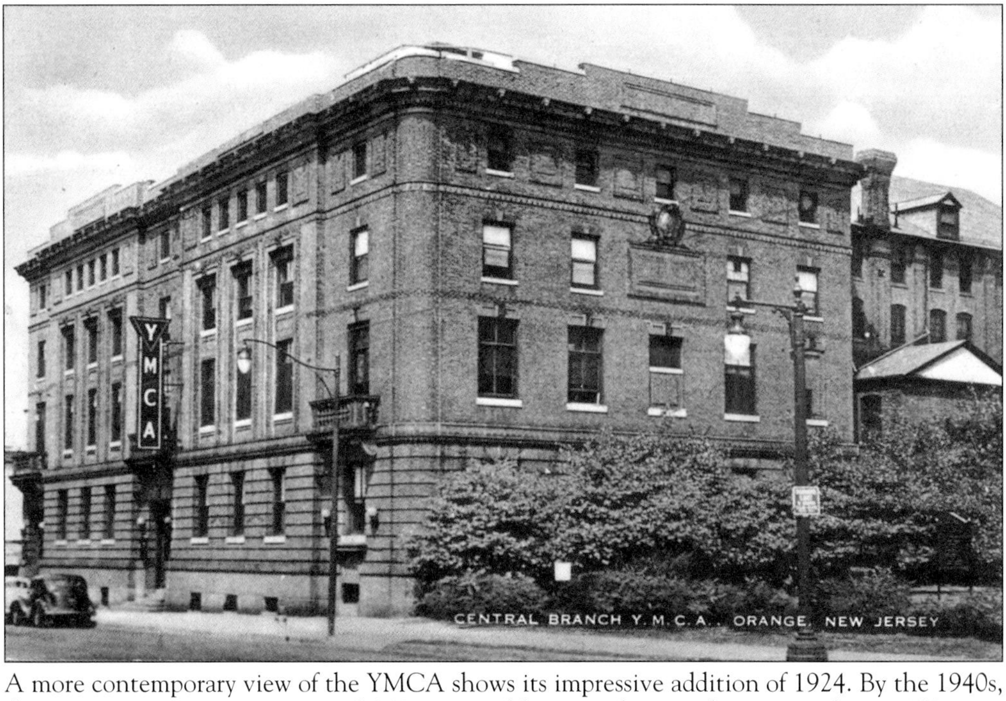

A more contemporary view of the YMCA shows its impressive addition of 1924. By the 1940s, the association was serving over 5,000 men and boy members, and accommodating 150 in its residence halls. Sadly, today, the building is abandoned.

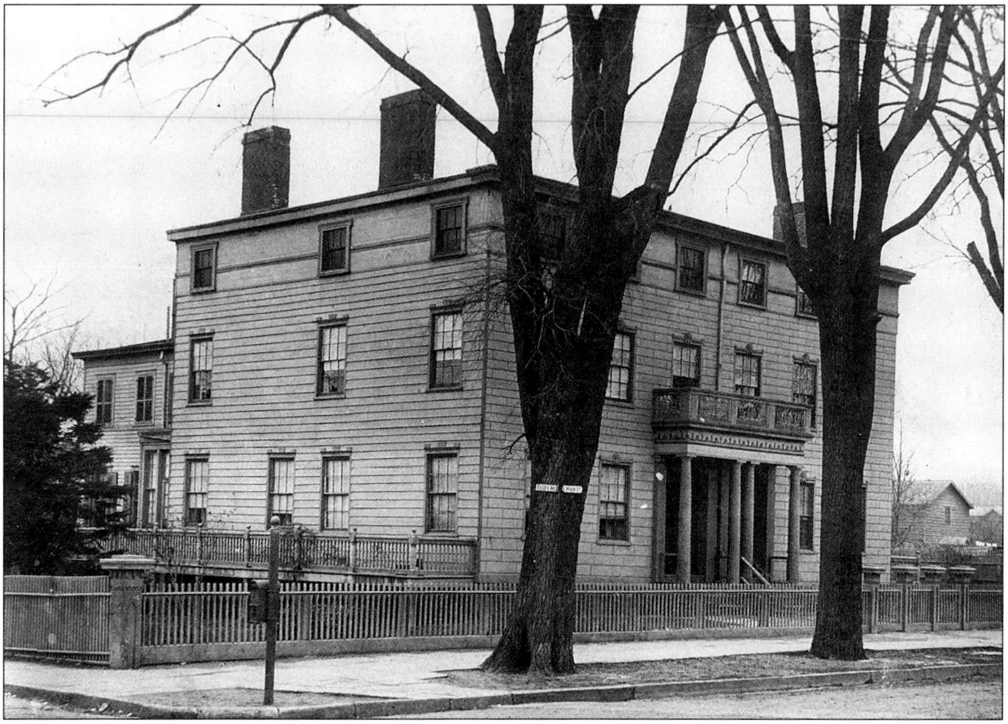

The Orange Free Public Library traces its roots to Sarah Martin, who assembled 169 volumes in a reading room at Central Hall, Main Street on December 7, 1883. On December 30, 1884, a charter was obtained, and Miss Martin became its first president. In 1891, the organization occupied the Bailey House on the southwest corner of Essex Avenue and Main Street. (Photo Courtesy of the First Presbyterian Church.)

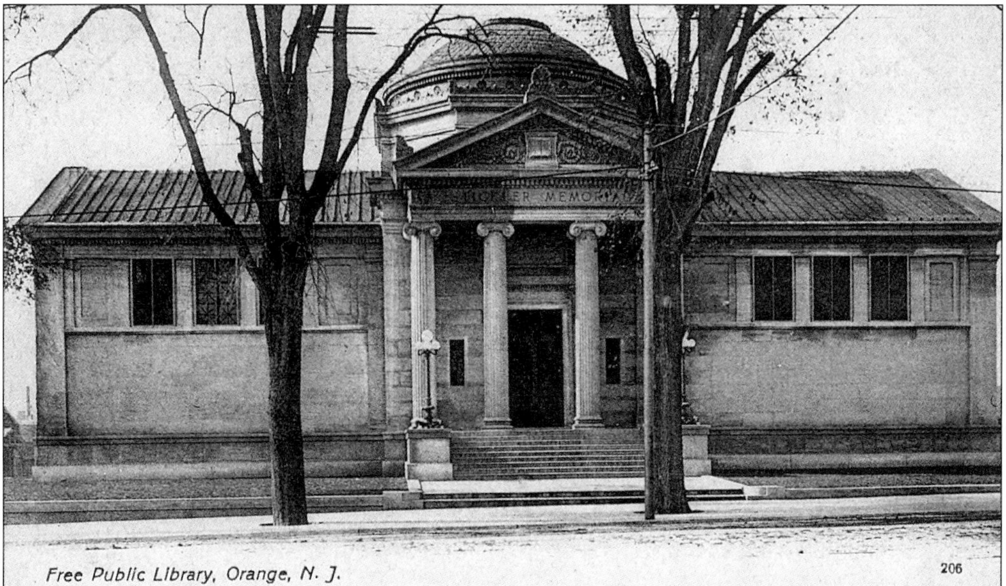

When the time came to construct a modern library, the Bailey house was razed and the new Orange Public Library was built at the same location.

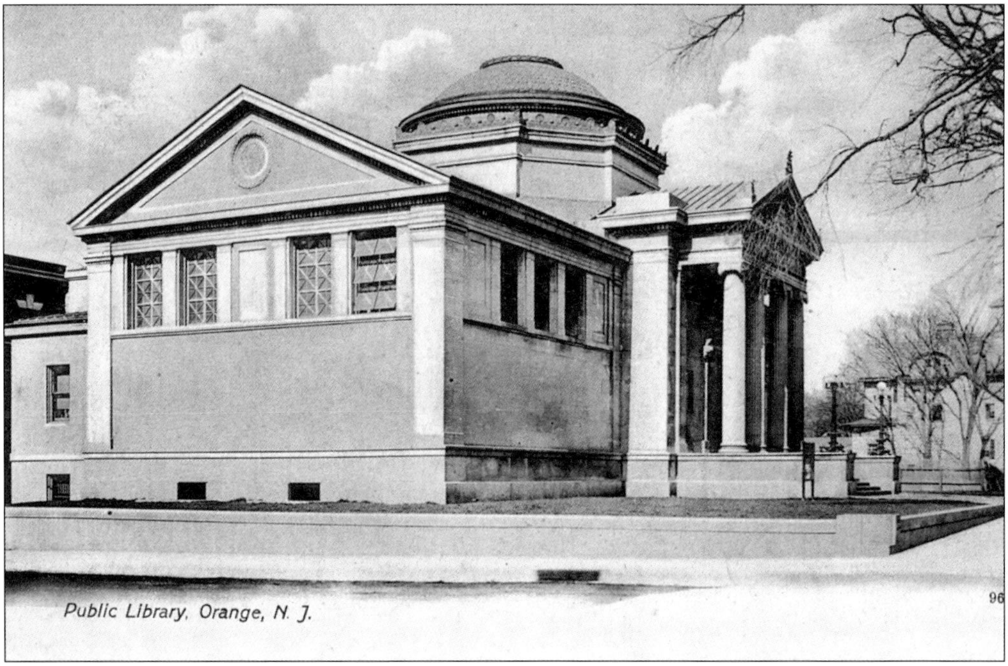

By the time this picture was taken, the Orange Public Library had been completed in classic Greek design with Indiana limestone at a cost of over $100,000. The building was a gift of Mr. and Mrs. Joseph Whipple Stickler, as a memorial to their son, Dr. Joseph W. Stickler. The announced capacity was 50,000 volumes.

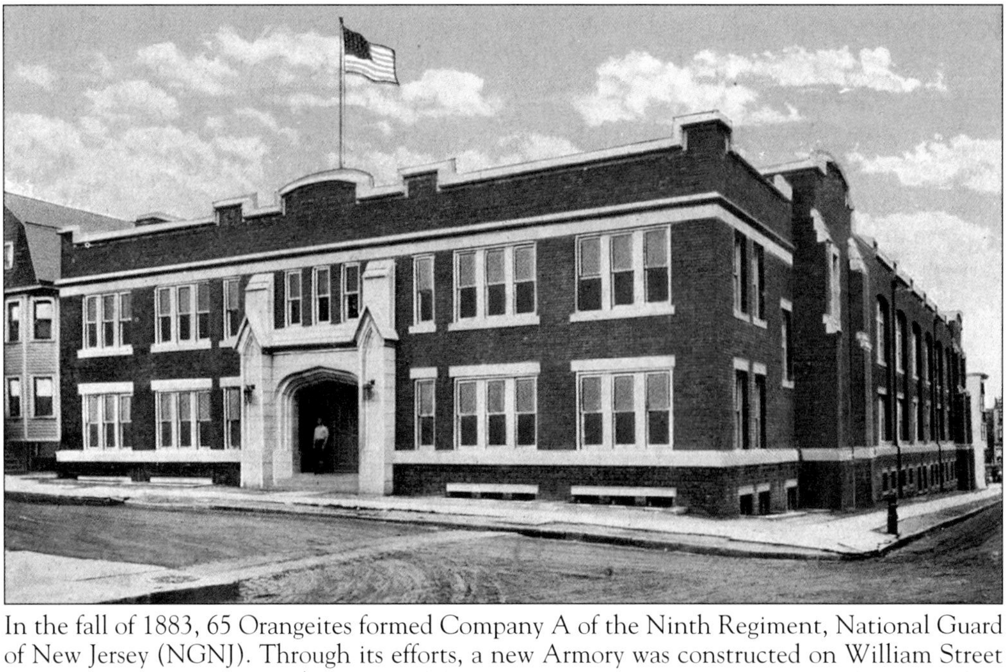

In the fall of 1883, 65 Orangeites formed Company A of the Ninth Regiment, National Guard of New Jersey (NGNJ). Through its efforts, a new Armory was constructed on William Street at North Center at a cost of $25,000 and dedicated January 29, 1888. Its large drill area made it popular with local clubs and societies for social activities. Elementary school graduations were often held here. The Company eventually was merged into the Second Regiment, NGNJ.

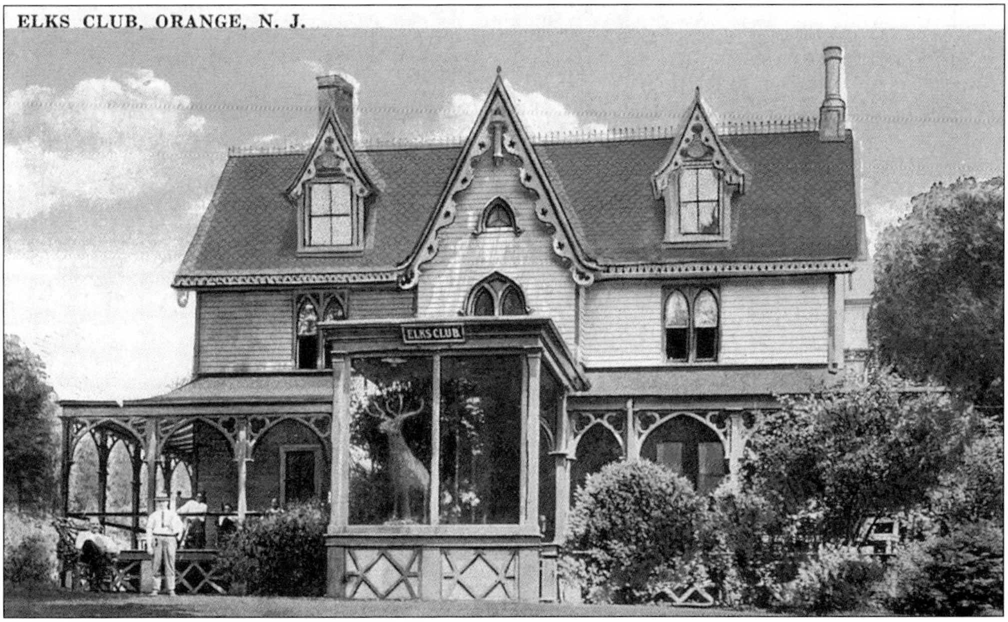

The Orange Lodge No. 132 of the Benevolent and Protective Order of Elks was chartered in August 1889, and originally encompassed the Oranges, Bloomfield, and Montclair. Its first headquarters were located in the Post Building at Main and Washington Streets, East Orange. Eventually, as further lodges split off, the Orange group moved in 1907 into this handsome 1852 Victorian structure on Main Street between Ridge Street and Manor Terrace.

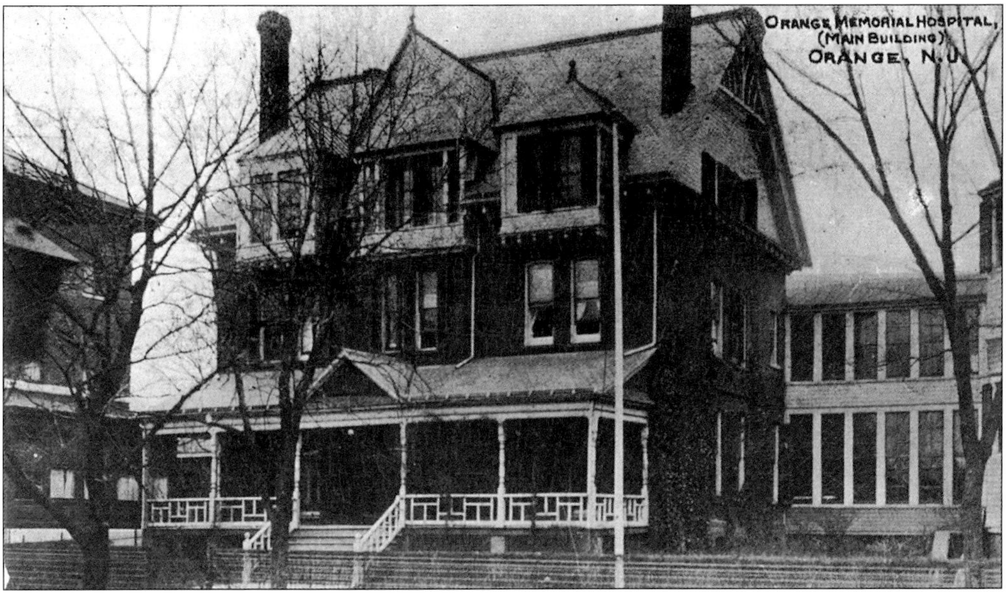

Dr. William Pierson and John G. Vose were the driving forces behind the founding of the Orange Memorial Hospital. The hospital was incorporated on March 4, 1873, initially operating out of an unused firehouse on Lincoln Avenue near the railroad. Joseph W. Stickler donated property on Essex Avenue near Henry Street. Additional land on the corner of Henry was secured by 1881, and on June 27 of that year, ground was broken for this $31,000 facility which was dedicated on May 25, 1882.

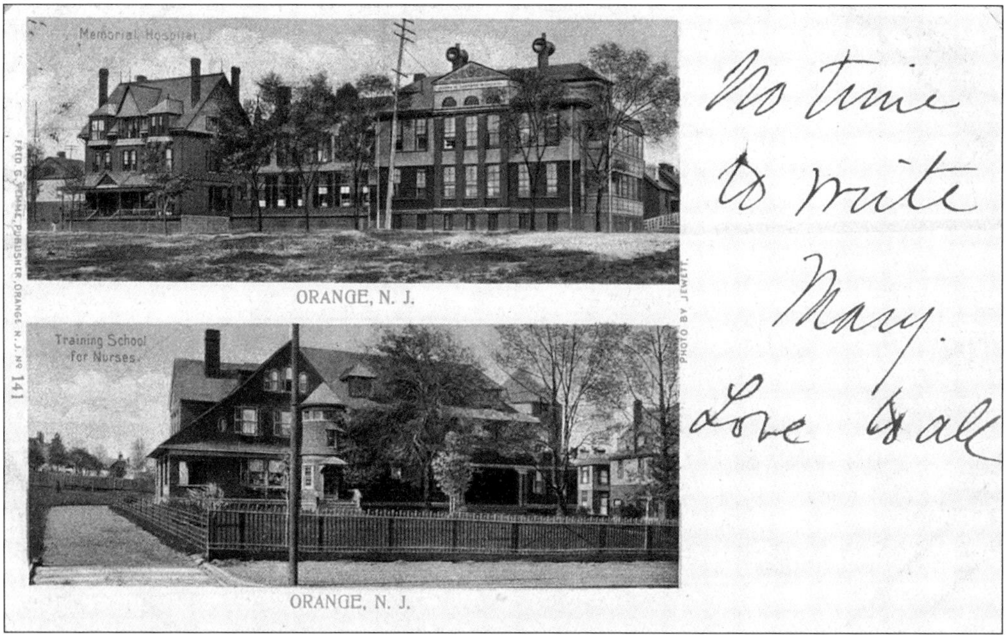

This unusual "split" card shows two views. The top is a 1904 view of the Memorial Hospital complex, with the original building at the left. The Training School for Nurses, located on Henry Street, is at the bottom.

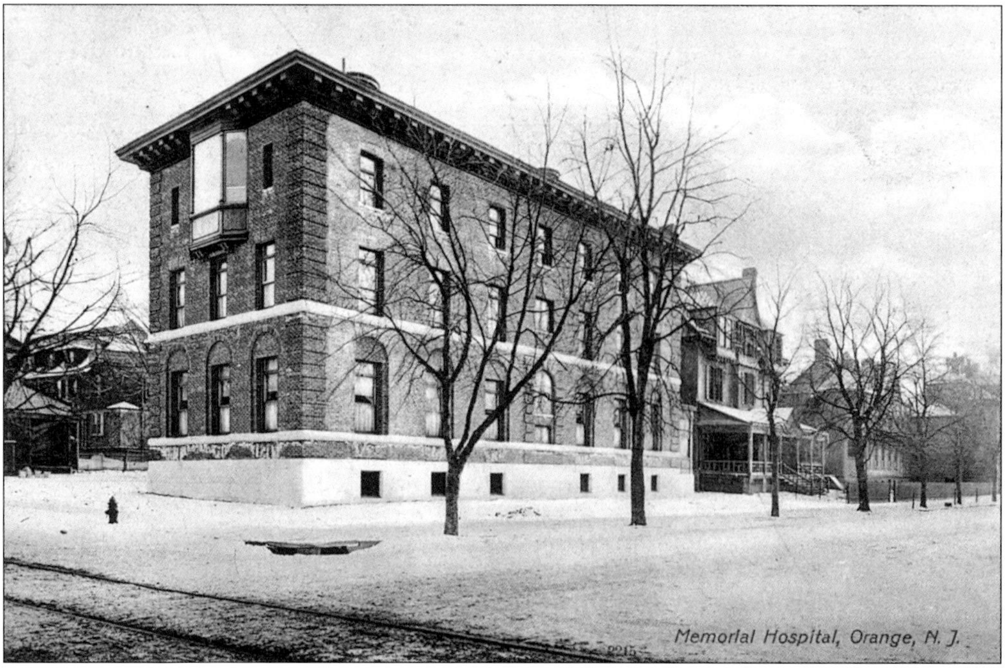

The North Building, viewed in this snowy winter scene from 1907, is located at the corner of Henry Street and Essex Avenue. The original Queen Anne–style hospital building is directly adjacent to the right, and the nursing school is just visible to the left. The trolley tracks in the foreground belong to the Crosstown Line.

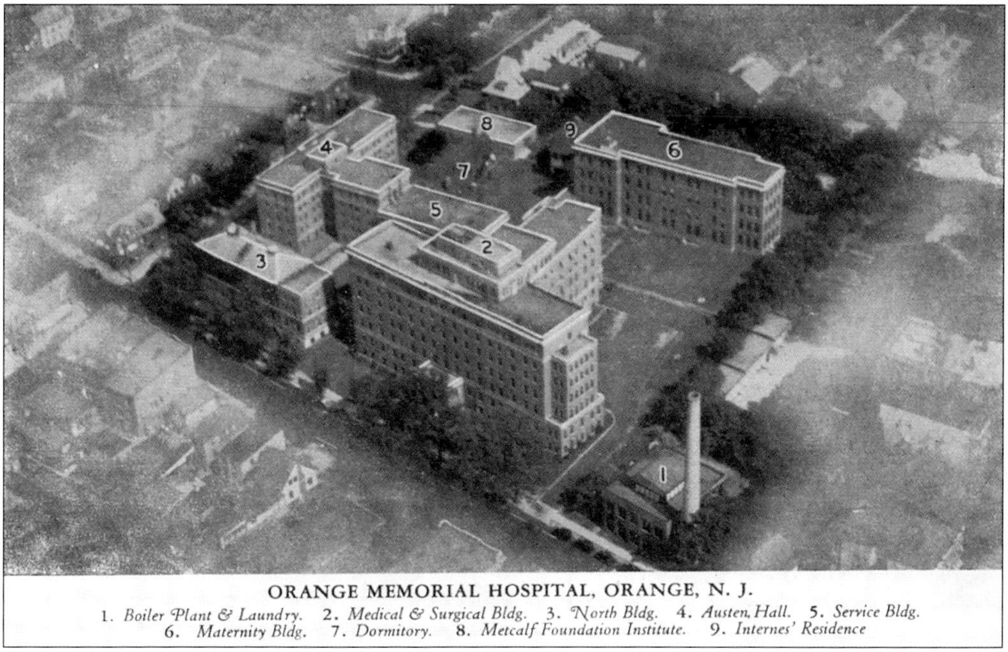

The only visible link to the past in this *c.* 1945 aerial view of the Memorial Hospital Complex is the North Building (number three). With a minor addition, it still sits nobly at the corner of Essex Avenue and Henry Street.

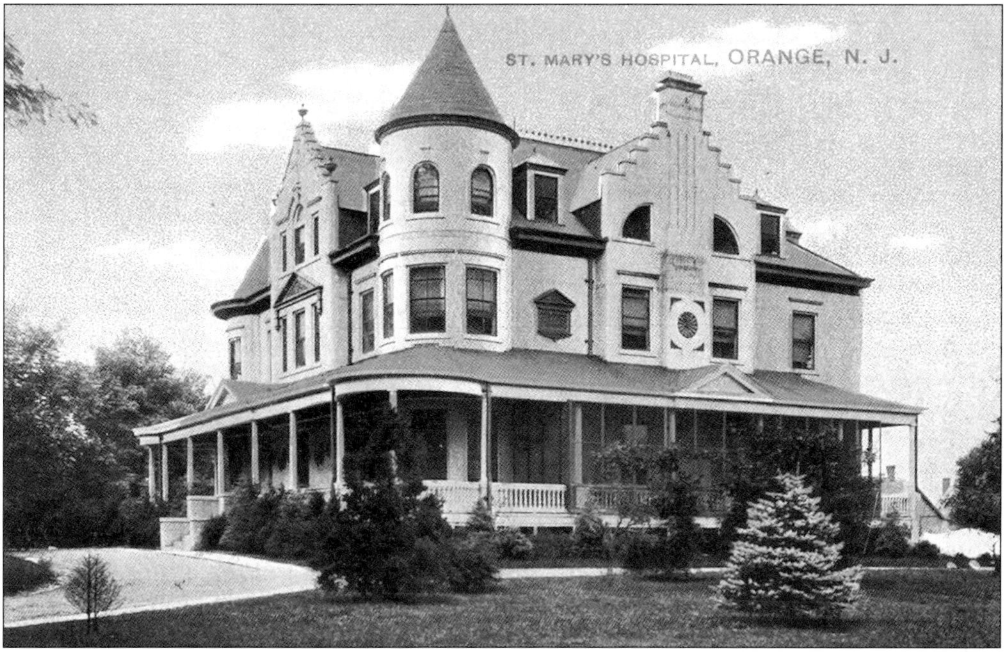

Rev. Victor Romanelli, pastor of Our Lady of Mount Carmel, founded St. Mary's Hospital in 1904, intending it primarily for parish use. The handsome mansion of Michael Winters on South Center Street was purchased and renovated. Community interest was so high, however, that the hospital was opened for general use and the operation of it turned over to the Sisters of Saint Francisco.

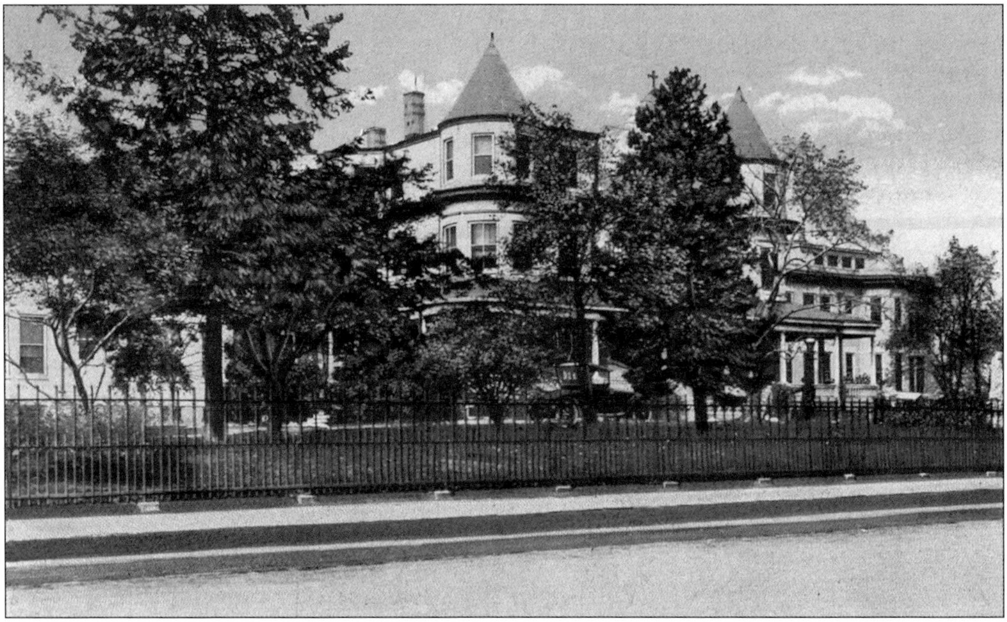

Taxed to capacity, St. Mary's solicited expansion plans in 1911, and the design was awarded to Hobart A. Walker of East Orange. He strategically placed large wings on either end of the original building, providing a total of 125 beds, 4 operating rooms, large solariums, and an elevator. A chapel was added near the main entrance.

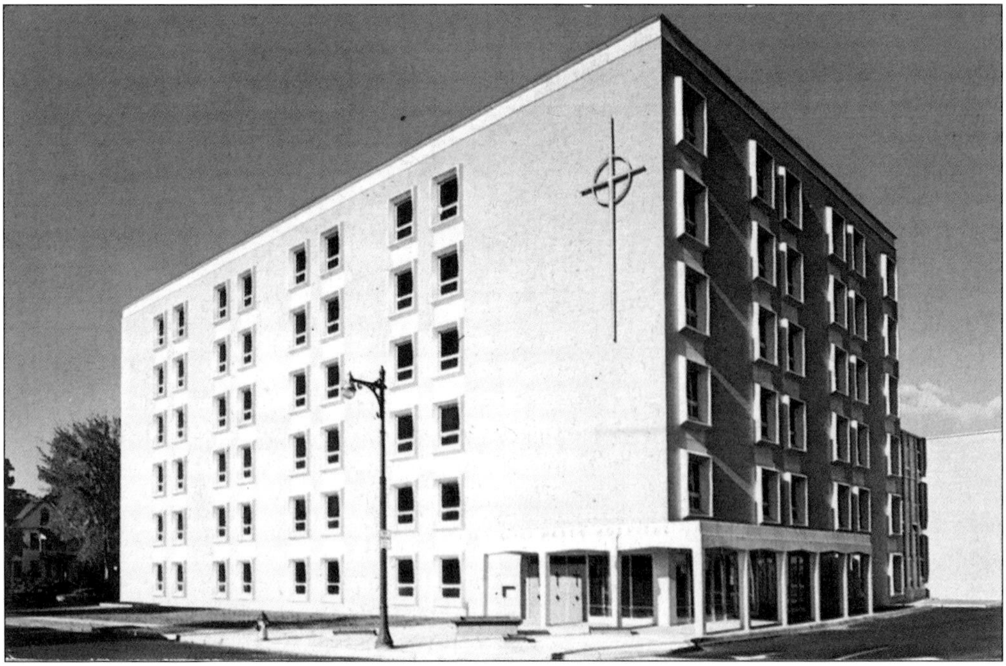

St. Mary's ultimately reached its apex with the construction of this six-story addition on the corner of South Center and Henry Streets in 1966. The hospital came under the management of Cathedral Healthcare in the 1980s, but was closed and converted to a long-term care facility in 1989 as part of Cathedral's economic downsizing.

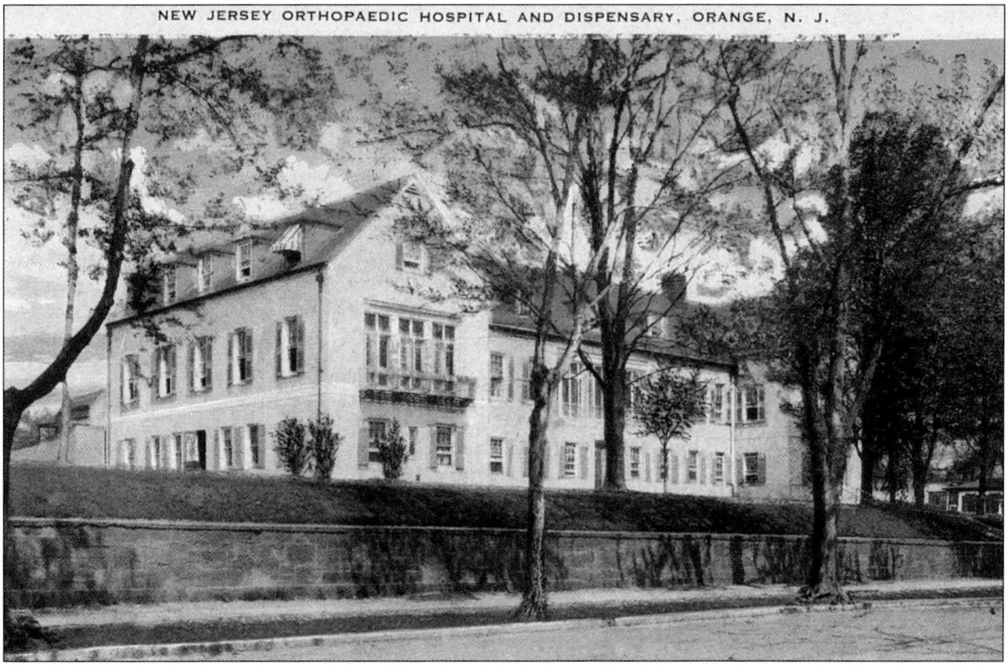

Dr. Russell A. Hibbs founded the New Jersey Orthopedic Hospital on October 3, 1903, at the Visiting Nurses' Settlement at 24 Valley Street. Incorporation occurred on December 17. In May 1904, the hospital moved to a house at 148 Scotland Street, and when that facility became outmoded, property at 141 Lincoln Avenue was purchased in February 1915. By 1917, $150,000 had been raised for the construction of a dispensary and main building.

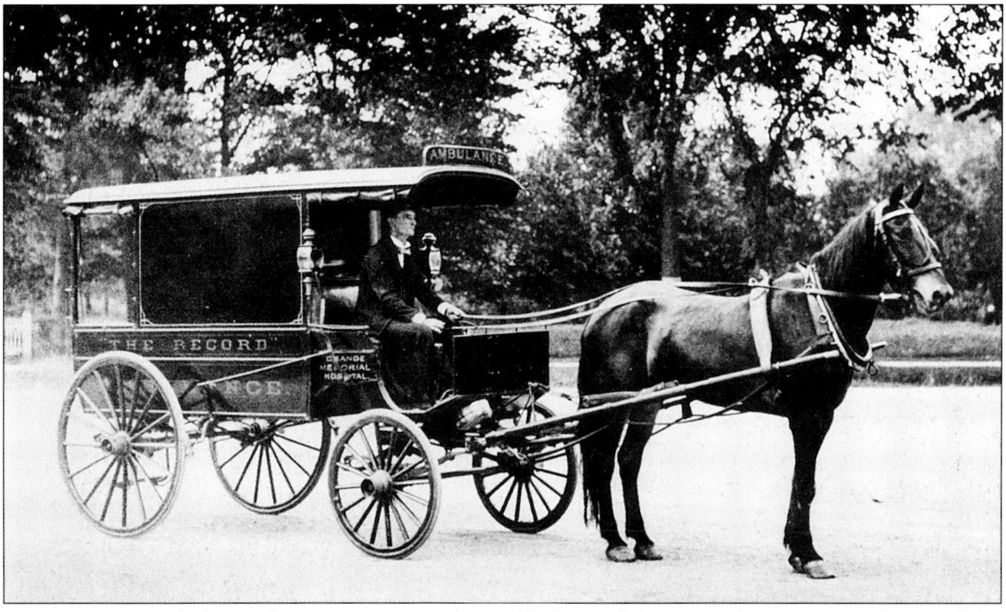

The Record Ambulance began in 1888. The publishers of the *Record* newspaper clamored for such a conveyance and raised $550 for it by seeking subscriptions and running concerts and theatrical productions. The first ambulance was stored in Colt's Express stable on Day Street, and the horse rented from that company. (Photo Courtesy Orange Fire Department.)

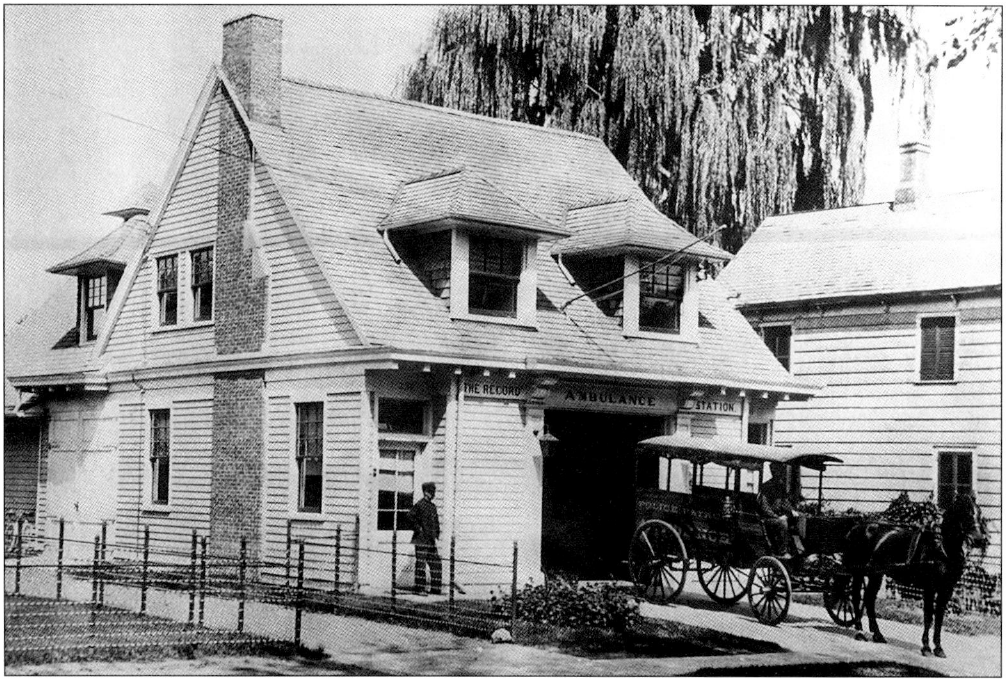

The ambulance moved into its permanent home on South Essex Avenue opposite Orange Memorial Hospital on November 26, 1904. The ambulance shown in this photograph actually belongs to the Orange Police Department. (Photo Courtesy Orange Fire Department.)

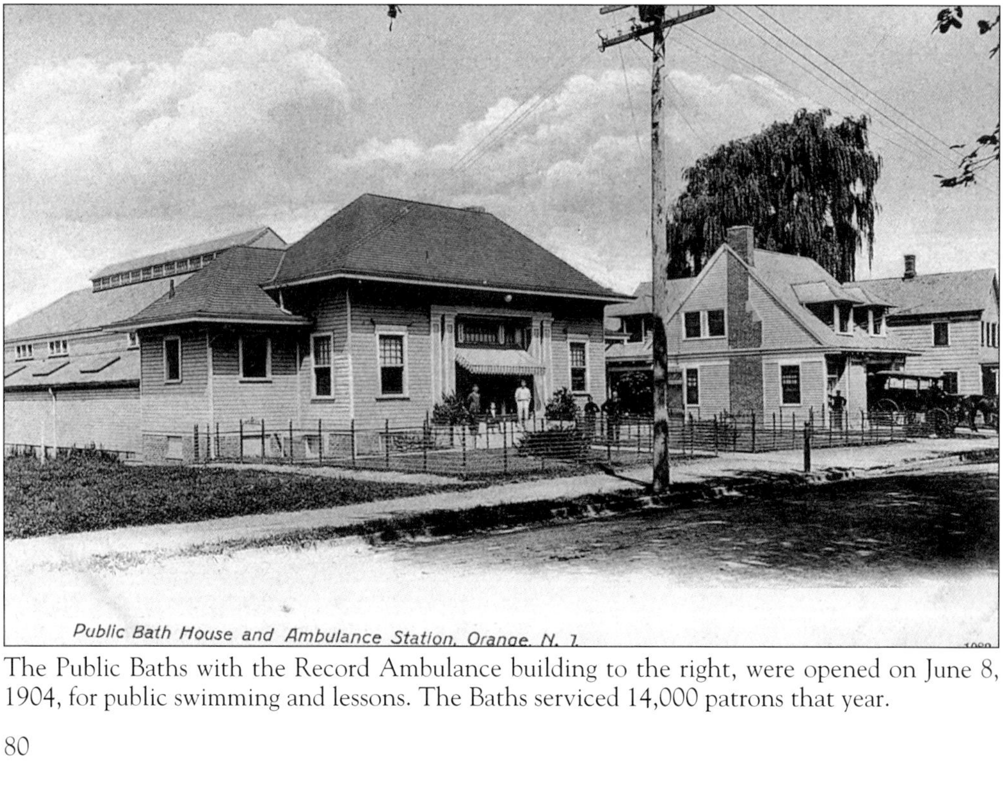

The Public Baths with the Record Ambulance building to the right, were opened on June 8, 1904, for public swimming and lessons. The Baths serviced 14,000 patrons that year.

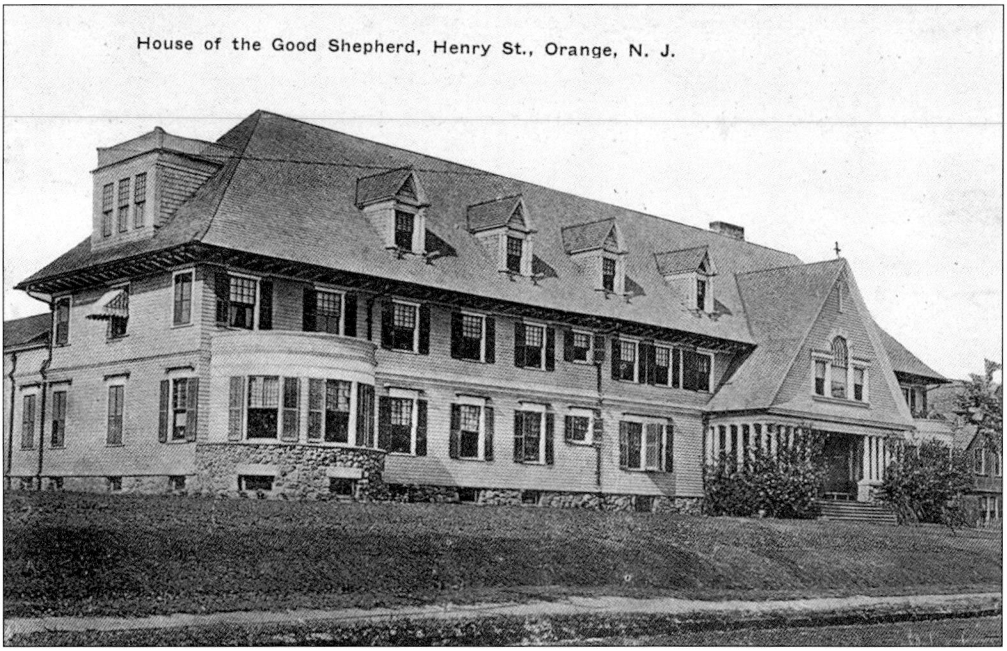

The House of the Good Shepherd was dedicated to the care of elderly and infirm women, and can properly be called Orange's first nursing home. It was founded in 1892 under the auspices of four local parishes (St. Mark's, West Orange; Grace, Orange; Holy Communion, South Orange; and Christ, East Orange), which purchased a lot on Henry Street, near Cone, for $4,000 in 1891. An additional $12,000 was paid for the construction of this frame building.

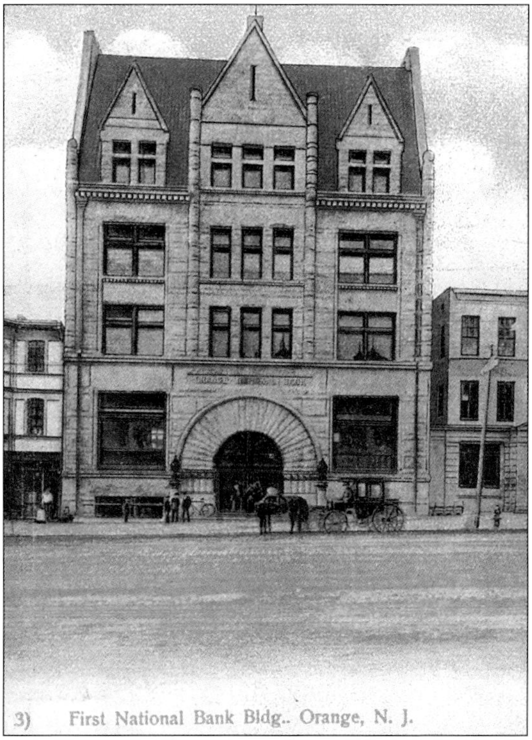

The Orange (First) National Bank was first incorporated on February 26, 1826. It opened for business on August 1, 1828, in the home of Ephraim Perry on Main Street by the Military Common. A more central site on the south side of Main near Cone Street was purchased in March 1829 for $300. A 60-by-100-foot brick structure was erected at a cost of $4,184.42. This handsome structure replaced it on February 23, 1892, at a cost of $100,000. It was constructed of Indiana limestone, and boasted the first elevator in Orange.

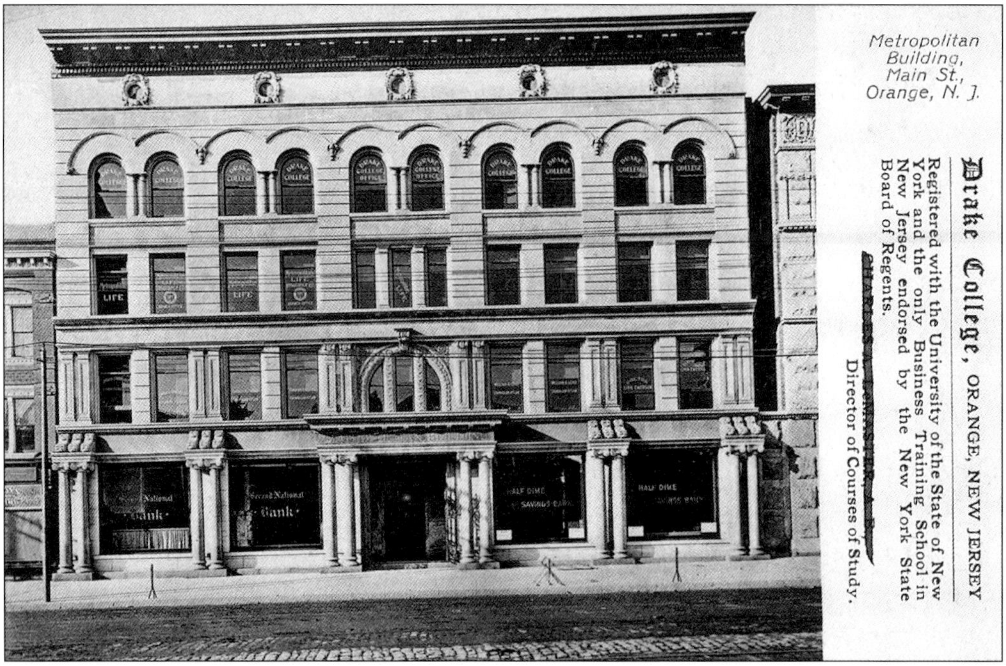

The Second National Bank (first floor left) and the Half Dime Savings Bank (first floor right), competed in the Metropolitan Building. The Second National was incorporated in January 1892, and first had offices in the Lindsley Building on Main Street before moving here on June 20, 1904, just after the building's completion. The Half-Dime dated to April 11, 1870. Other tenants, beside the namesake life insurance company included Drake Business College, Dr. Linn Emerson, and William A. Lord, Counselor-At-Law.

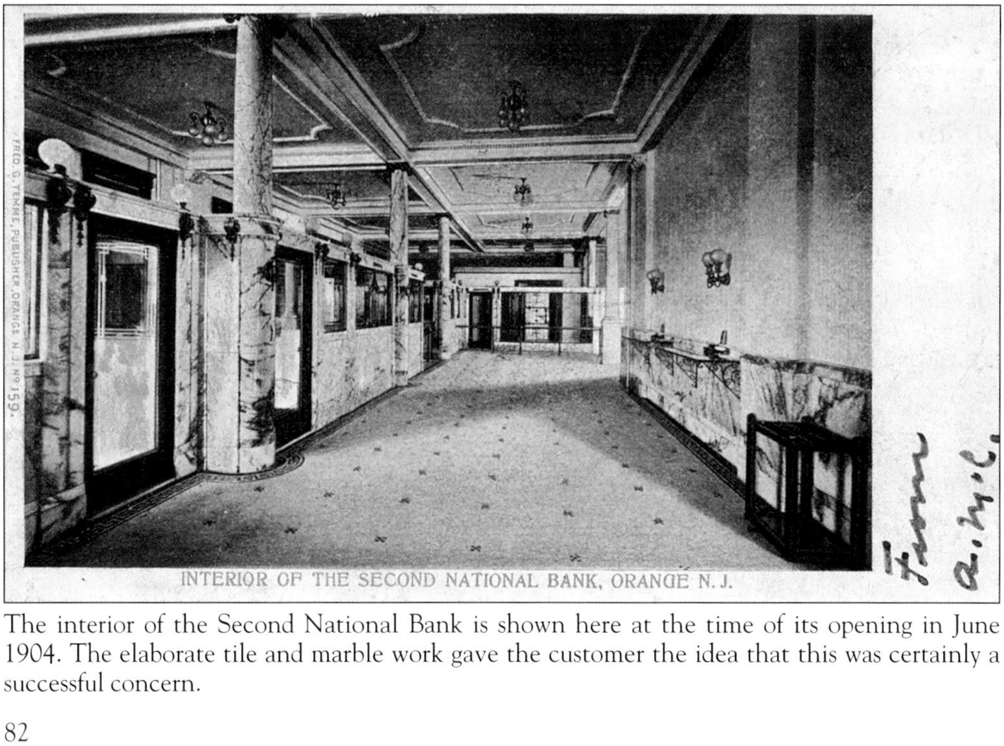

The interior of the Second National Bank is shown here at the time of its opening in June 1904. The elaborate tile and marble work gave the customer the idea that this was certainly a successful concern.

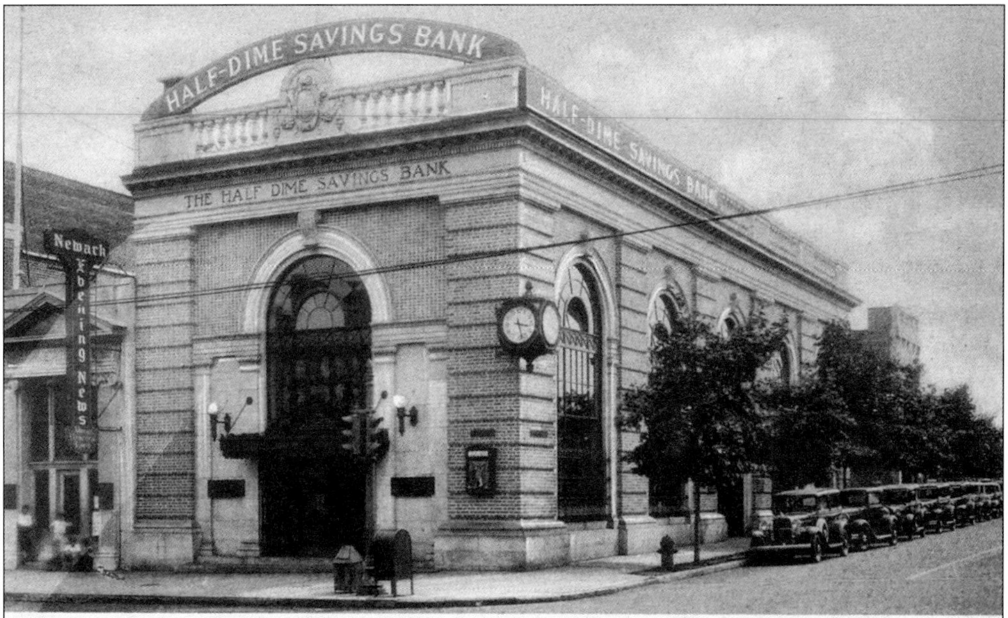

THE HALF-DIME SAVINGS BANK, 356-358 MAIN STREET, COR, LACKAWANNA PLAZA, ORANGE, N. J.

The Half-Dime Savings Bank ultimately moved to its own impressive facility on the corner of Main Street and Lackawanna Plaza. The building to its left houses the local office of the Newark "Evening News," so the photo dates to the 1930s. It is 3:30 p.m. and, no doubt, the bank is closed for the day.

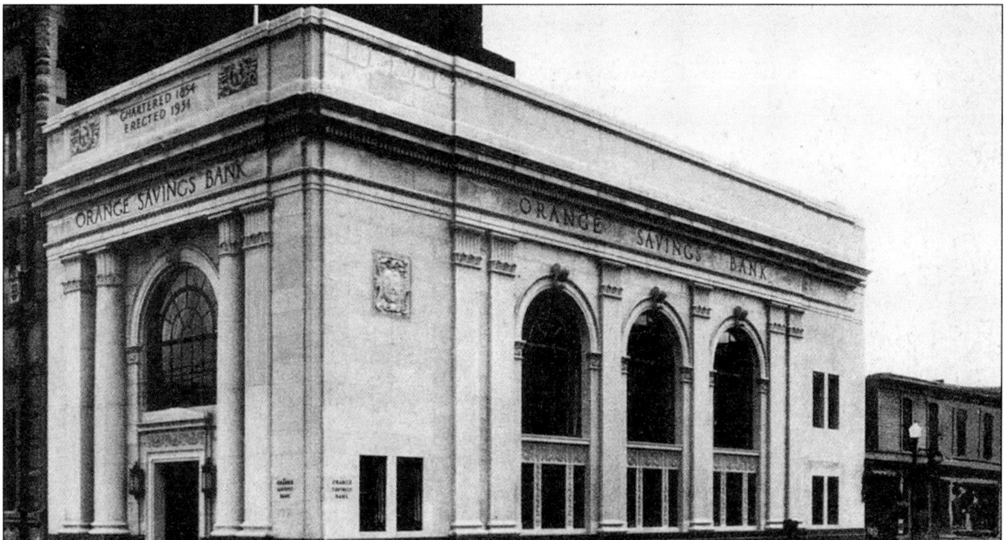

ORANGE SAVINGS BANK, MAIN AND SOUTH DAY STREETS, ORANGE, N. J.

The Orange Savings Bank, second oldest in the city, was chartered on April 10, 1854, and occupied the location at the corner of Main and Cone (later South Day) Streets. This handsome building was constructed of Indiana limestone in 1931, not a great era for banking.

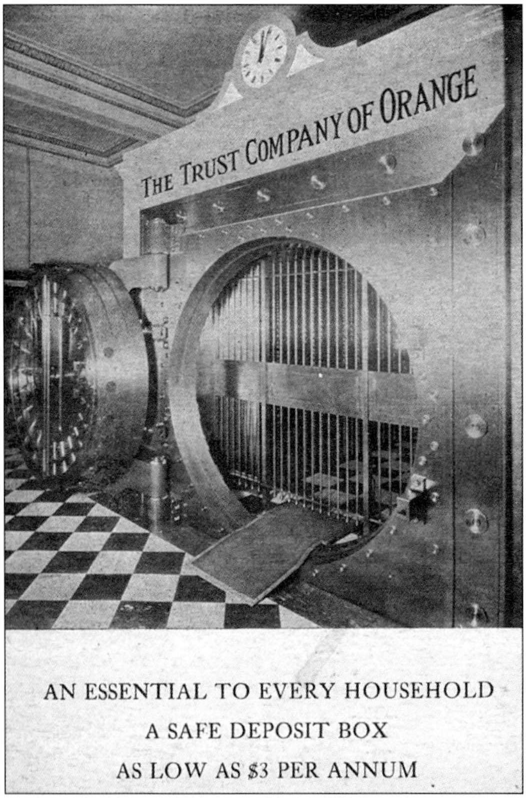

If the sight of this vault at The Trust Company of Orange on Main Street did not inspire confidence, nothing would! The company was located in the Orange National Bank Building.

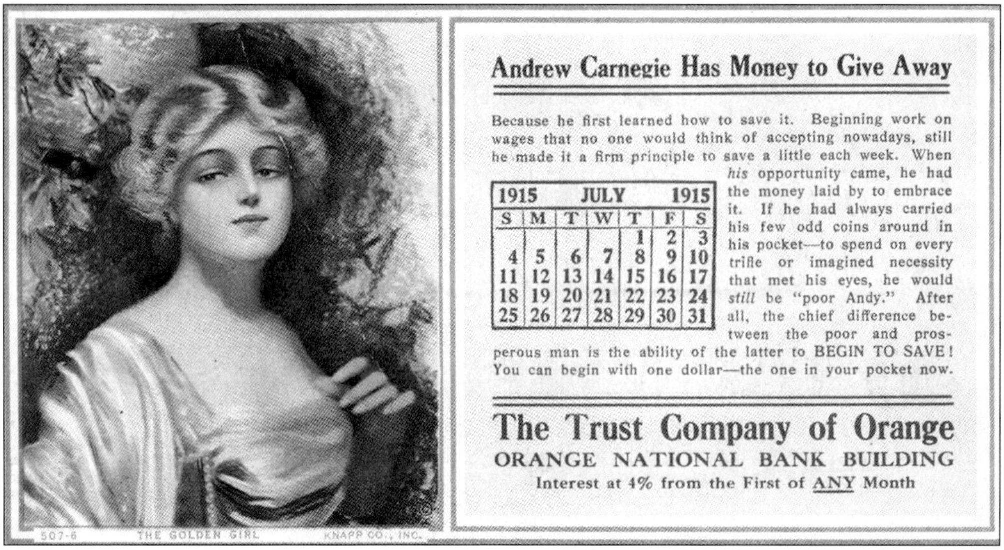

This July 1915 advertising blotter from the Trust Company of Orange admonished the reader to save for the day they would be rich like Andrew Carnegie. Four percent interest was not bad for that era!

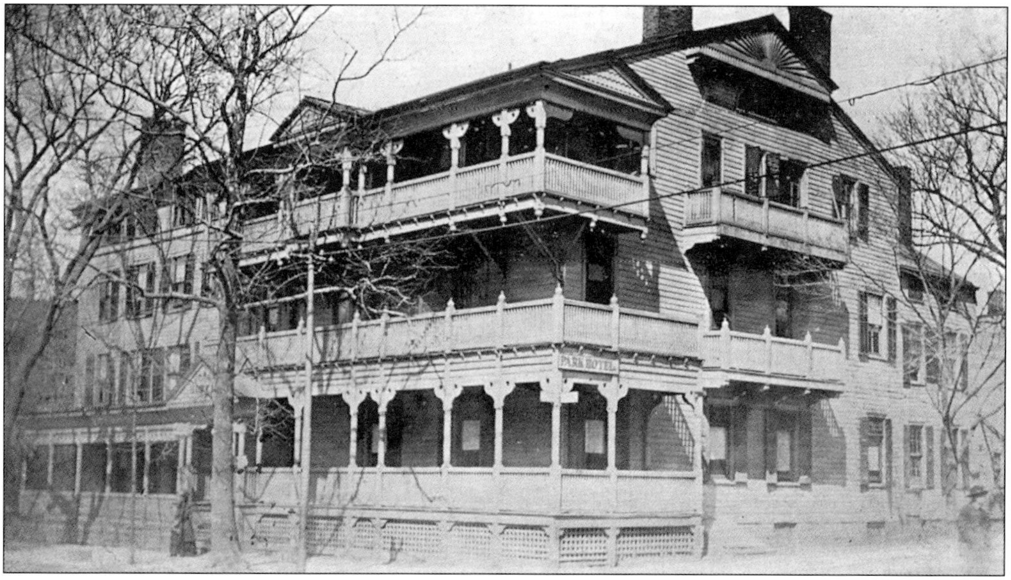

In the nineteenth century, several hotels catered to the needs of the traveling public in Orange, which was on the main road from Newark to Morristown and Dover, NJ, and Easton, PA. The Park Hotel, shown here, was located at the corner of Main and Park Streets. It could trace its roots as a hostelry back to 1758, when the Park House was opened by John Munn. For a while it was known as the Kilborn or the Plaza. The hotel closed about 1925.

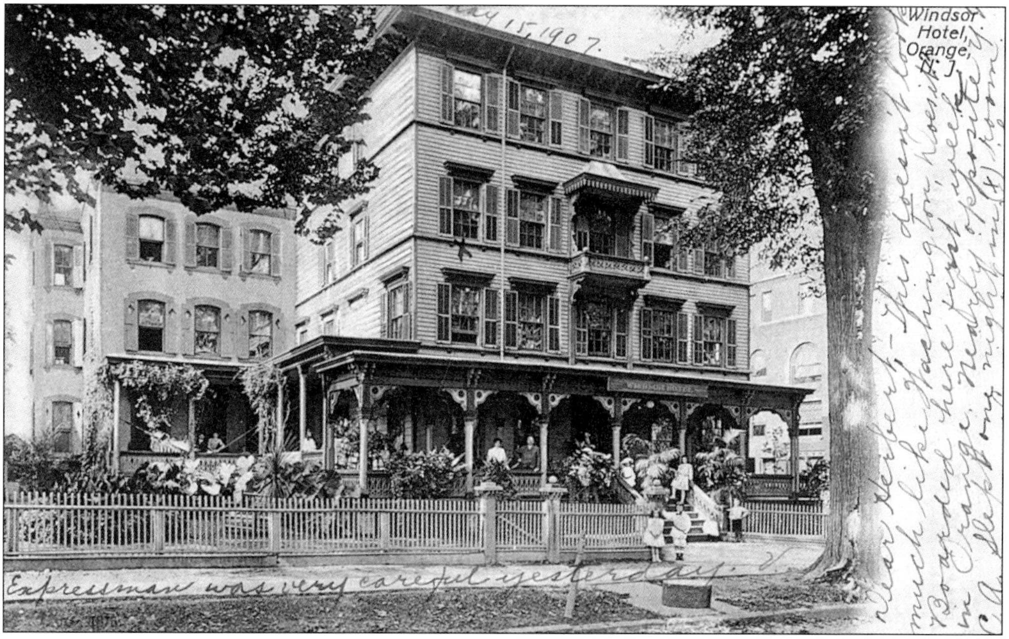

Originally the "Mansion House," the Windsor Hotel on Main Street was run as a boarding house until 1876 and then sold to Roswell Holmes, who added the two wings. The card writer notes, "Dear Herbert. This doesn't look much like Washington, does it? Boarded here first week in Orange. Nearly opposite YMCA. Slept one night (x) room. Lovingly, Viola." Note the window where Viola was accommodated. This postcard dates to about 1907, and the Holmes family sold the operation in 1910.

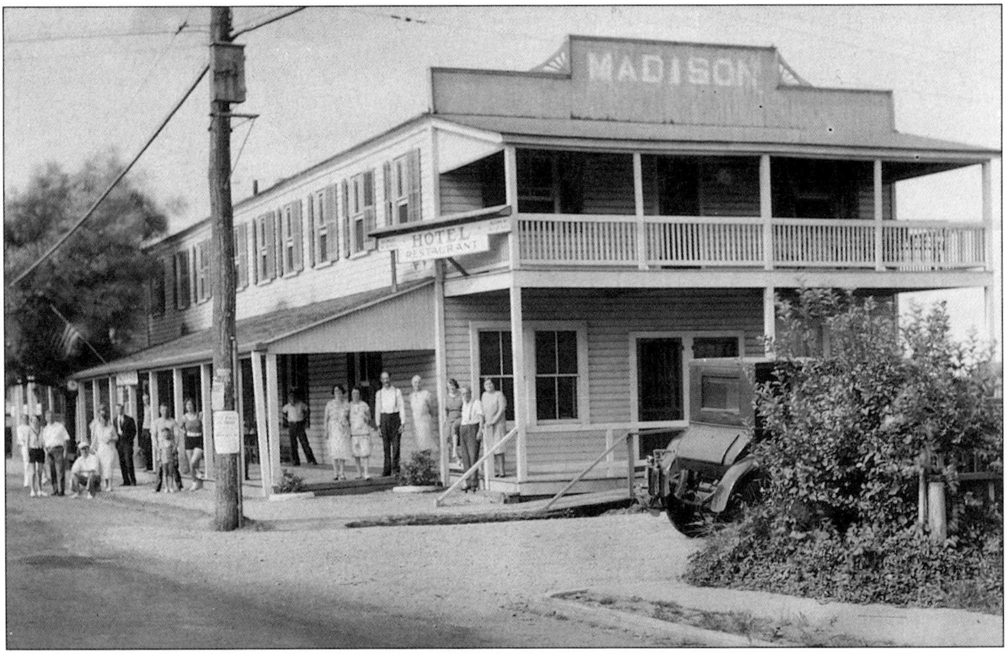

The note on the back of this postcard of the Madison Hotel reads: "Susan and Tom Henry used to run this place in Orange, NJ." Attire of the guests dates the scene around 1930. No one, however, is familiar with this establishment, and we place it here only as a curiosity.

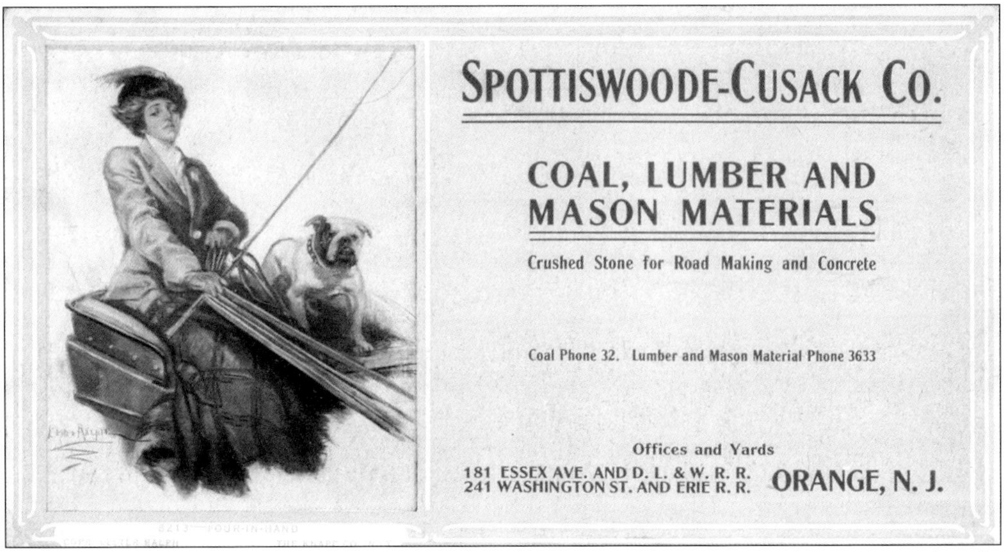

Numerous coal and lumber yards dotted the areas around the Erie and Lackawanna Railroads. Spottiswoode-Cusack was one of the best known, with facilities on both lines to serve the entire town.

Charles Decker was truly a "grocer for the Oranges." He established his first store in 1871, and by 1920, Decker and his brothers had eight stores dotting the Essex County area. The Orange facility was located in his building at 222 Main Street. Artistic advertising cards such as this were the business promotions of their day.

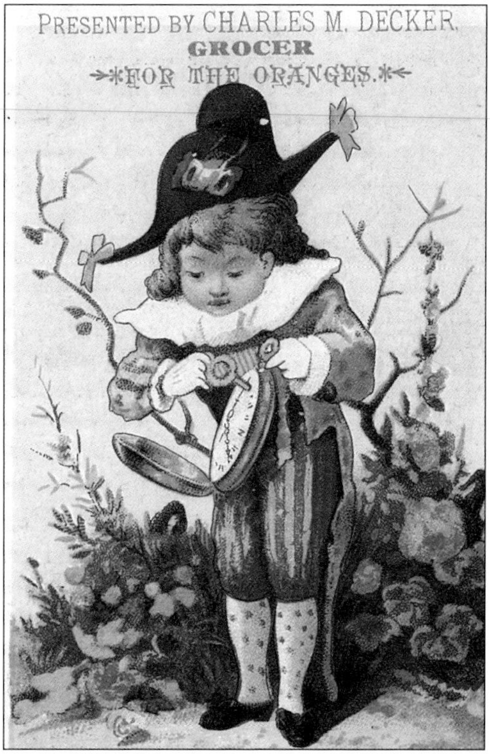

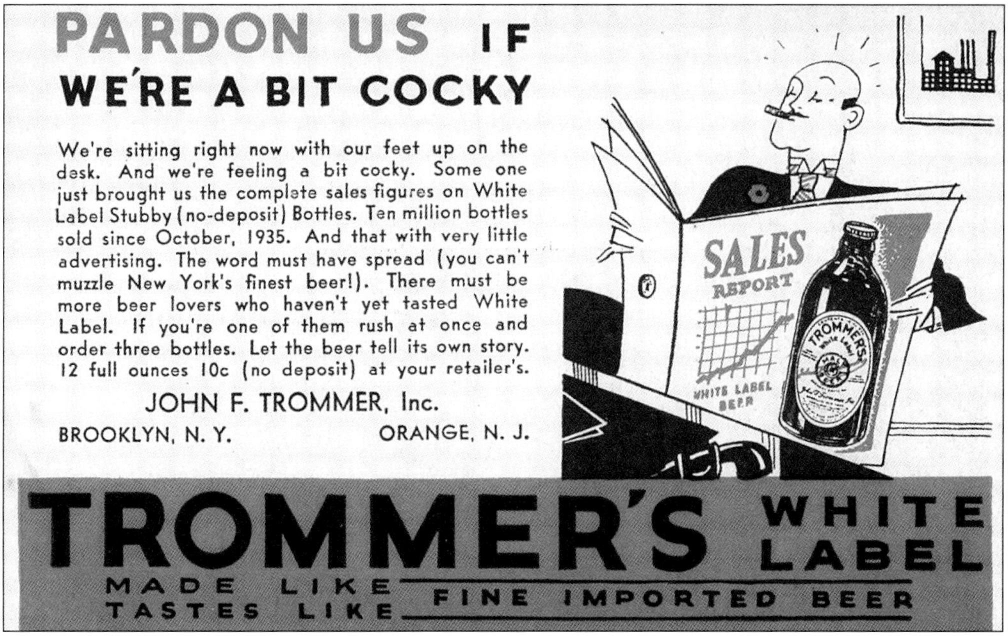

Beer was first brewed in Orange in 1890 by the Winter Brothers of Pittsburgh, Pennsylvania. The Orange Brewing Company built a major plant in 1901 at a cost of $350,000, and sold it to John F. Trommers in 1935. Trommers expanded production, but sold the plant in 1950 to Liebmann Breweries, makers of Rheingold. In 1977, Liebmann was bought by Christian Schmidt and Sons, who permanently closed the plant shortly thereafter.

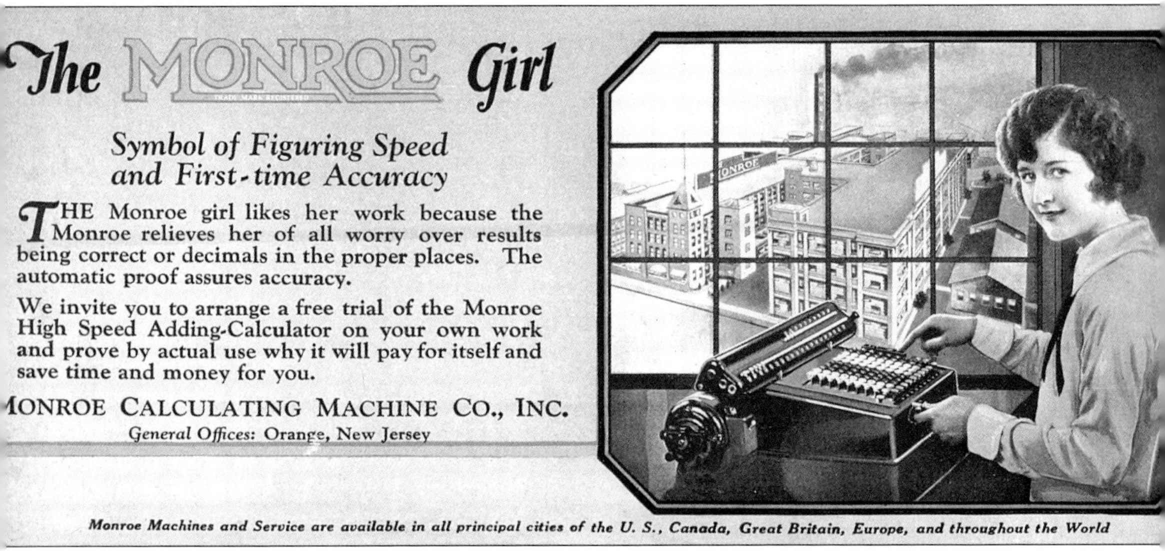

The "Monroe Girl" gazes wistfully from her machine in an office that looks out over the sprawling plant in the Orange Valley. Patented by Frank Baldwin in 1874, the device reached prominence through the business efforts of Jay Randolph Monroe, who organized the company in 1911. The four-story addition to the original facility was completed in 1920.

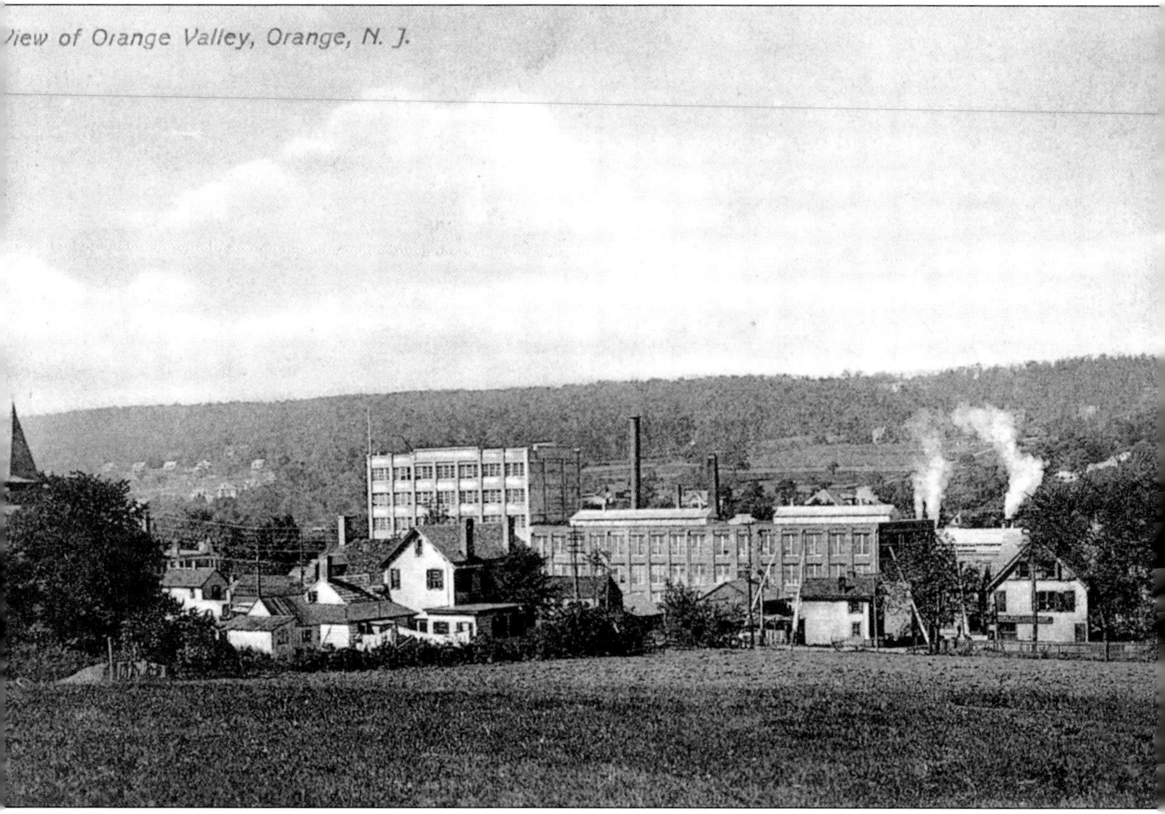

The Orange Valley was the gold buckle of the city's industrial belt. In addition to calculating machines and beer, Orange is probably best known for its hat-making plants. Hat-making traced its roots to the 1790s, but the industry reached its height in the 1870s when 33 different manufacturers were busily at work. Most notable among them were the plants of F. Berg and Company (shown above), and the No Name Hat Co. No Name, located for years at the corner of Mitchell and South Jefferson Streets, had its roots in East Orange around 1820 with the Stephen Stetson Family. In 1882, unable to agree upon a name, Stephen's sons Napoleon and John, and Napoleon's son Henry, called it No Name. John later moved to Philadelphia and began making hats under the well-known family name. By 1920, only five hat-makers remained. The note on the back of this card is of interest. "Went thro' this factory with one of the owners Henry Berg, March 12, 1909."

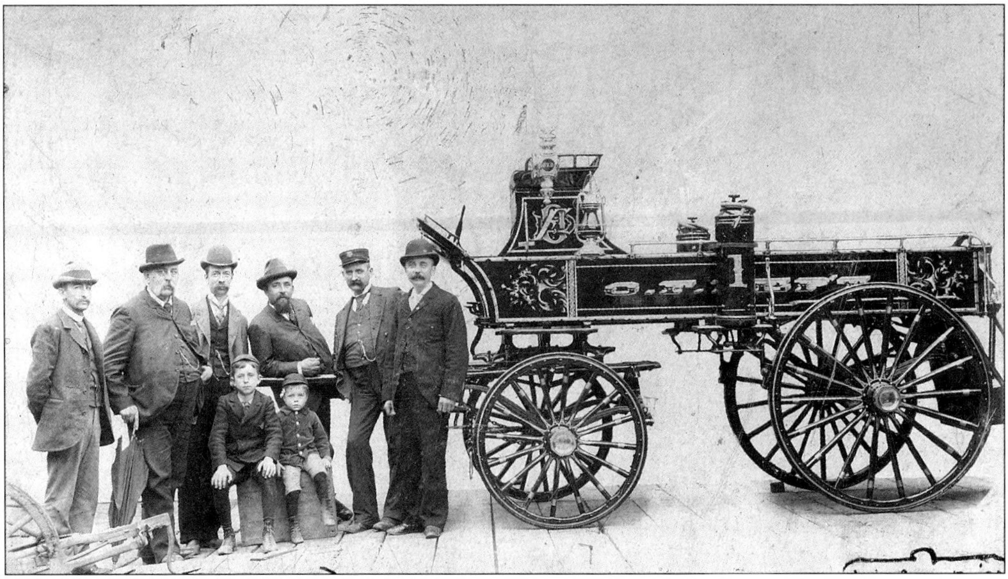

An enthusiastic crew of department members and politicians poses here in 1894 with an early fire wagon of the Orange Fire Department. This was taken just after the unit was overhauled and repainted. The wagon boasts hose canisters instead of the more traditional reels. Chief James W. Hodgkinson is second from the right. (Photo courtesy Orange Fire Department.)

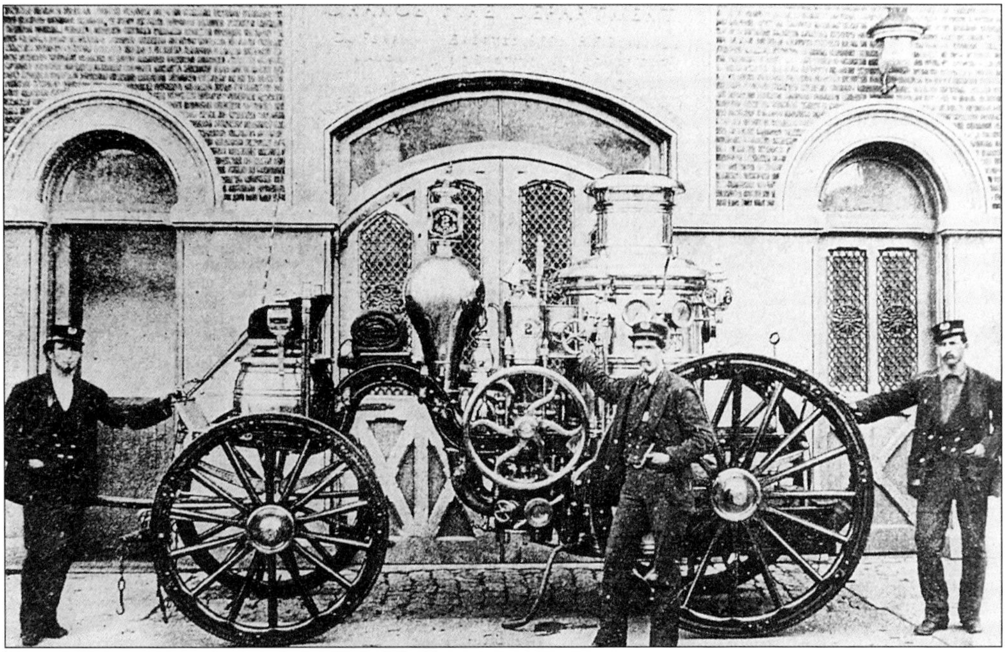

A steam-powered chemical pumper stands in front of the first permanent Fire House on Canfield Street in 1873. The cornerstone for the building was laid on August 2, 1869. Pictured here are, from left to right: August Wilson, Henry Hulenback, and Charles Irmis. (Photo courtesy Orange Fire Department.)

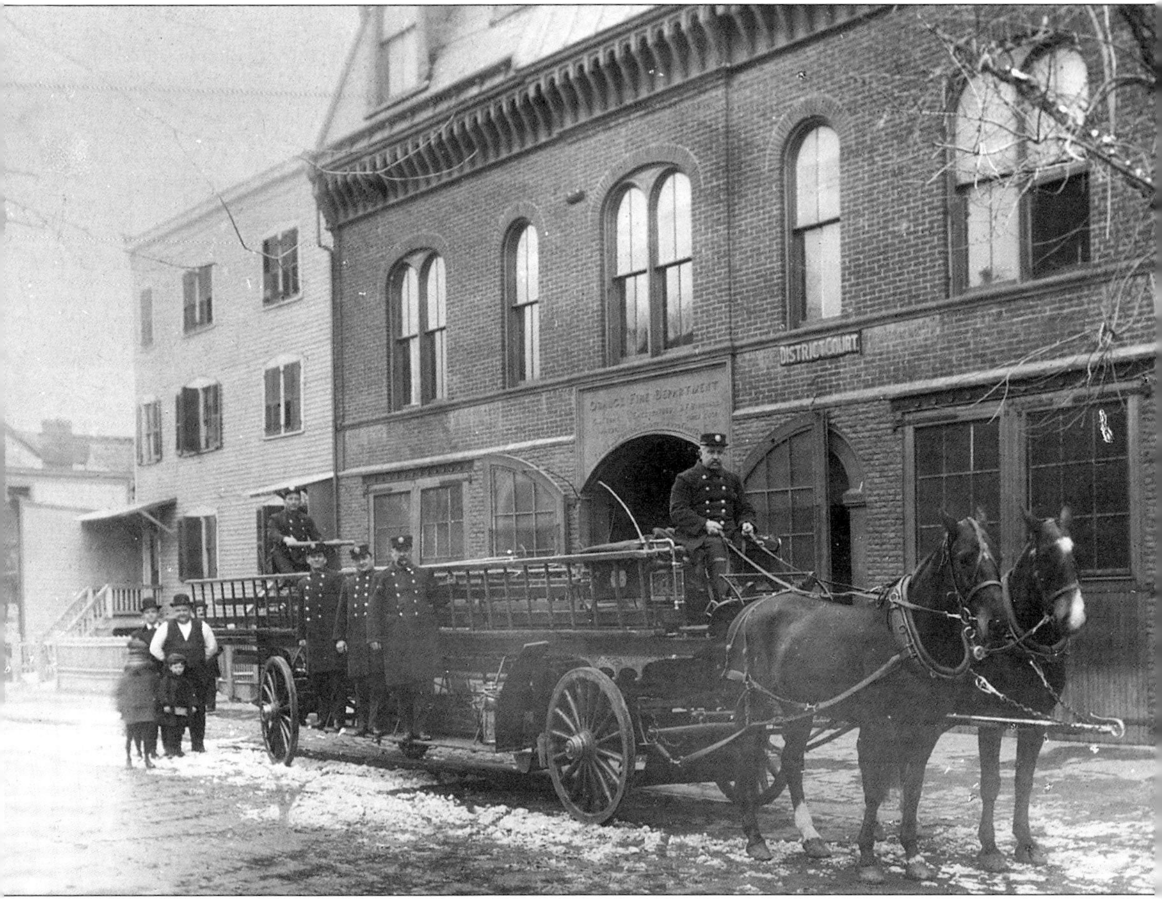

The department went from hand-drawn to horse-drawn in 1873, as this view attests. The department traced its origins to an all volunteer crew in 1857. In 1867, the common council appropriated $1,150 for the first truck, a Dennison. The truck was delivered on April 30 and christened "O'Neill" in honor of a New York City firefighter who resided in Orange. The truck performed so badly that it was returned to the manufacturer and rebuilt in 1869. Beginning in 1887 members were partially paid, and in 1908, a fully paid department was authorized with three houses. The headquarters remained on Canfield Street and additional equipment was located on Forest Street and Washington Street. (Photo courtesy of Orange Fire Department.)

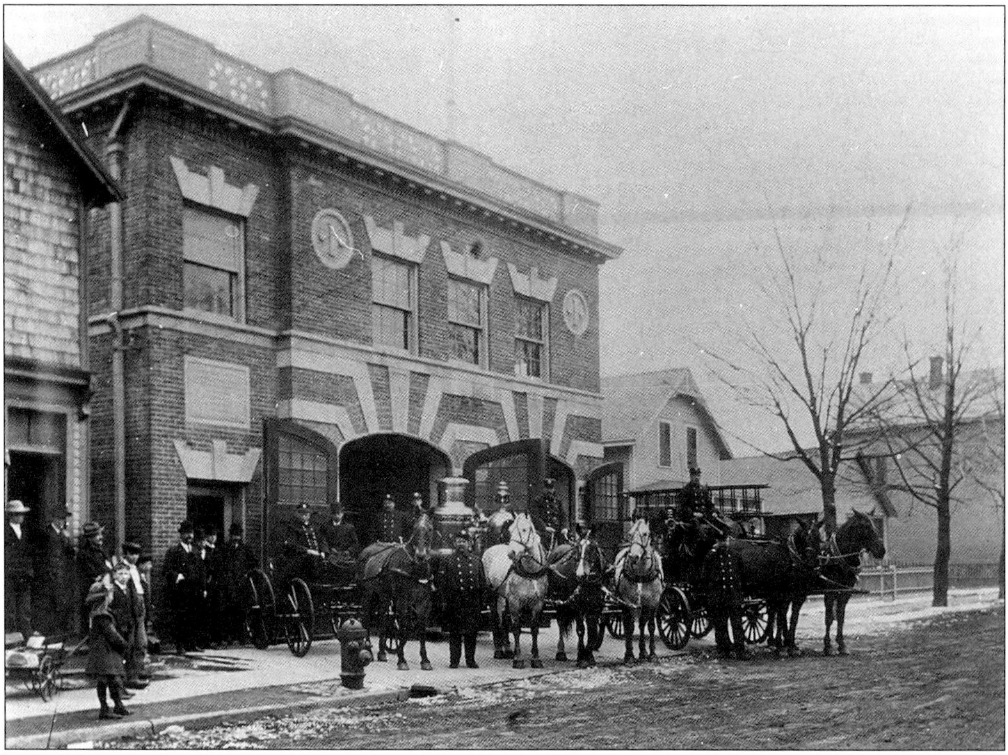

The Forest Street Firehouse was built in 1890 and is still standing, although no longer used for that purpose. Horsepower is still in vogue in this 1905 view as the entire house poses for the photographer. (Photo courtesy Orange Fire Department.)

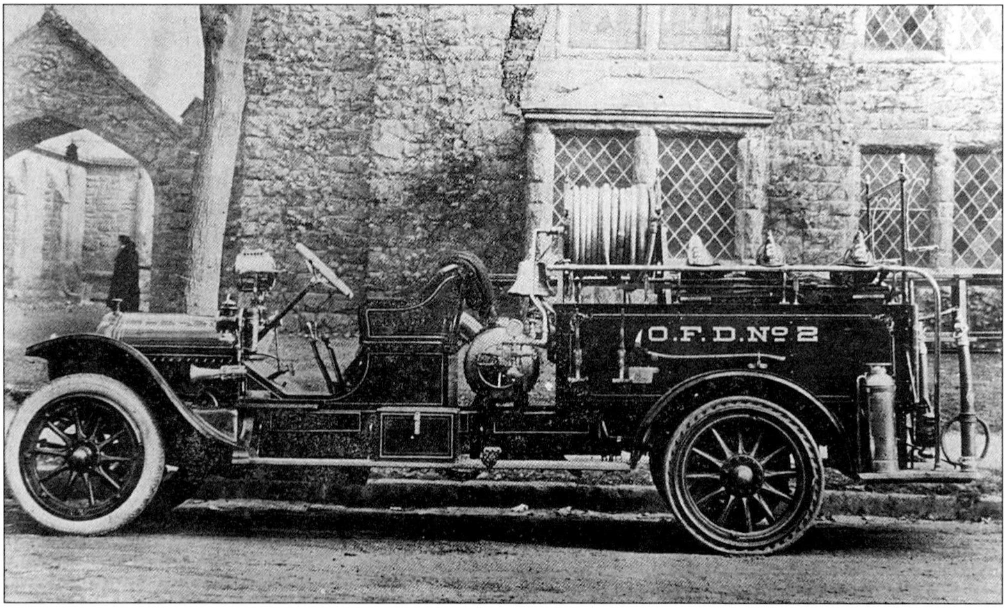

The Orange Fire Department became completely motorized in 1914 with the delivery of six White trucks. Here, brand new combination chemical and hose truck No. 2 poses for the camera, probably somewhere near the White Plant. (Photo courtesy Orange Fire Department.)

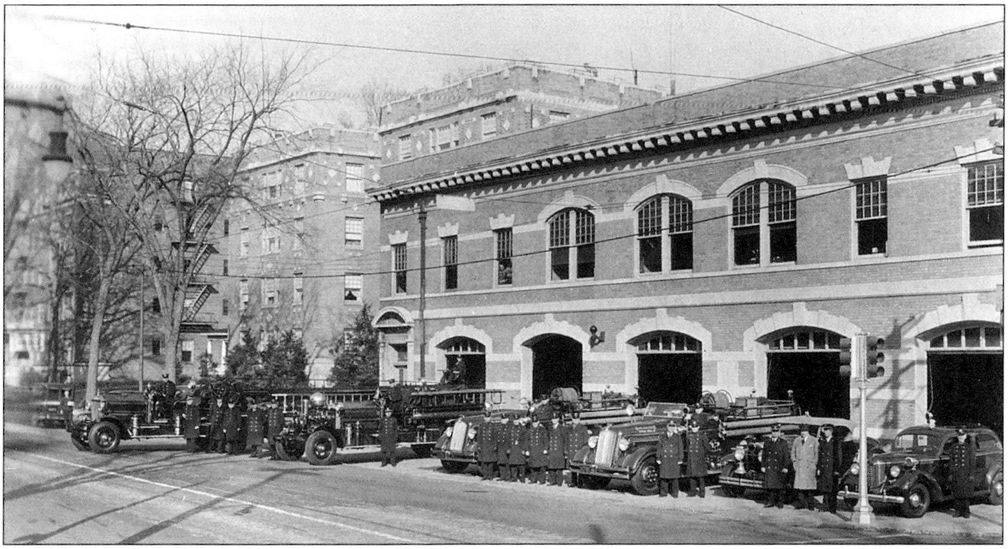

The Central Fire House was constructed in 1917 at the northwest corner of Central and Lincoln Avenues. At that time, all of the other houses were closed and the building designated as "Fire Headquarters," which it remains. This photo dates to about 1940. The original fire house on Washington Street was reopened in 1950 and houses one truck. (Photo courtesy Orange Fire Department.)

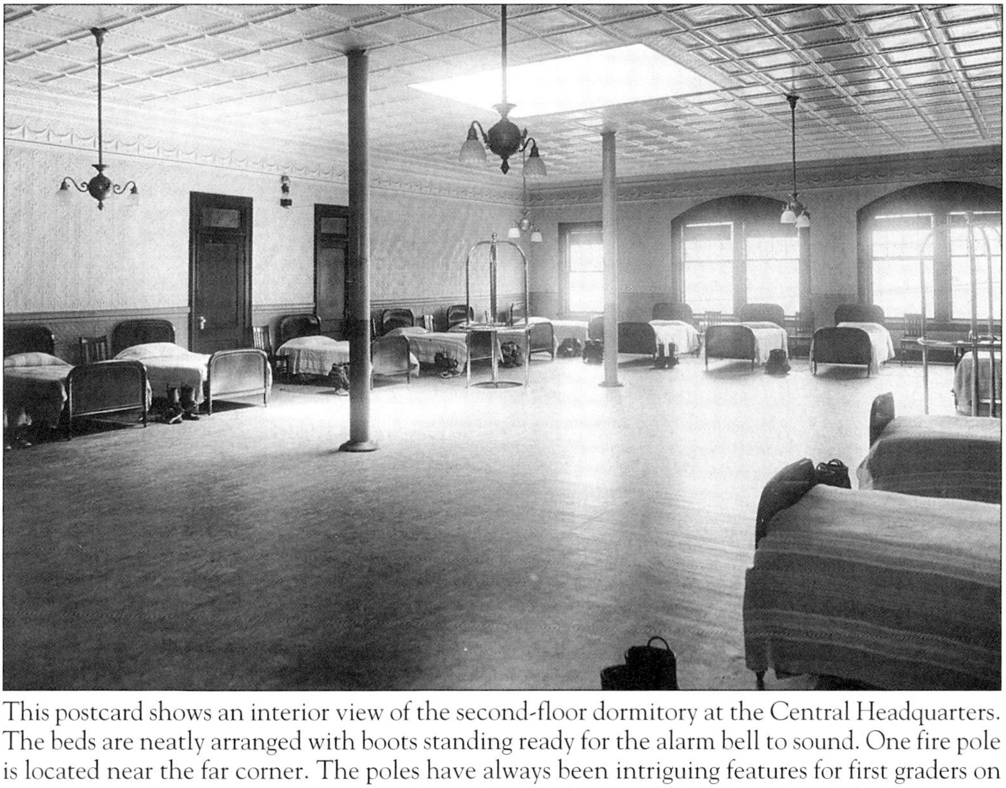

This postcard shows an interior view of the second-floor dormitory at the Central Headquarters. The beds are neatly arranged with boots standing ready for the alarm bell to sound. One fire pole is located near the far corner. The poles have always been intriguing features for first graders on field trips to the Central Fire House. All wondered if they would be allowed to slide down them. They weren't! (Photo courtesy Orange Fire Department.)

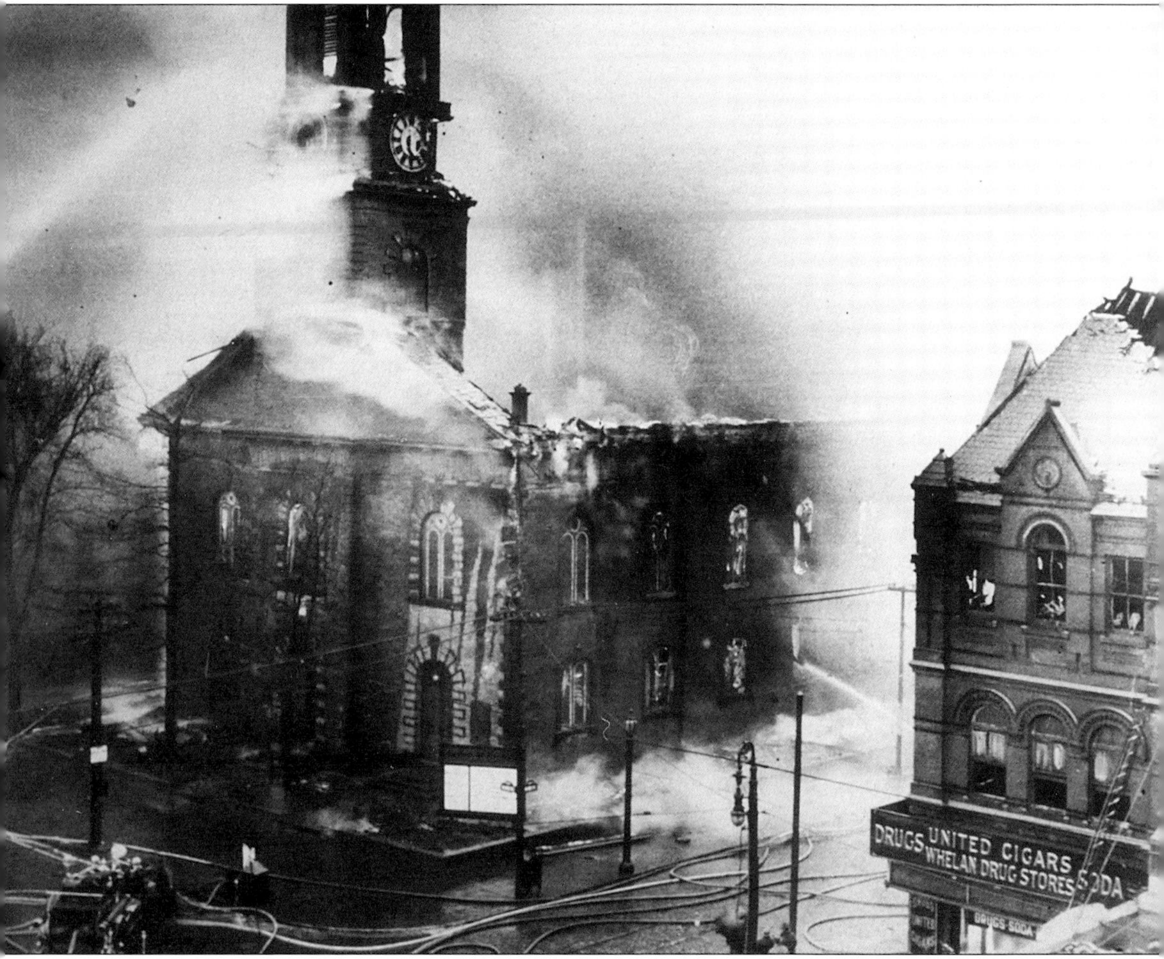

One of the most tragic conflagrations in the history of Orange occurred on April 5, 1927, when fire broke out on the second floor of the Music Hall (then the Royal Theatre) at the corner of Main and Day Streets. A witness noted, "A swift east wind howled and the snow and rain pounded down, which handicapped the firemen. This made it miserable for them. The flames shot high into the air sending sparks onto the roof of the old (First Presbyterian) church which then started to burn. It rapidly spread until the entire roof was ablaze . . ." As darkness fell, the smoldering spire was described as looking like ". . . a sparkling jewel." Soon the roof collapsed and the church passed into history. A new church was constructed the following year at the Old Burying Ground at Main and Scotland Streets, but the Music Hall was gone forever. (Photo courtesy Orange Fire Department.)

Six

Around the Neighborhoods

The Allen House, built about 1850, originally stood in "the first of a row of small houses in a lane east of the property of David Ropes." When Ropes was the mayor in 1865, he engaged in the opening and extension of several streets, including High Street from White Street to Park Avenue, and this little saltbox stood in the way. The house was moved to White Street and purchased by a Mr. Garrabrandt, whose descendants still occupied it at the time this picture was taken in 1913. This is one of many homes in this chapter, which serves as a tour of some of Orange's tree-lined streets. Perhaps you will spot your home!

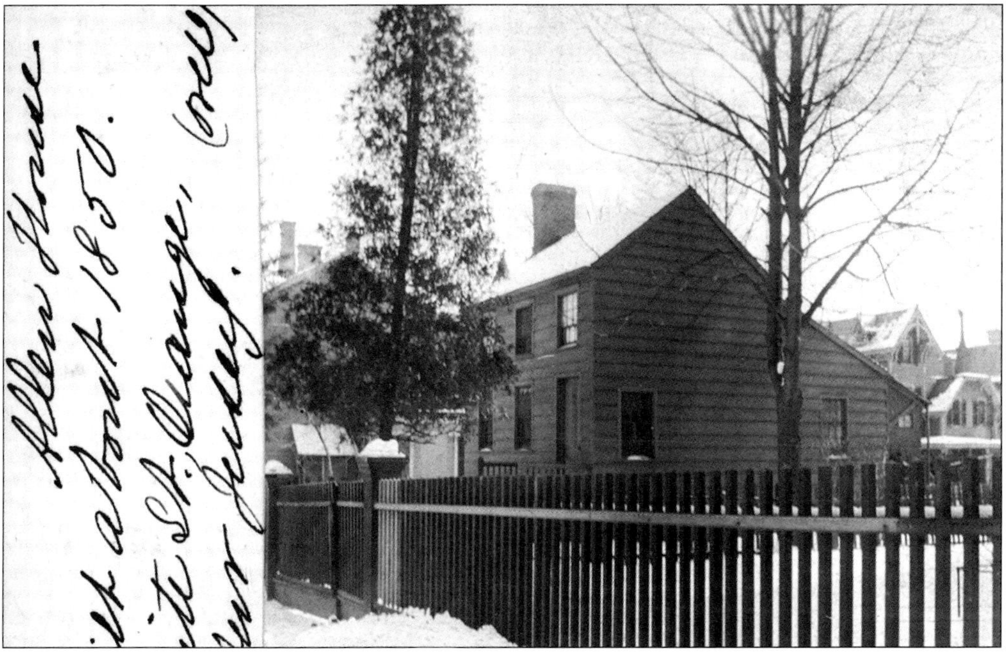

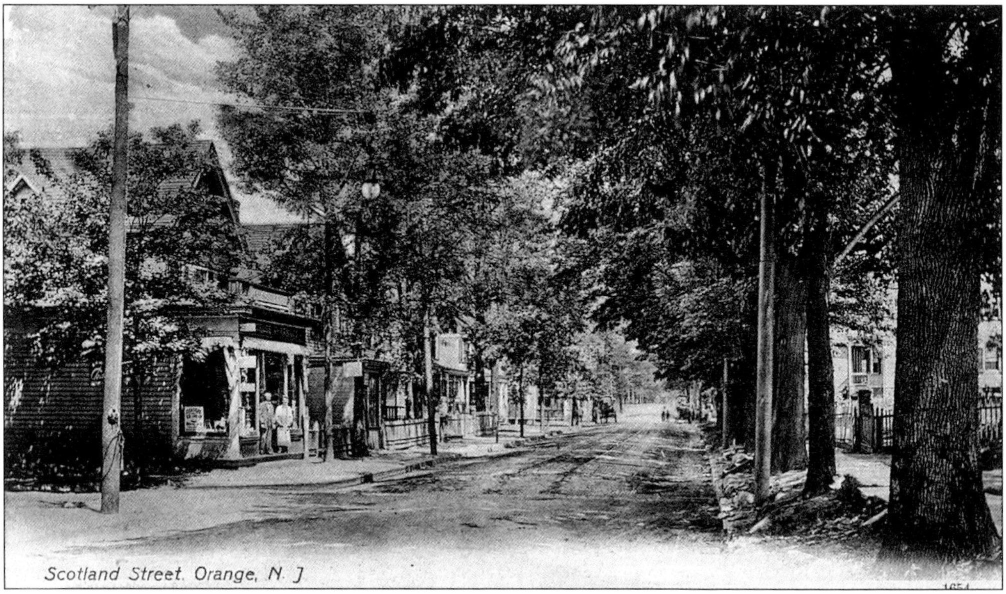

Scotland Street (later Scotland Road) provides a tranquil setting in this view looking north near Nassau Street. If you ever heard the term "Mom and Pop Store," you can now see its origin in the flesh, as J. Edward Keeler and his wife pose for the photographer in front of their Montrose Pharmacy. The trolley tracks ending in the road mark the southern extension of the Crosstown Line, which would eventually reach Morris Street.

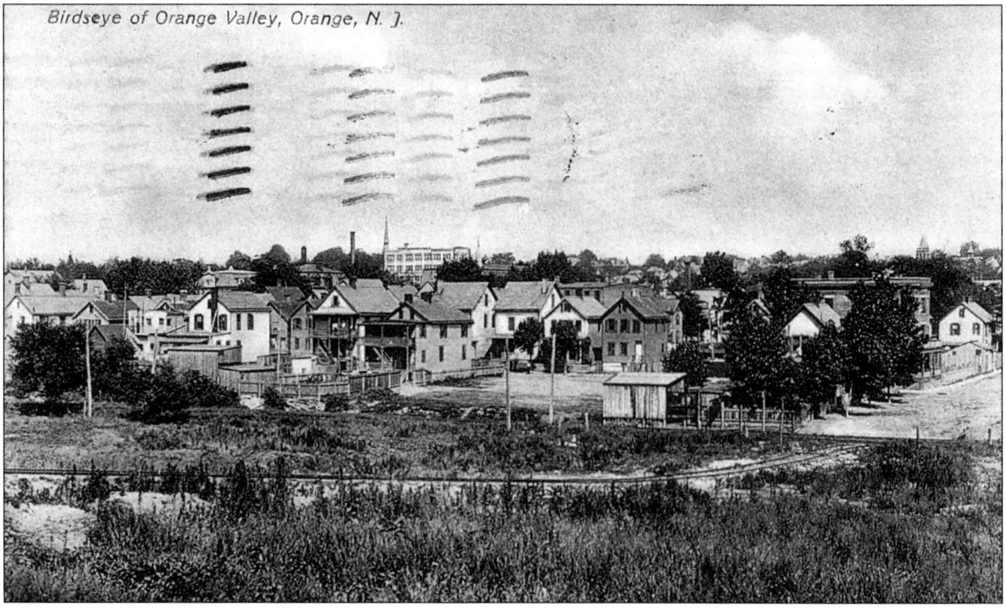

That part of the Orange Valley originally called Freemantown was the industrial heart of the city. The 12 square blocks bounded by Central Avenue to the north, Valley Street to the west, Nassau Street to the south, and the Lackawanna Railroad tracks and Scotland Street to the east provided jobs and housing for hundreds of residents. In this bird's-eye view, a more residential valley north of Central Avenue is pictured with the trolley tracks of the Montrose ("Swamp") Line passing in the foreground.

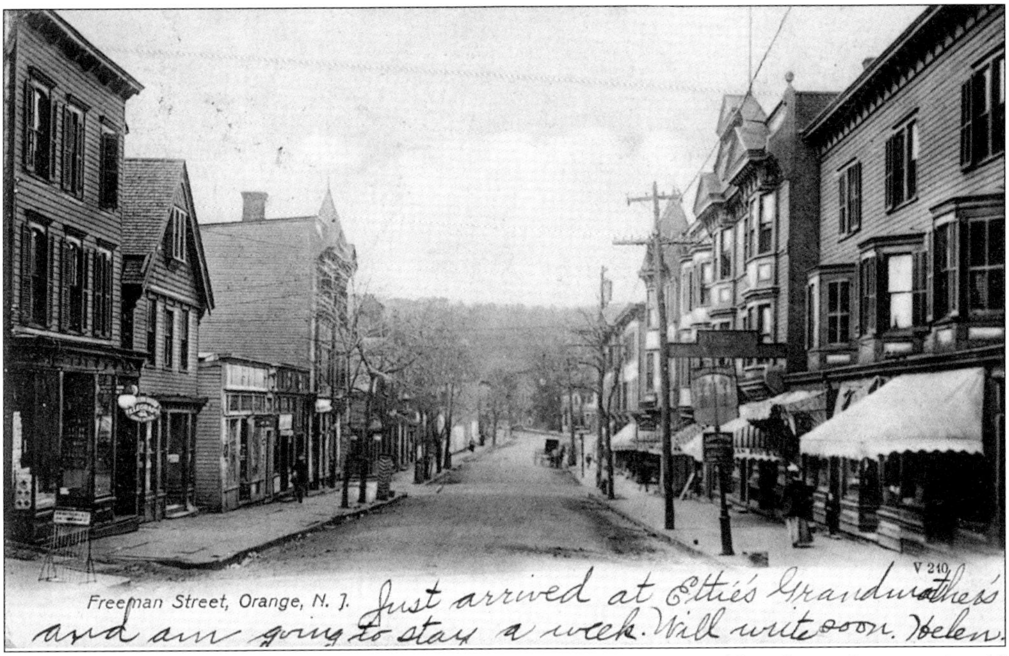

Freeman Street, looking west from the DL&W crossing, was a jumble of storefronts and cold water flats that typified the "other side of the tracks," but it was a gateway to the manufacturing area that was Orange's lifeblood.

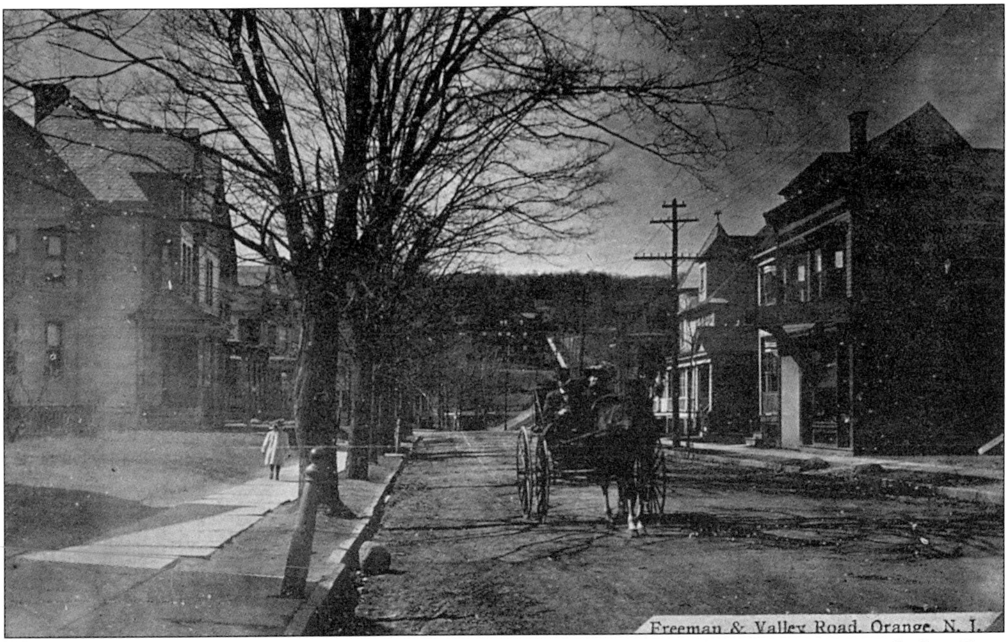

This "quieter" image is of Freeman Street and Valley Road looking west toward the First Mountain. The street, at this point, was the physical border between Orange on the left, and West Orange on the right. Just a quarter mile to the north of here was the base and house of the Essex County Toboggan Club run that delighted Orangeites of all ages each winter.

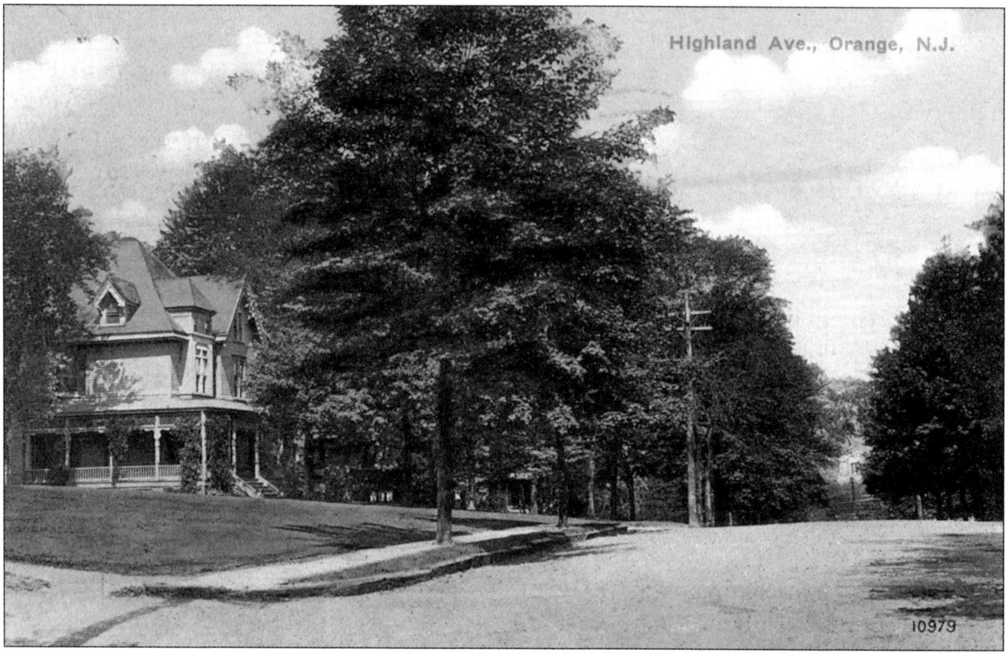

Highland Avenue ran east to west from Orange Park to Scotland Road and boasted a wide thoroughfare and large Victorian- and colonial-style homes. In this view, looking west from the crest of the hill near Lincoln Avenue, the First Mountain can be seen in the distance. Today, apartment houses have largely replaced the single-family residences.

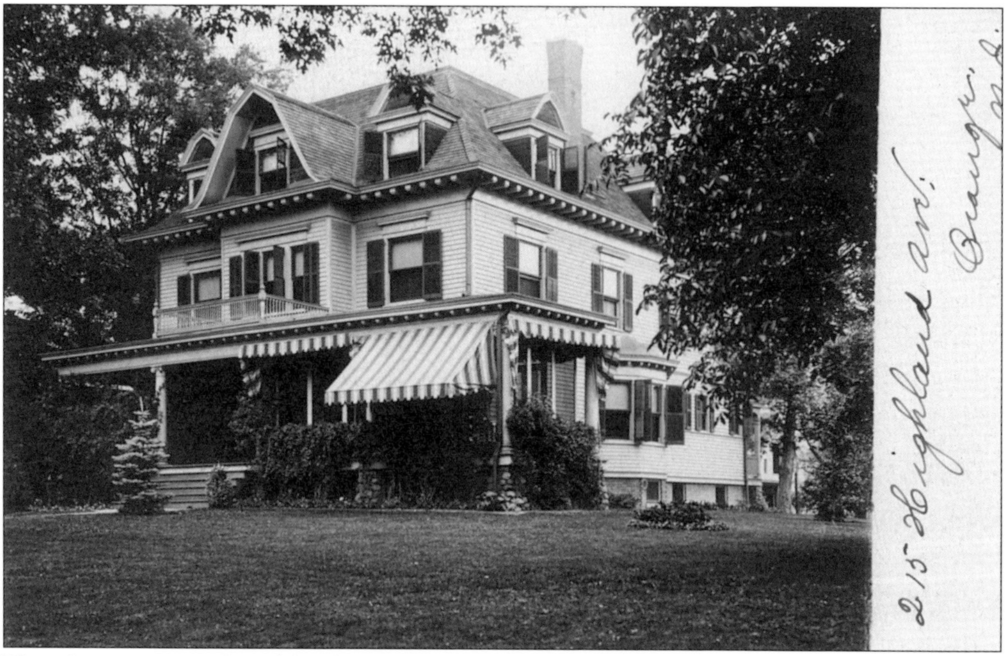

The plantings at 215 Highland Avenue, 1912, belie a house that is probably not more than 15 years old. The typical full-length verandah looks quite inviting. Chances are good that the awnings and shutters are dark green. The house was owned by the Berg family.

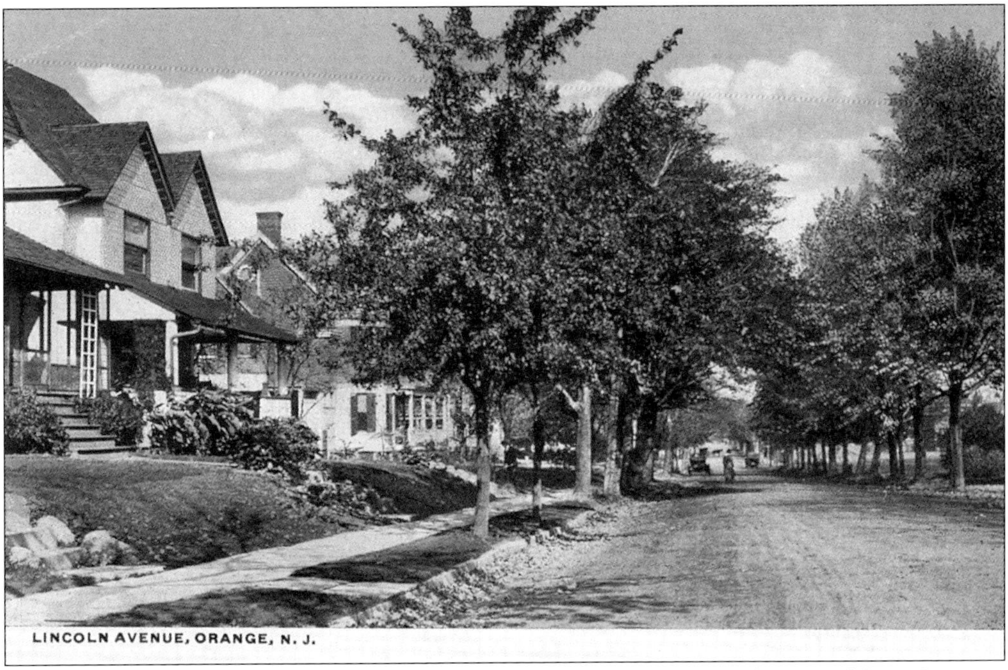

Lincoln Avenue appears tranquil in this 1908 view looking north towards Central from Conover Terrace. The open land visible in the distant background will soon be occupied by Central Playground, when Colonel Austen Colgate donates it to the city in 1912. The "third" high school building will be erected at the near corner in 1925. In 1999, the houses to the left are still standing, and the "fourth" high school is directly on the right.

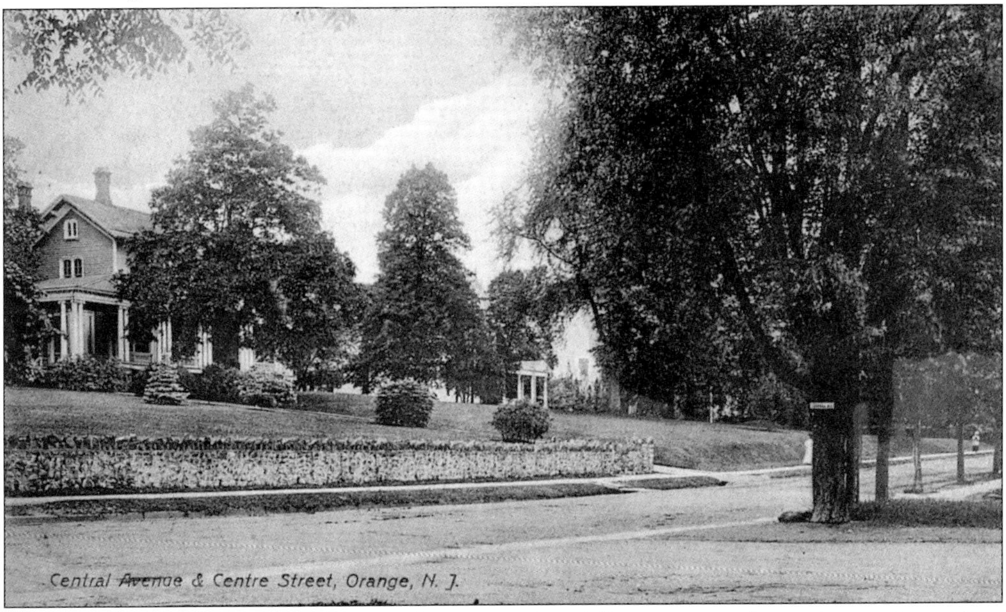

Central Avenue and South Centre Street is a far different scene here than today, when apartment houses, row stores, and a large pharmacy exist. In 1910, the road is still dirt, and the trolley line has yet to be constructed. The wall marks the location of St. Venantius Church and School property.

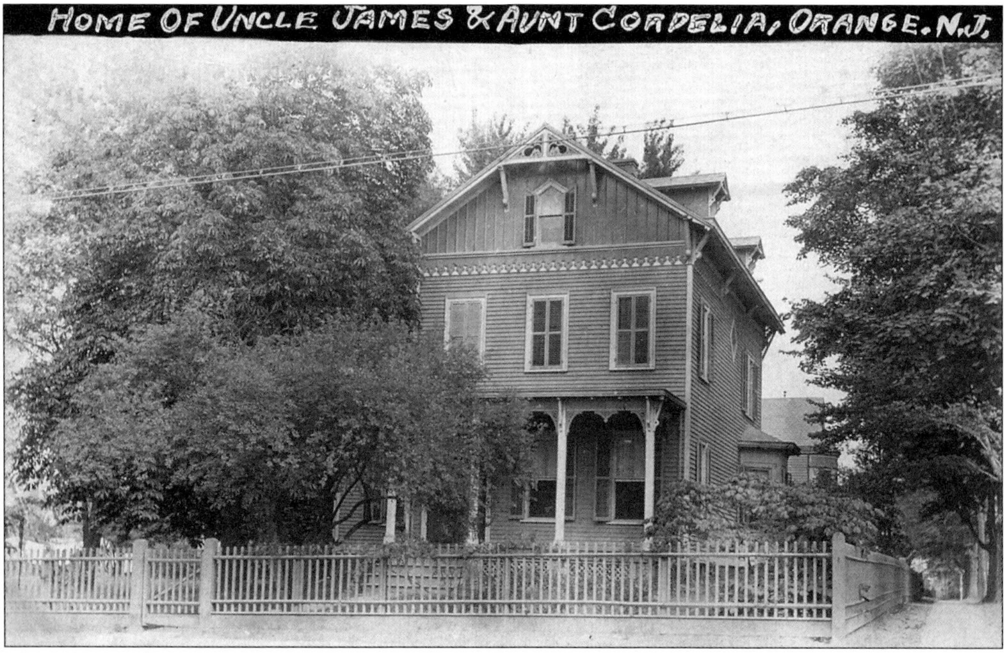

Identified only as the "Home of Uncle James and Aunt Cordelia, Orange, NJ," this residence stands proudly on some unknown corner of the city. No other identification helps to place this structure, although the photograph dates to 1910.

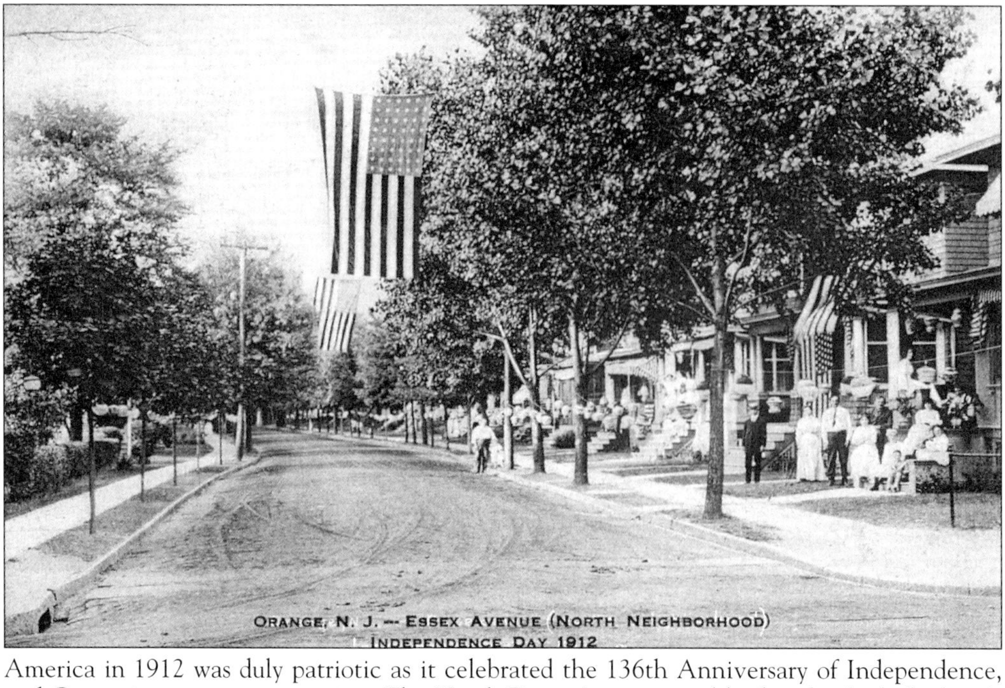

America in 1912 was duly patriotic as it celebrated the 136th Anniversary of Independence, and Orangeites were no exception. The North Essex Avenue neighborhood is bedecked with flags, bunting, and Japanese lanterns, as its residents anxiously await a day of picnics, band concerts, and a fireworks display. Thoughts of the recent sinking of the *Titanic* and the bubbling unrest in Europe are miles away.

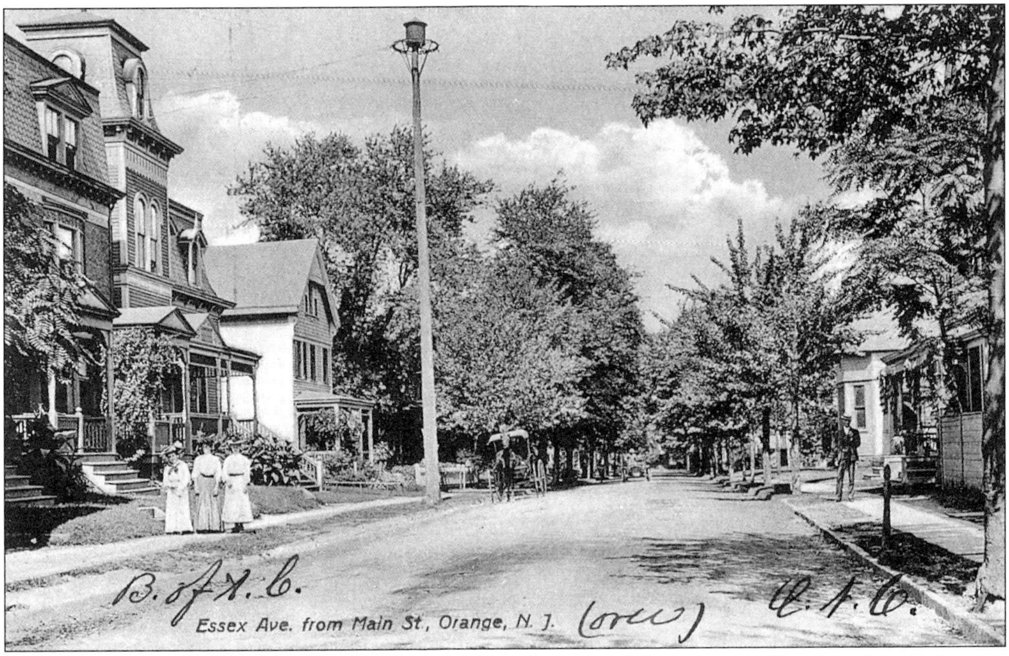

Three young ladies are standing in front of the Bureau of Associated Charities house in this shot of Essex Avenue from Main Street. Built in 1872 by Charles J. Prescott as a private school, the building was sold to the organization in June 1883.

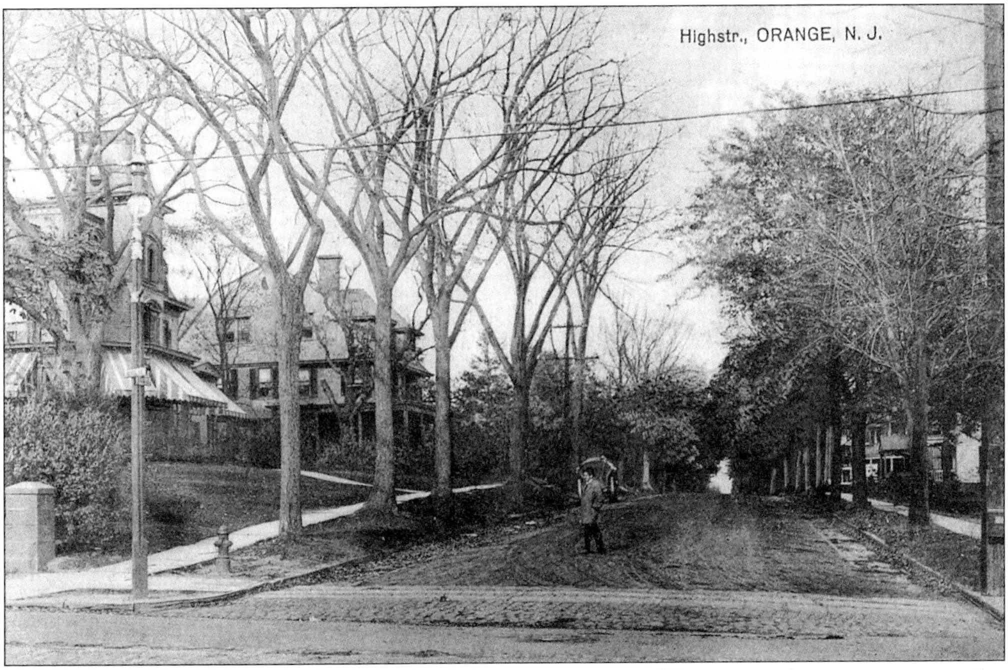

In 1909, a solitary pedestrian crosses High Street at Main, oblivious to the cameraman, who often caught local subjects unaware as they went about their business. Today, the left corner is occupied by a bank, but the house behind it still stands under a brick facade. The right corner houses a gas station-turned-coffee shop. The trees on the left are strangely bare.

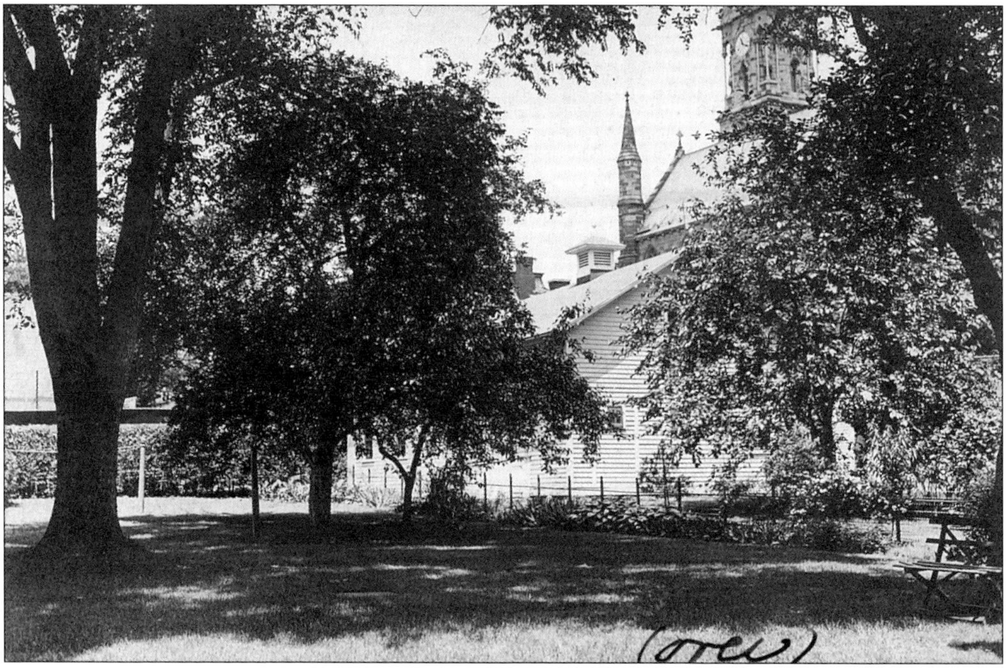

A rare backyard scene by noted Orange photographer Frank P. Jewett in 1916 shows the property at 75 High Street. The residence was owned by the C.J. Prescott family, who had purchased it in 1881. The illuminated electric chime clock, visible in the steeple of St. John's Church, had been installed barely a year before and tells us that it is 11:20 a.m.

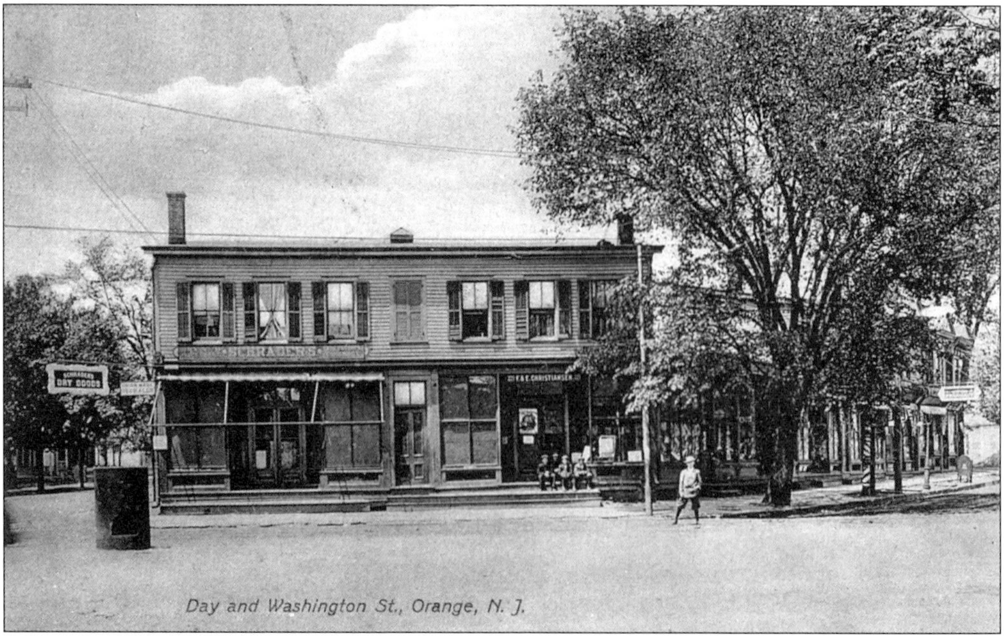

Schrader's Dry Goods and F&F Christiansen occupy opposite ends of this duplex at the intersection of North Day and Washington Streets, 1908. The view to the right looks toward the Erie Railroad station. The lack of activity and the children's clothing surely signal a Sunday morning.

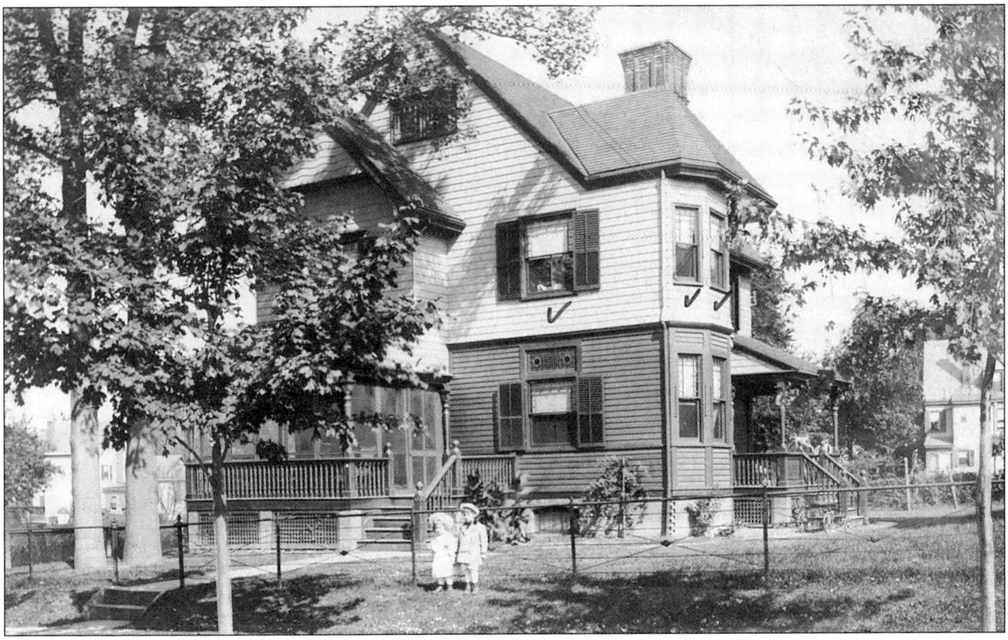

The caption on the rear of this postcard reads simply, "18 Berwyn Street, Orange, NJ. Where Robert Dodge Merrill was born. June 9, 1904." This might have been the home of John Lenord Merrill, amateur playwright of Orange's "Paint & Powder Club," and a member of the city's Centennial Committee.

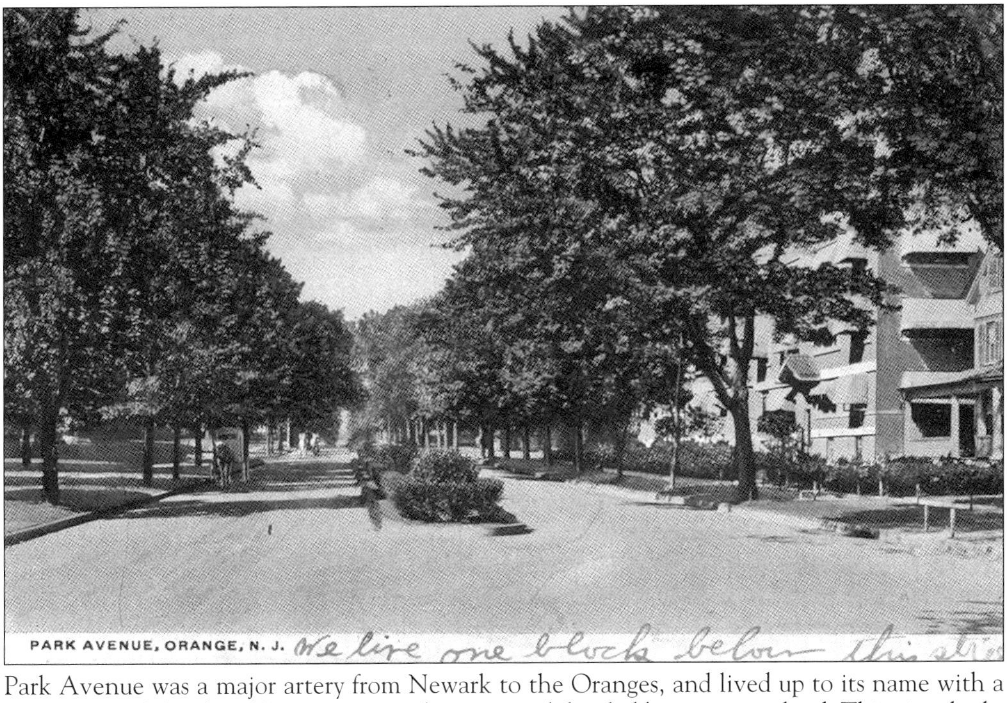

Park Avenue was a major artery from Newark to the Oranges, and lived up to its name with a wide thoroughfare lined by impressive plantings and divided by a center island. This view looks west near Cleveland Street.

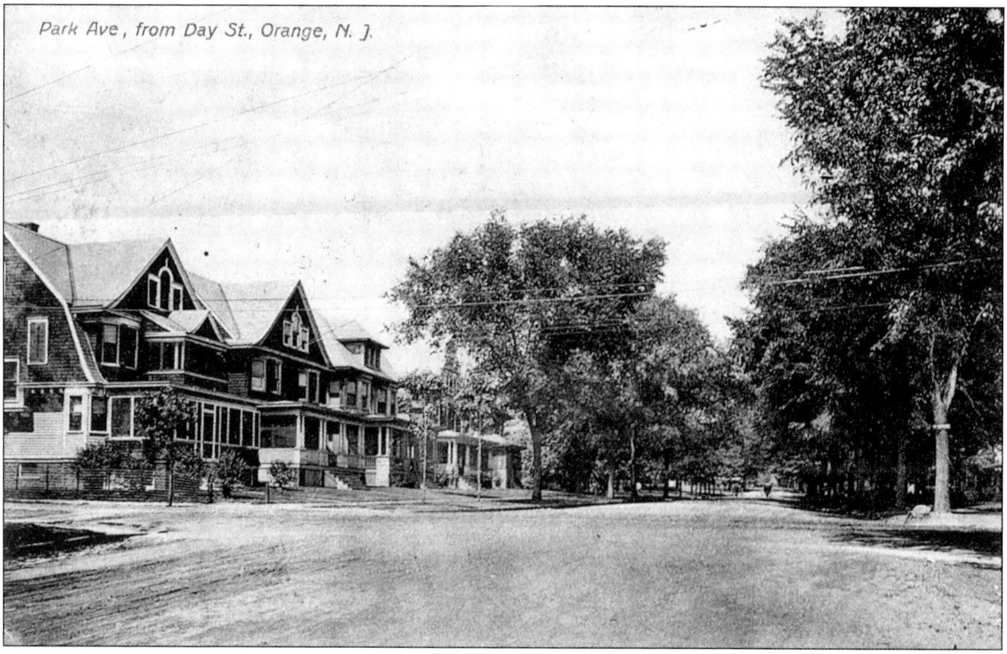

These large, spacious houses on Park Avenue at Day Street are still standing today. They demonstrate a great deal of symmetry, with only minor variations on roof lines, dormers, etc.

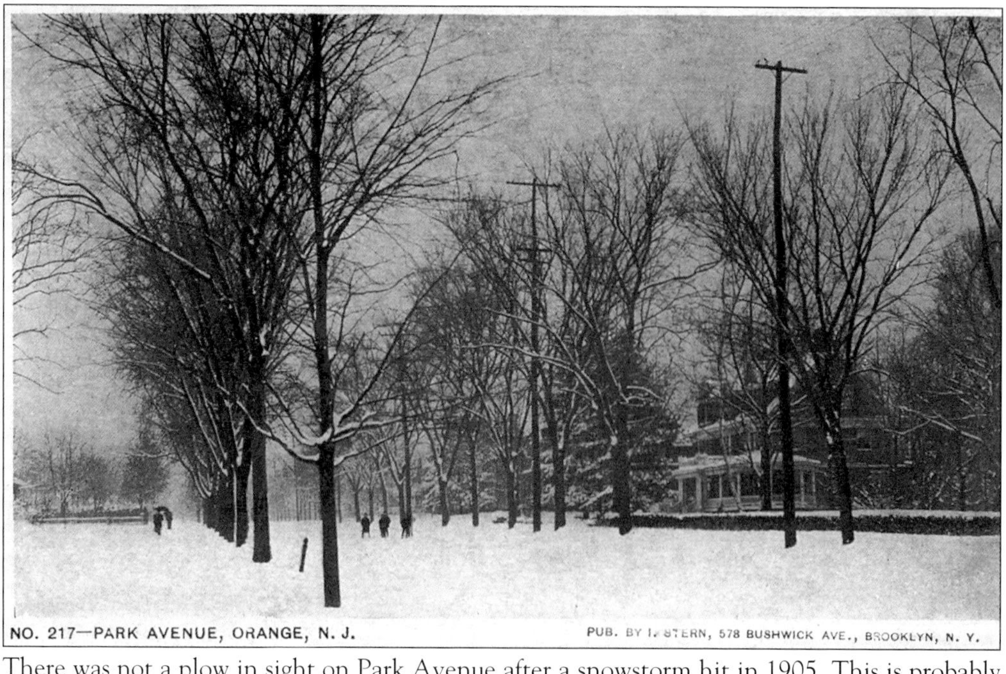

There was not a plow in sight on Park Avenue after a snowstorm hit in 1905. This is probably because there *were* no plows, nor any cars to dig out! If you lived on a street with a trolley line, you were fortunate, as the traction companies had special sweeper units to take care of the snow. However, here it was muscle power that got you out, or you were snowbound! The kids in the road look happy since school is, no doubt, closed for the day?

Seven

Leisure Time

On June 18, 1872, Mayor David N. Ropes offered a resolution stating that ". . . the speedy erection of a first class building embracing a large hall for musical and other entertainment, and smaller rooms for use of various societies is a public necessity." The Orange Music Hall Association organized on June 16, 1879, and began construction of this building on the northeast corner of Main and Day Streets on August 14, 1879, on land formerly owned by Stephen Day. A total expenditure of $51,000 included $15,000 for the lot. The facility opened to the public on March 4, 1880. By 1915, it had become the Bijou Vaudeville. This busy holiday scene probably signals some special occasion, such as Memorial Day or the Fourth of July. Known at various times as the Music Hall, Orange Theatre, Bijou Vaudeville, and Royal Vaudeville, the structure was destroyed in a spectacular fire on April 5, 1927. The inferno started on the second floor, and sparks ultimately spread to the roof of the First Presbyterian Church across Day Street, destroying it as well.

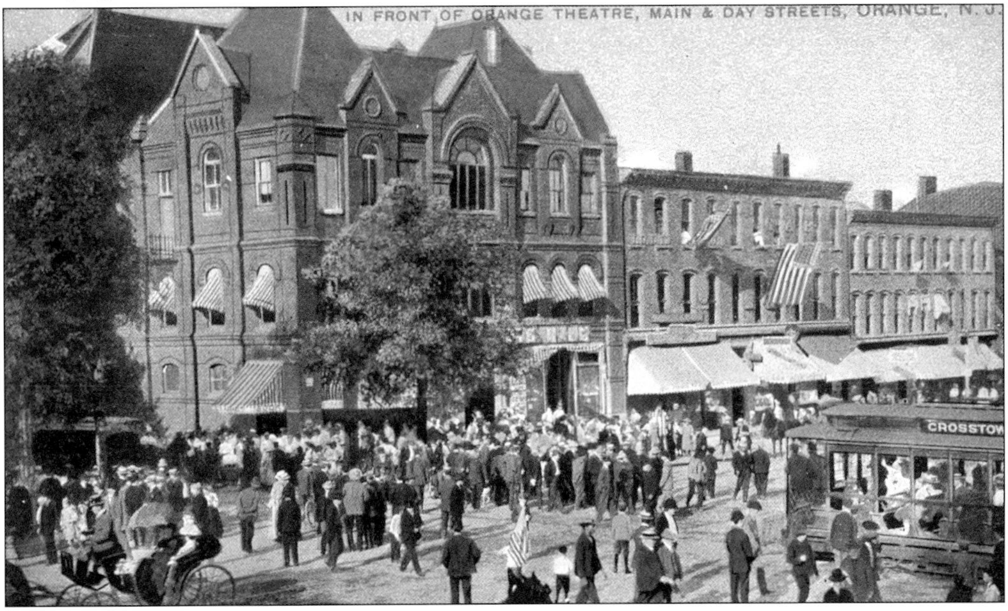

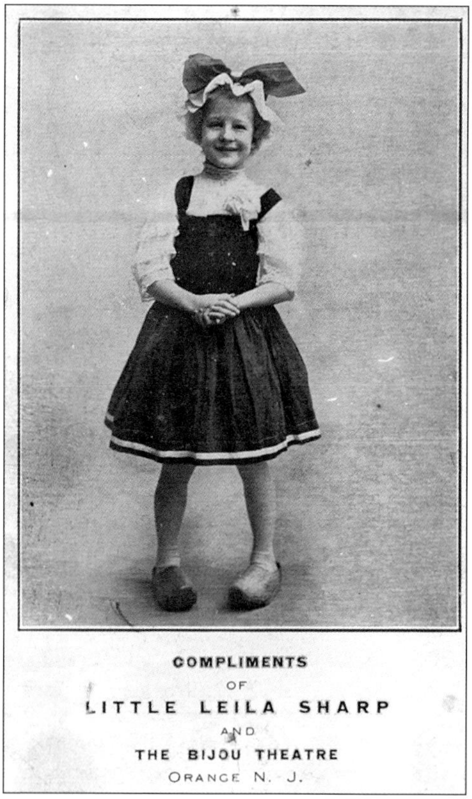

Little Leila Sharp wowed 'em at the Bijou Theatre and handed out these souvenir cards, ensuring that nobody would forget her. Pigeon-toed Leila must really have kept the fans awake with those wooden shoes! And check that grin. If Peck's Bad Boy had a sister, it would, no doubt, be Leila!

NEW ENGLAND SOCIETY, OF ORANGE.

Orange, N. J., June 7th, 1883.

DEAR SIR:

The last regular meeting of the Society, for the season, will be held on Monday Evening next, June 11*th, at* 8 *o'clock.*

Yours respectfully,

WM. READ HOWE, Secretary.

The New England Society was the driving force in the construction of the Music Hall and was ultimately headquartered on its second floor. It was founded on May 25, 1870, to "sustain New England traditions, promote sociability, and guard the highest interests of the Oranges." Lowell Mason Jr. was its first president. This 1883 postcard, the oldest we have seen, announces their last meeting of the 1883 spring season.

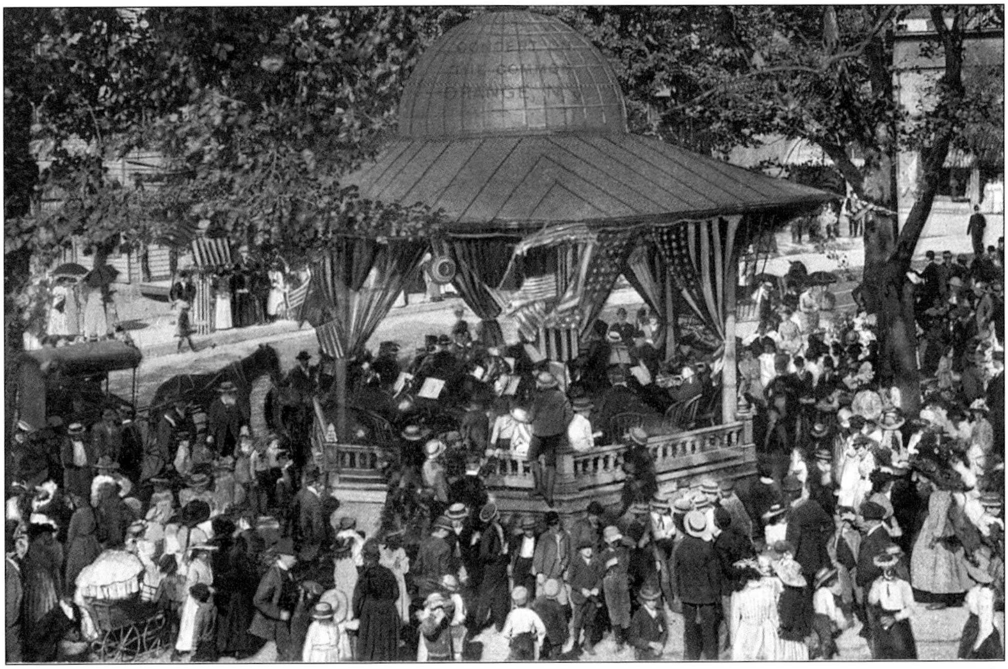

The bandstand at Military Common was the scene of many enjoyable open-air concerts such as this one, probably a Memorial Day or Fourth of July affair. Markwith's Band was a popular fixture in Orange that often played at special events. On October 26, 1900, William Jennings Bryan addressed a crowd of 10,000 from this spot as he campaigned unsuccessfully against William McKinley for President.

Second Grand Annual

BALL

OF THE

SCHLANGER FANGER P. C.

TO BE HELD AT

German-English School Hall

PARK AND WILLIAM STS., ORANGE

Monday Evening, January 27, 1908

Come and Have a Good Time

Songs by the Famous Harmony Four Quartette

TICKETS 25 CENTS

The New Century Press, 33 N. Centre St., Orange.

Orange's large German population enjoyed social activities of their own, such as this grand ball at the German School at Park and William Streets in 1908.

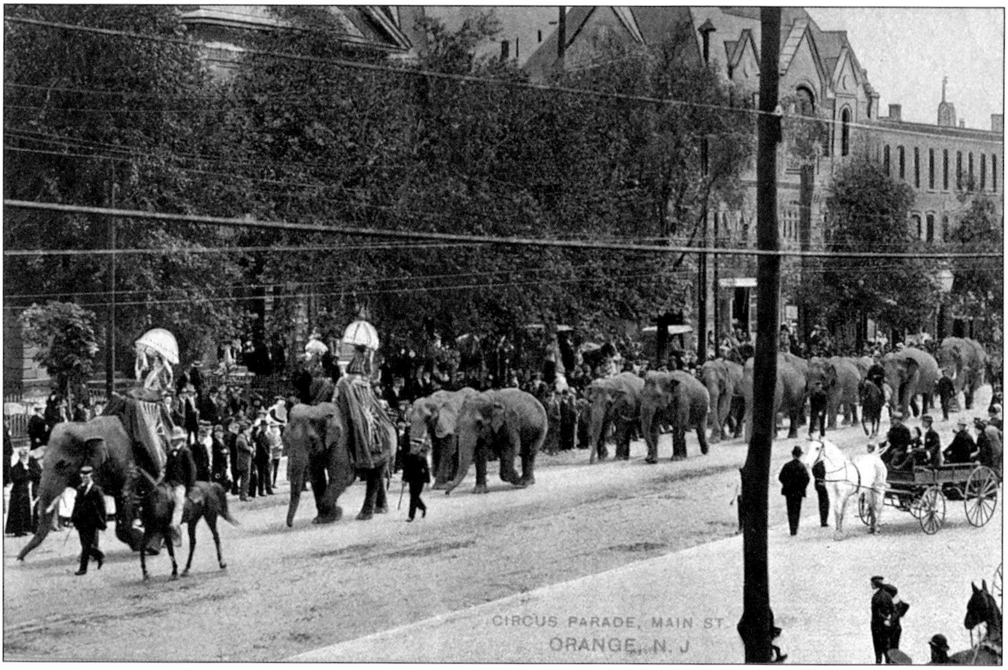

Circus parades were always a treat for Orange residents, but this one was extra special. Fourteen elephants, the first two carrying their drivers in ornate howdahs, lumber their way slowly past the First Presbyterian Church on May 25, 1897. The Paw and Sells Brothers Circus was in town!

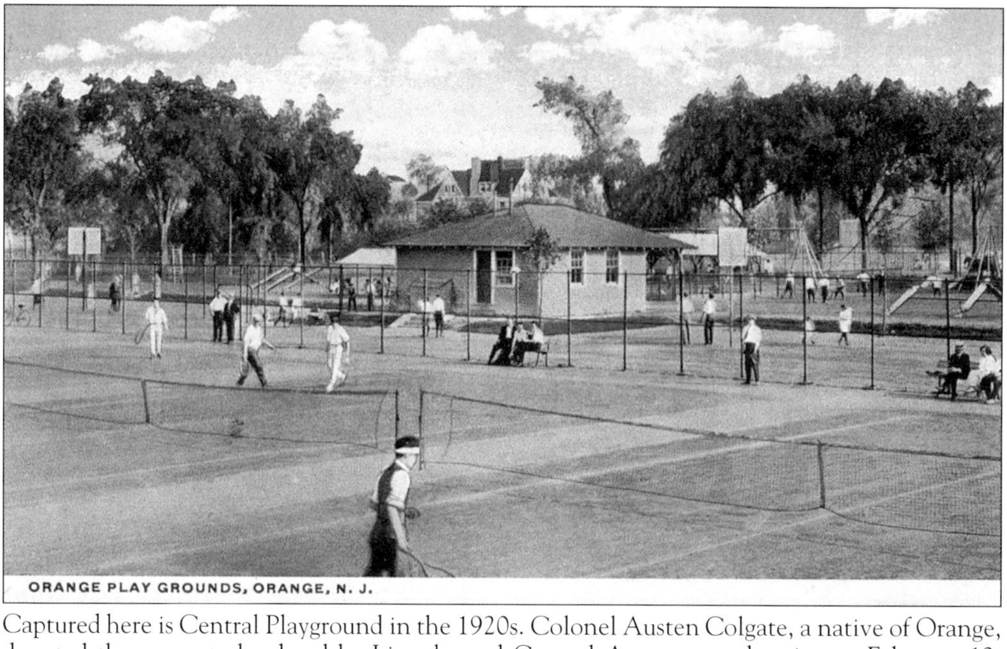

Captured here is Central Playground in the 1920s. Colonel Austen Colgate, a native of Orange, donated the property bordered by Lincoln and Central Avenues to the city on February 12, 1910, and it was dedicated that October 19. A grandstand was erected on the Lincoln Avenue side, and Orangeites were treated to band concerts and movies there. Each winter, a portion of the playground was flooded for ice skating.

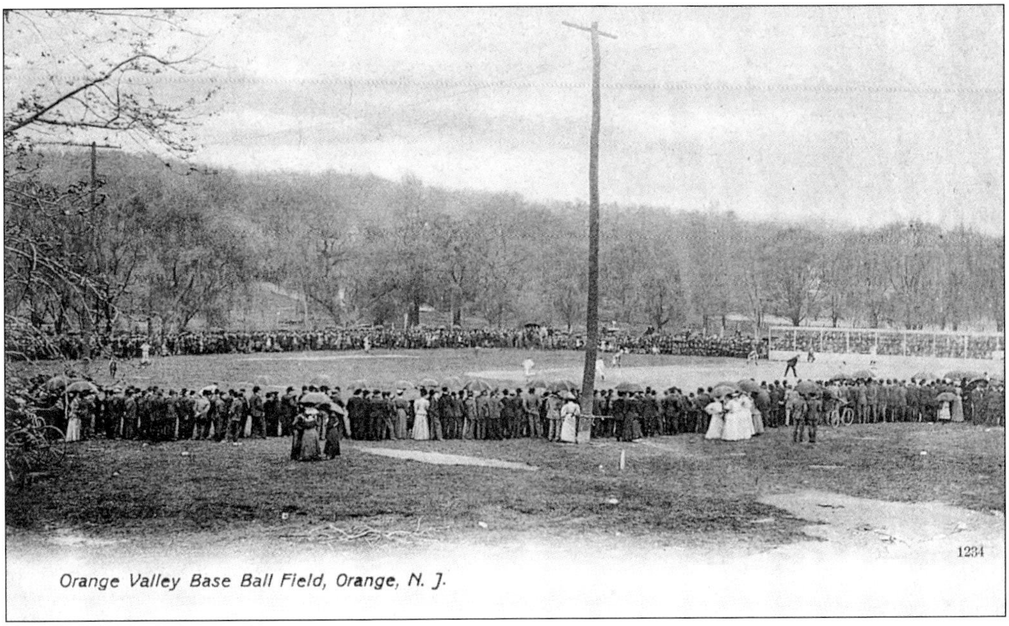

Baseball was quite popular in the Oranges, and taken quite seriously as this view from about 1905 shows. The grandstands at the Orange Valley field are filled to capacity and the overflow crowd rings the perimeter of the diamond, two and three deep in some places.

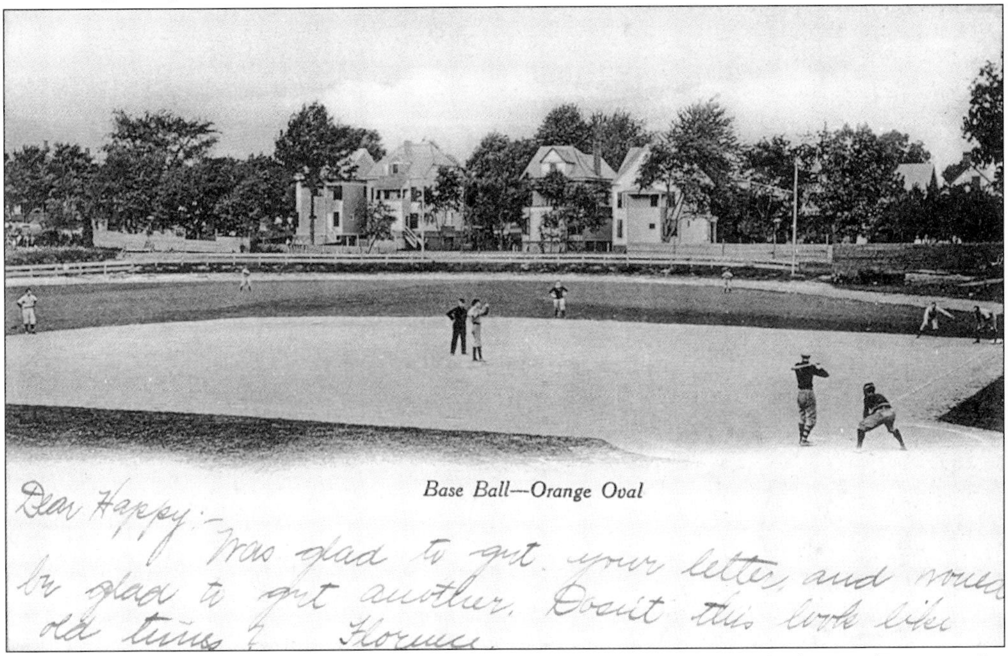

The pitcher checks the runner at first and goes into his stretch, while the batter digs in at the plate. The solitary umpire stands behind the mound in this great 1905 action scene at the Orange Oval, which was owned by the Orange Athletic Club and actually located in East Orange at Grove Street. Note the pole in right field. The short fence dimensions necessitated its placement, and balls hit over the fence to its right were ground rule doubles. Balls hit over to the left were home runs.

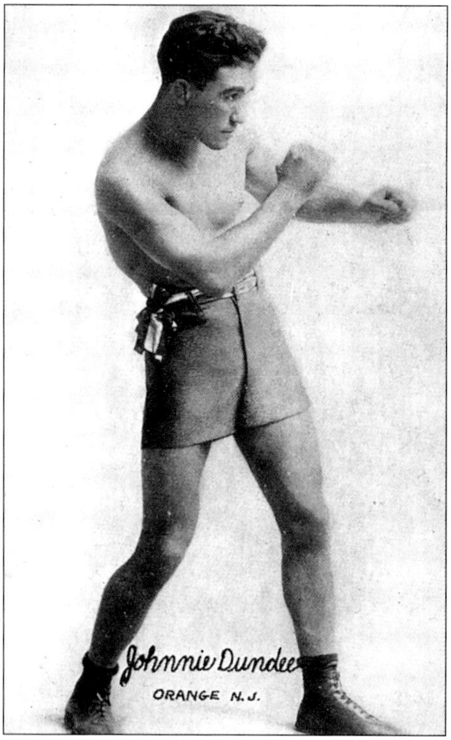

Boxing was another popular recreational pastime. Orangeite Johnny Dundee was a lightweight contender in the days when the 20-round bout was still in vogue. In 1920, Johnnie had 15 fights, winning 3, losing 1, and battling to 4 draws and 7 "no decisions."

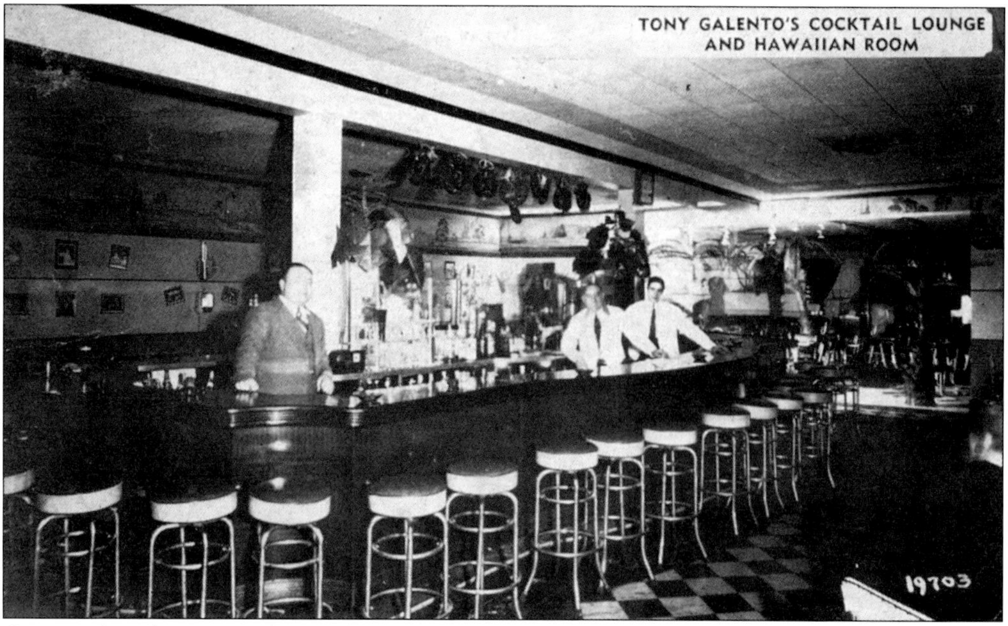

Orange's best known professional boxer was the legendary "Two-Ton" Tony Galento. Galento fought Joe Louis for the heavyweight championship at Yankee Stadium in 1939. He knocked the "Brown Bomber" down before eventually losing by a TKO in Round 4. In an 11-year career and 97 fights, it was the only time that Tony was knocked down. Tony retired to the bar and raconteur business and greets the customers in this 1941 view of his Hawaiian Room on South Day Street.

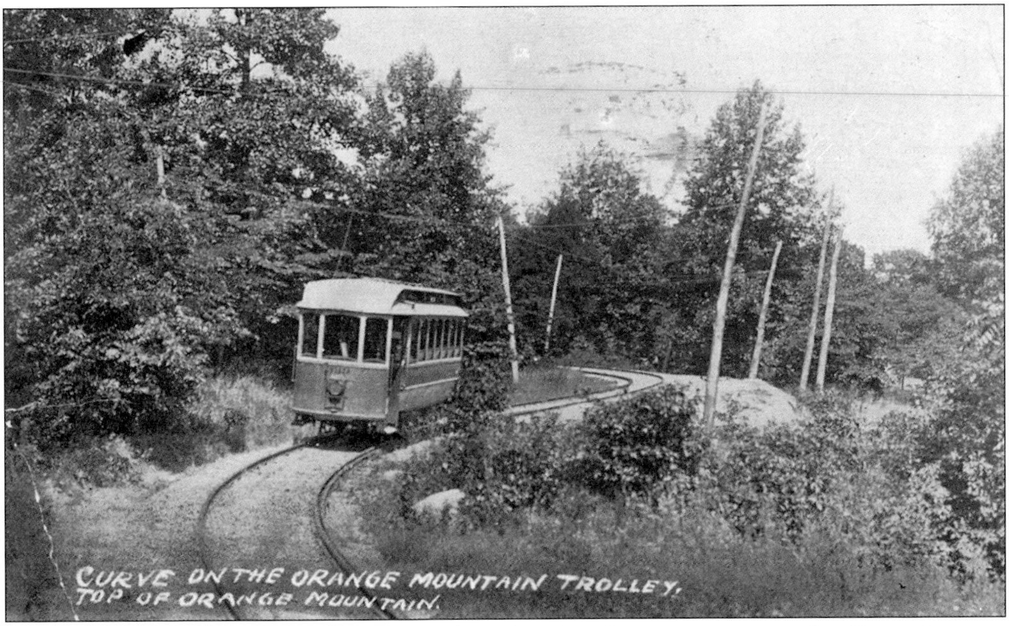

An extremely popular and well-patronized weekend and summer getaway for Orangeites was actually across the border at Eagle Rock in West Orange. On June 20, 1894, trolley service made the "Rock" more accessible. The line was completed from Scotland Street and Tremont Avenue to a terminus at Undercliff Avenue, adjacent to a stairway that had been constructed to reach the picnic grounds and observation point above.

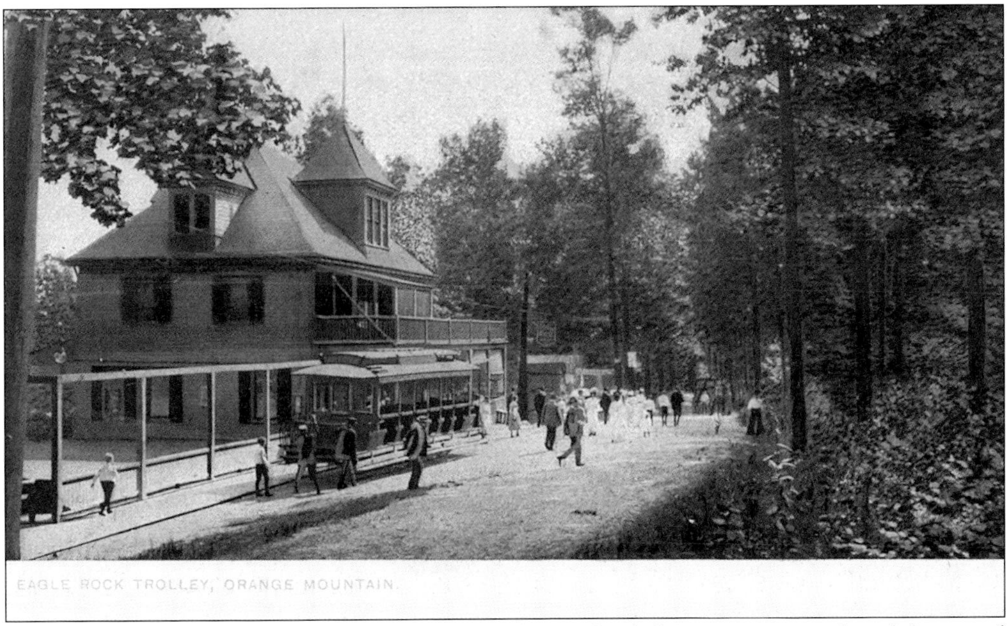

An open car has just discharged its passengers at the Undercliff Avenue terminal, and the crowd is headed to the stairway that will take them to the observation area, picnic groves, and ice cream pavilion. (This area was the former vantage point for George Washington's troops during the Revolutionary War.) The namesake rock commemorated the mighty birds that once built aeries there, and the view of the Hudson River and New York was spectacular.

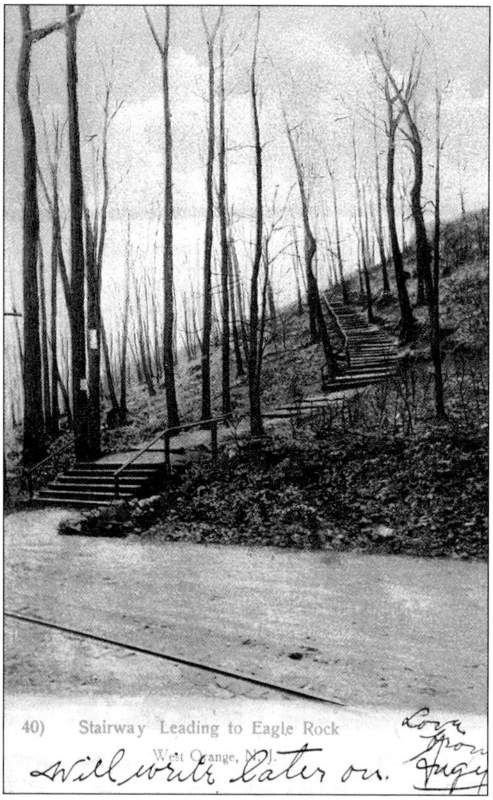

The steps leading to the observation area were not for the faint hearted, as seen in this winter view with barren trees. Disembarking from the trolley, whose tracks are visible in the foreground, visitors ascended these crude wooden stairs to sample the wonders above.

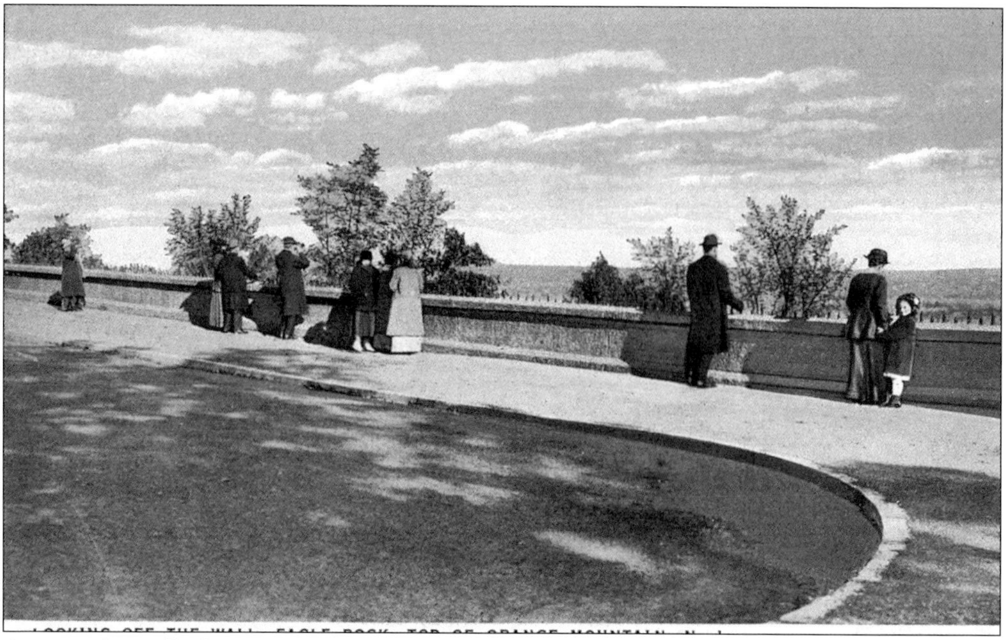

Once at the wall, the view to the east was wonderful! Eventually, large binocular devices were placed here, and, by dropping a nickel into the slot, you were treated to all the sights for miles, until your one minute of time ran out.

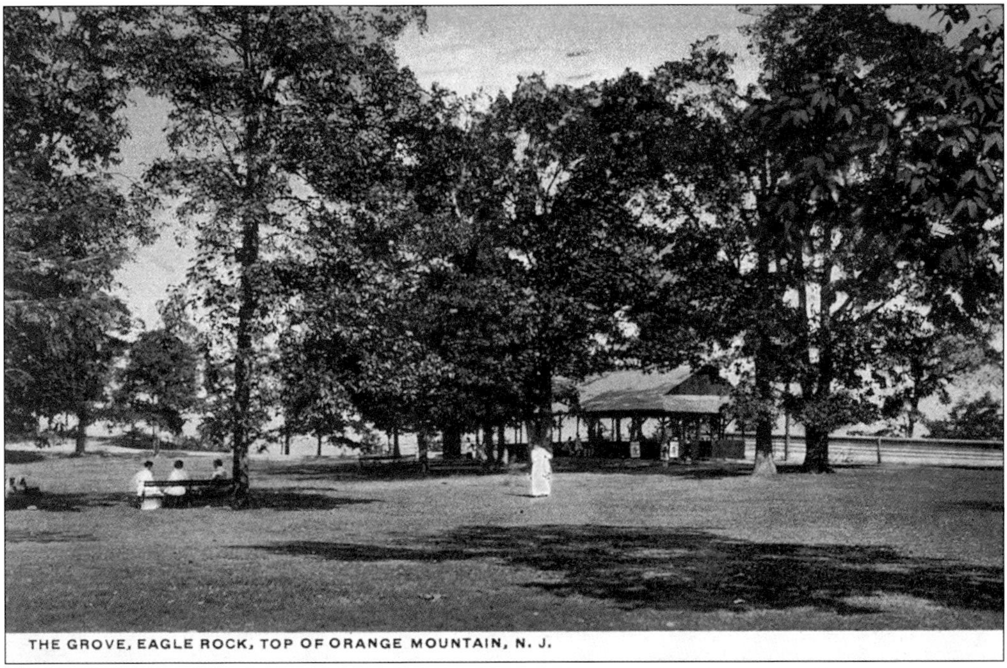

Picnic groves and pavilions dotted the landscape at the top of Eagle Rock. The property today is under the jurisdiction of the Essex County Park Commission and is still packed on weekends. Now, however, the trolley is long gone and the picnickers come by automobile.

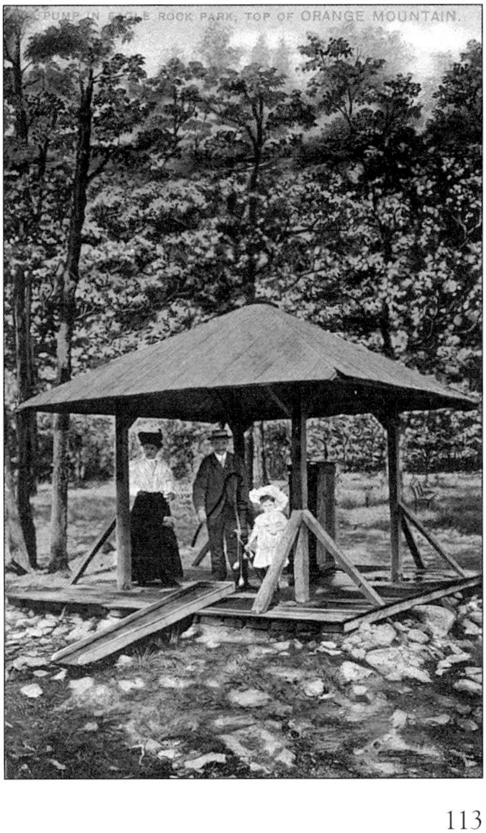

Cold water was available from this wonderful old pump at the picnic grove. Here, mother, father, and little Louise test the sparkling beverage. Dad has a grip on the handle while Lou dutifully holds the cup . . . and our photographer captures the moment for posterity.

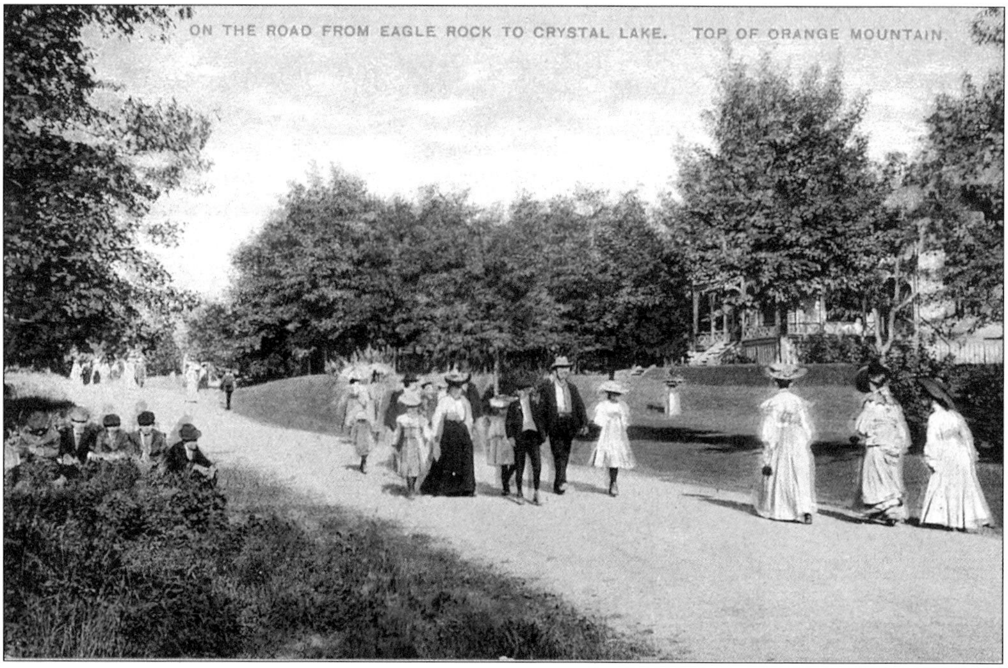

If things got too boring at Eagle Rock, you could always saunter about a half mile down the road to Crystal Lake, where the spring-fed attraction was ringed by refreshment stands, boat docks, and a small amusement park.

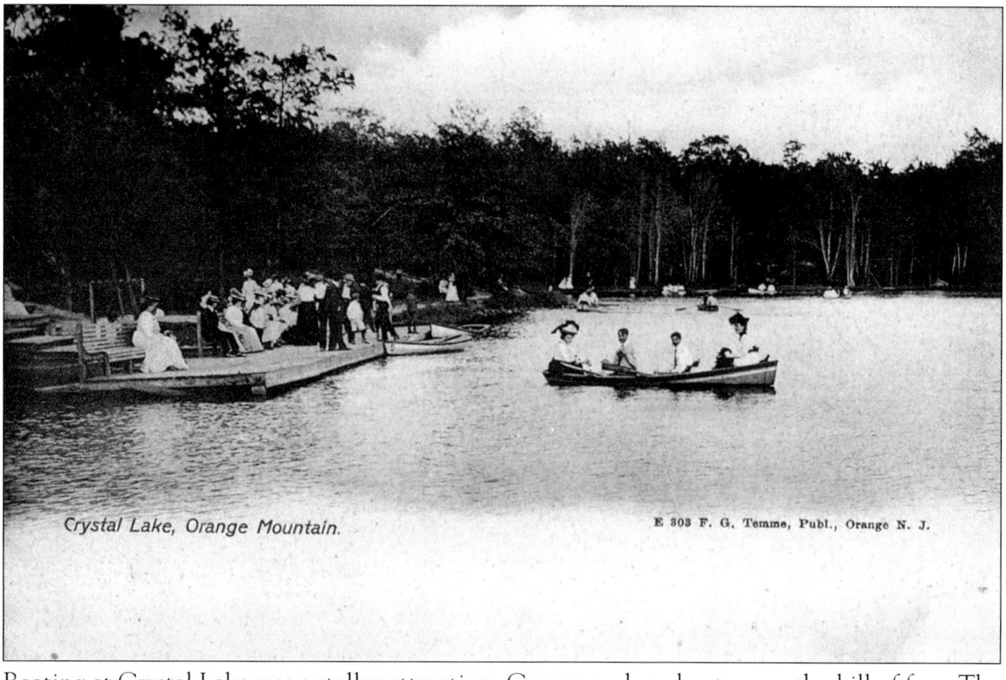

Boating at Crystal Lake was a stellar attraction. Canoes and rowboats were the bill of fare. The more hearty swains embarked with their sweethearts (and a ukulele) in the former, and father loaded mother and the kids in the latter. It was not long before some foolish soul stood up, and got a quick dip in the cold water.

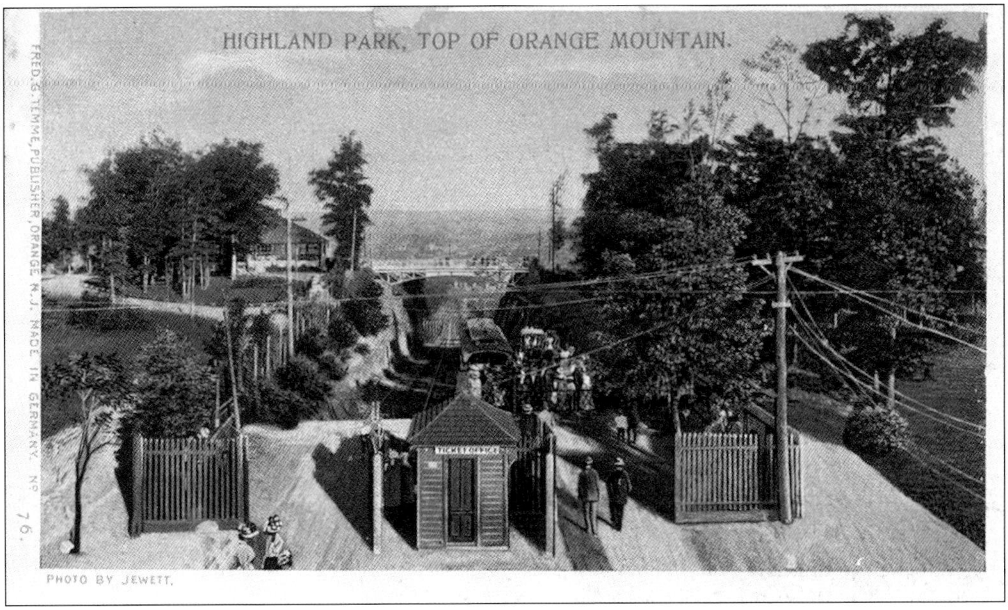

The cable road is virtually forgotten today, although most residents can tell you that a cable car once operated up Orange Mountain to an amusement facility called Highland Park at Cable Lake. Ground was broken for the roadbed on October 3, 1892, and the line was completed April 29, 1893. In addition to excursions, its secondary purpose was to carry prospective buyers to lots at the top of Northfield Avenue.

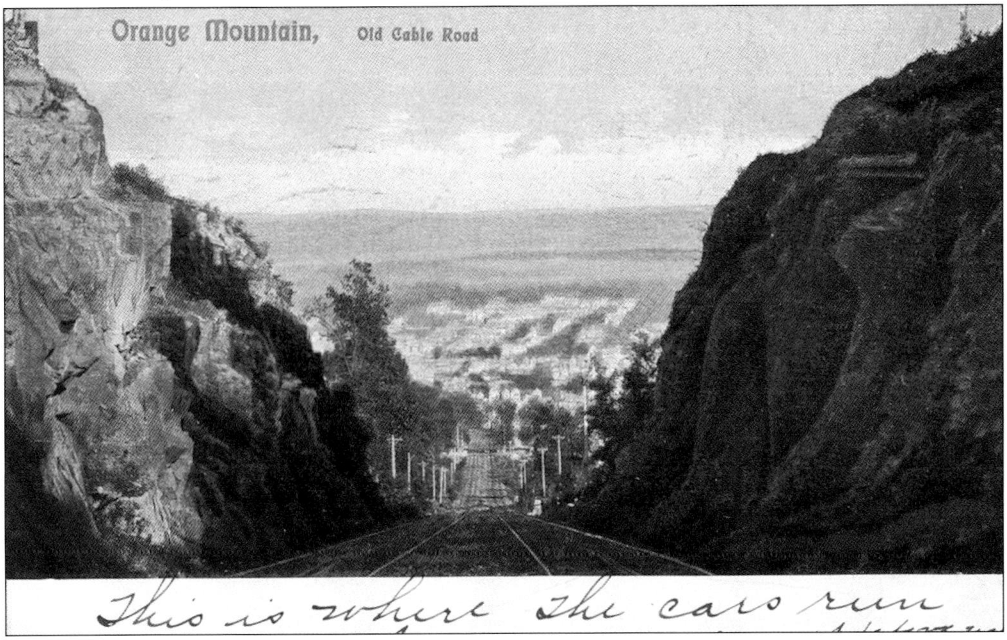

The Cable Road ran from Valley Road to a terminus at Cable Lake. Fares were 5¢ for foot passengers, 15¢ for one-horse vehicles, and 25¢ for two-horse vehicles. This view looks down the mountain from the deepest point of the cut where the walls were 30 feet high. The road lost $1,000 the first season and was sold at foreclosure in October 1895. Reopened briefly, it ceased operations in the fall of 1896.

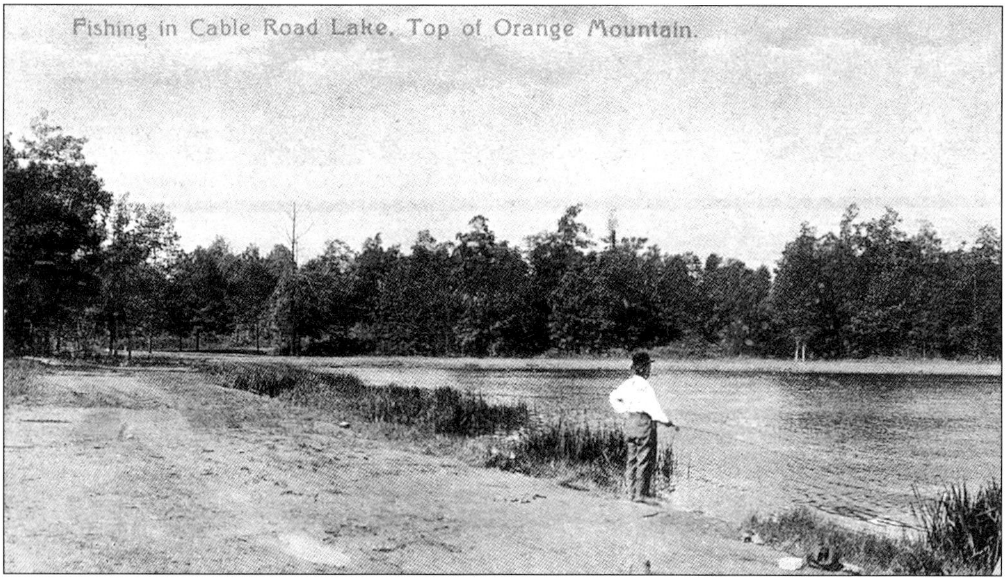

In 1906, a corporation headed by Frank Brewer tried to revive the operation to Cable Lake (pictured here) using regular trolleys instead of cable cars. Two ex-Public Service cars were purchased and outfitted with special brakes. On the test run on June 24, 1906, car number 102 got as far as the cut before losing traction and running away down the mountain and crashing into number 101, which was parked at the bumper. One rider was killed as he jumped off at Gregory Avenue.

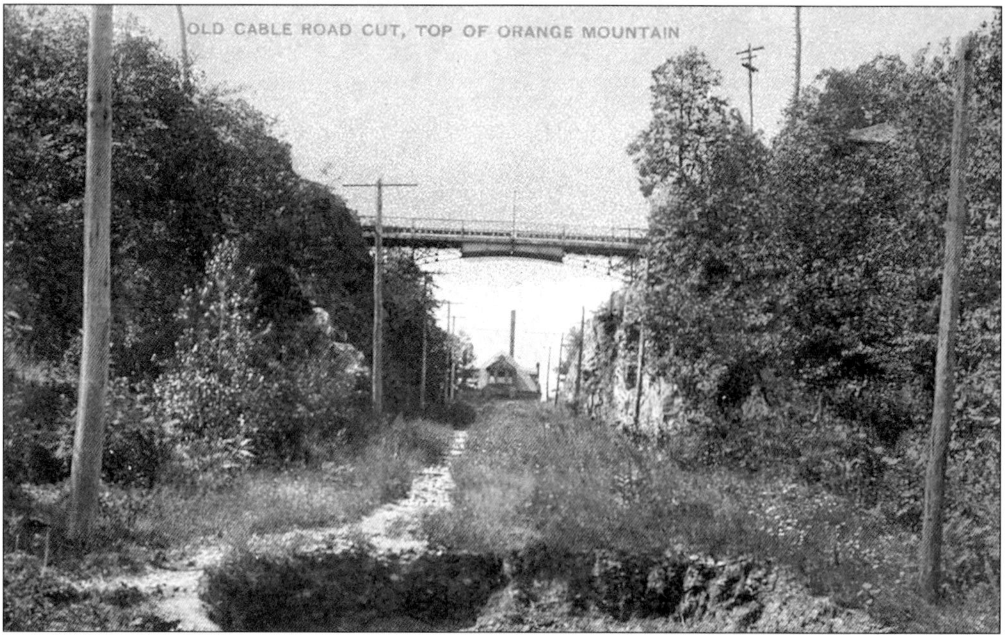

From this view of the abandoned roadbed c. 1915, it is hard to believe that the Cable Road once carried up to 13,000 passengers in a week. Despite the lake, free band concerts, and dancing, the operation quietly died before 1910. In this photo, only the washed out gorge and powerhouse remain as evidence of the Cable Road, along with the spindly bridge that once allowed spectators a closer look at this mechanical marvel.

Eight

The Big Party

Orange was incorporated as a city on March 13, 1860, and, within a short time, began to fractionate into smaller municipalities. In January 1907, city historian David L. Pierson decided it was time for Orange to have a centennial celebration. Perhaps reflecting upon the 100th anniversary of the secession from Newark, which had passed with little fanfare, Pierson seized upon an idea. He made the decision to celebrate the 100th anniversary of the first Council elections (1807) as the "real" centennial of not only his city, but of the rest of Oranges as well. Pierson, with a hand-picked committee of local dignitaries, began to plan for a festival like no one had ever seen. What follows is a photographic record of that glorious week.

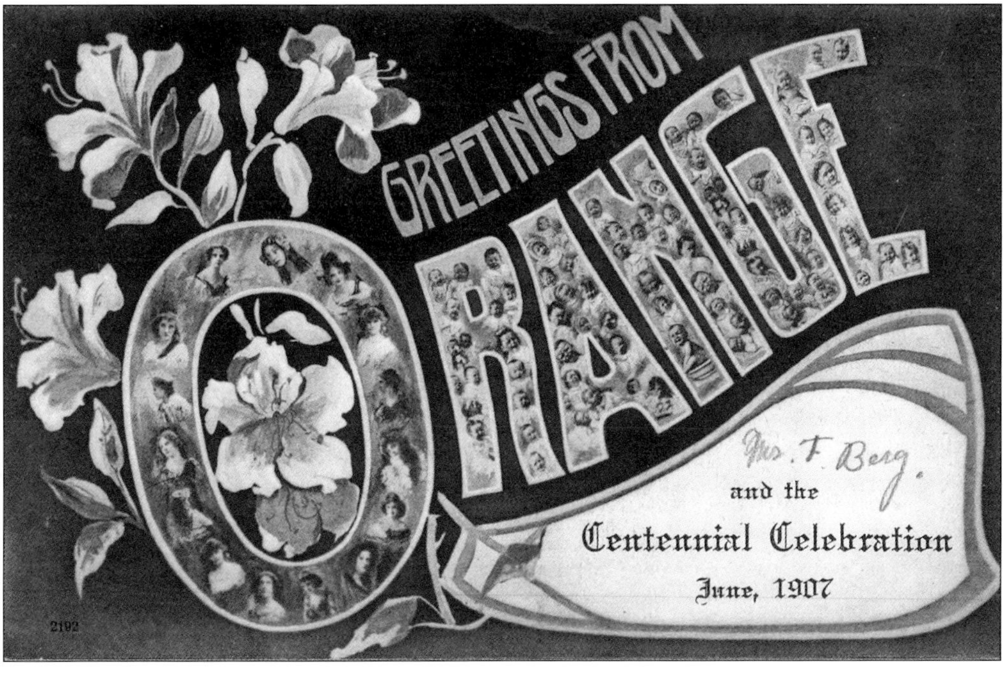

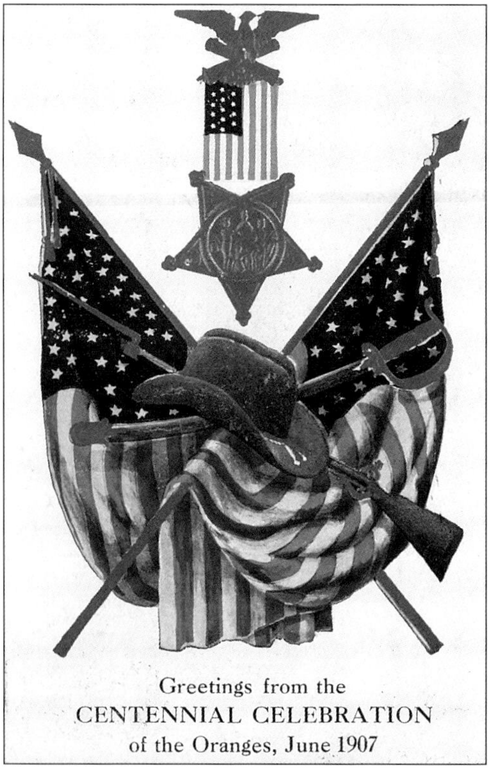

The celebration was deferred until the week of June 9, 1907, because of the concerns about the weather in early April, the actual time of the first elections. The festivities would include two distinct activities: "Old Home Week," and the dedication of a memorial statue to the "Dispatch Rider of the American Revolution" at the Old Burying Ground. This was to be followed by a giant parade. Commemorative cards such as this added to the festivities.

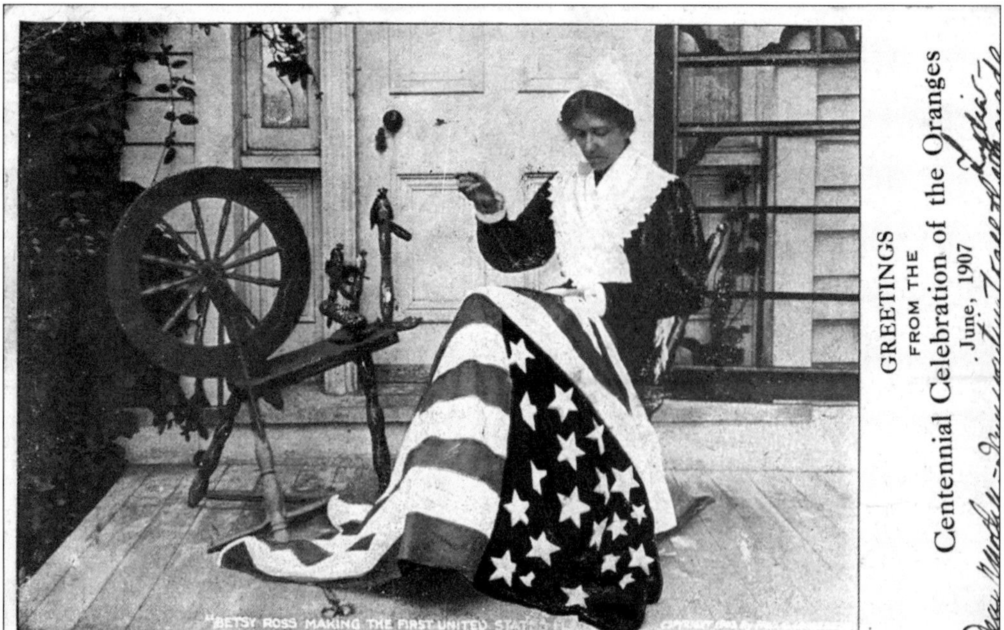

Dozens of special commemorative cards with all manners of design were produced for the celebration, along with pinbacks, buttons, ribbons, flags, and more. Sunday, June 9 dawned sunny and beautiful and the weather held for most of the week, but by Friday, June 14, the parade and dedication of the statue were carried out in a drizzling rain.

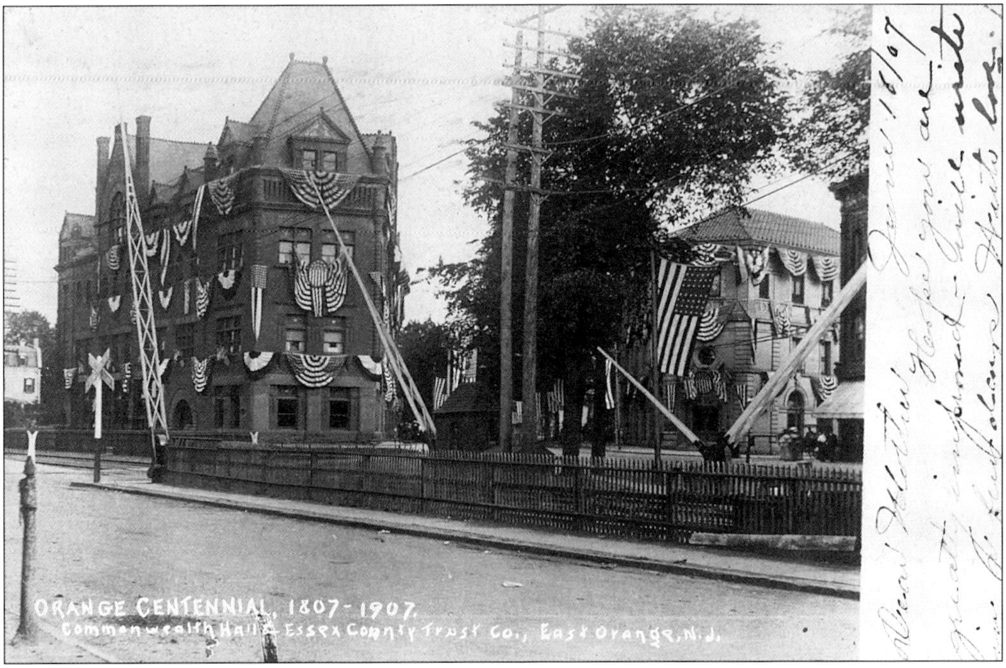

The two bunting-bedecked buildings are Commonwealth Hall and the Essex County Trust Company in this view of East Orange at the time of the Centennial. The Lackawanna Railroad tracks have yet to be elevated through the city, and manpower still cranks down the heavy wooden gates that protect vehicular traffic from the onrushing trains.

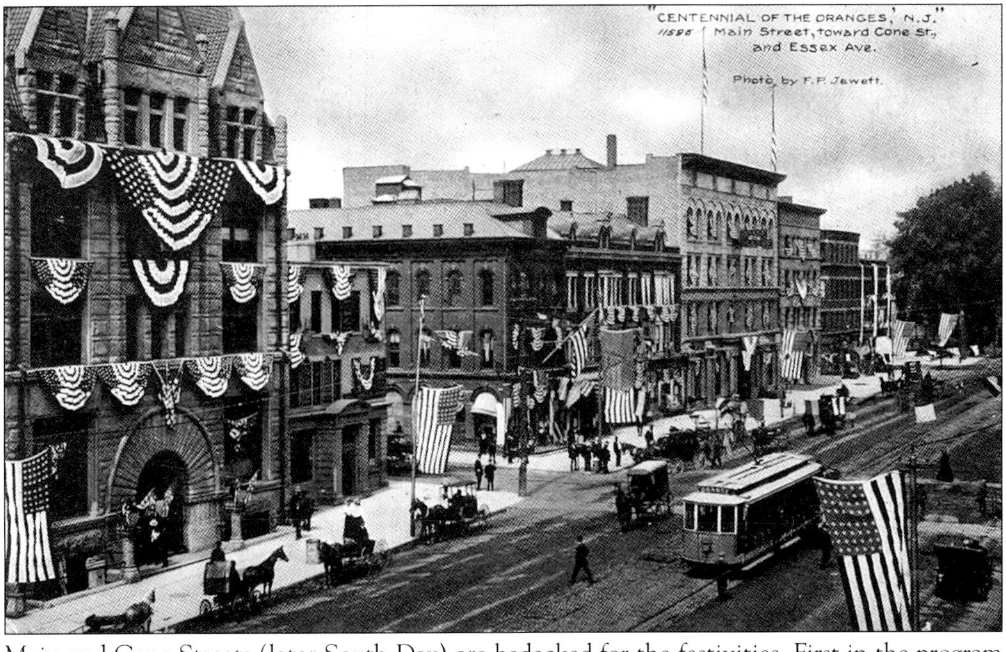

Main and Cone Streets (later South Day) are bedecked for the festivities. First in the program was the dedication of the new high school building at the corner of Main and Cleveland Streets. Numerous churches held special services, and the outpouring of patriotic oratory was overwhelming.

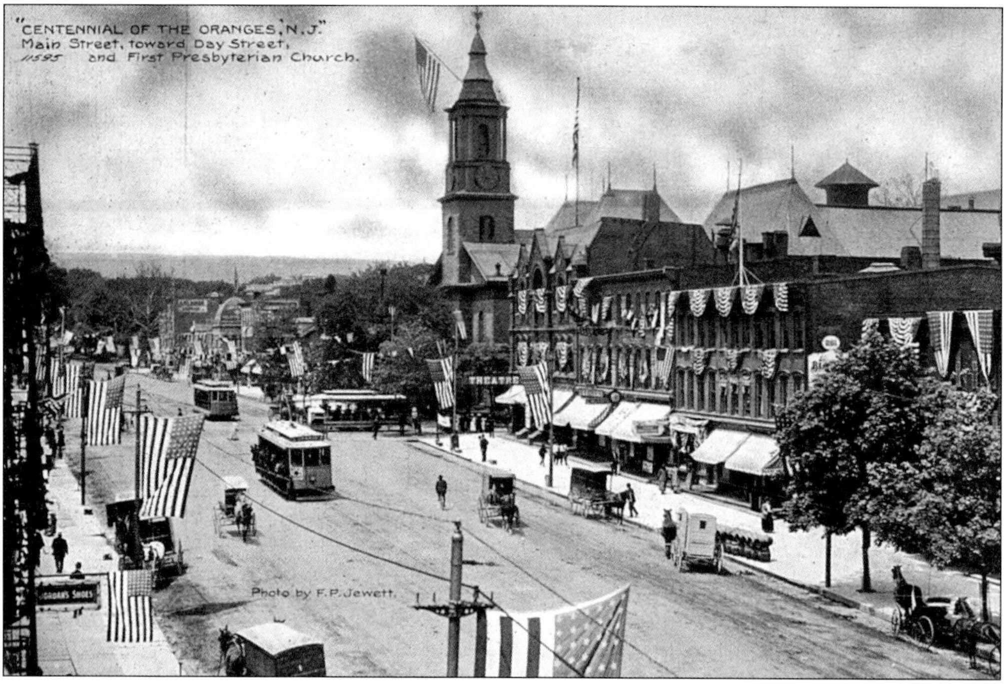

The formal opening of the Centennial took place at the Orange Theatre (Music Hall), which is visible at the corner of Main and Day Streets. Over 1,000 people jammed the facility to hear a speech by historian Pierson and an historical address by Rev. John Thomas, pastor of the Arlington Avenue Presbyterian Church in East Orange. The Orange Mannerchor provided the music.

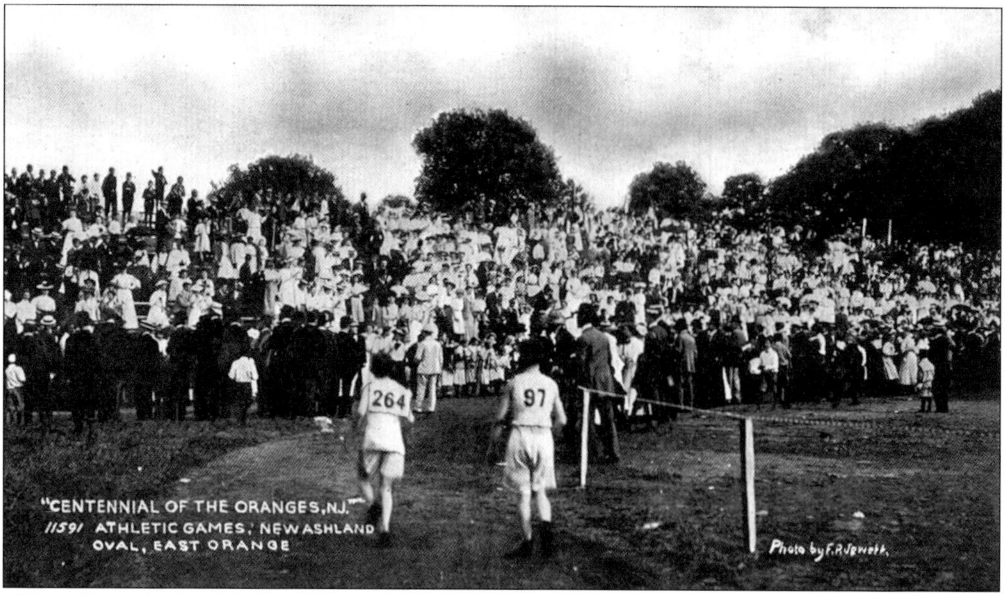

Throughout the week, numerous events took place, including receptions, luncheons, reunions, open houses, entertainment, and carnivals. Athletic competition was held at the new Ashland Oval in East Orange, and W. Courter won the 440- and 880-yard runs and the 100- and 220-yard dashes.

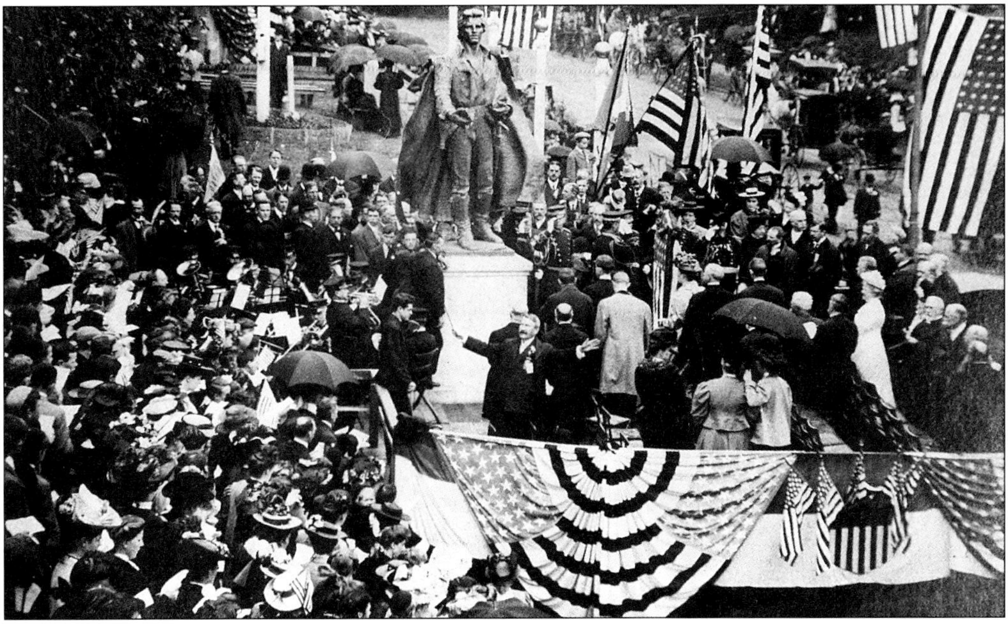

At exactly 1 p.m. in a drizzling rain, the Dispatch Rider statue was dedicated in the Old Burying Ground, with a throng of thousands in attendance. After a prayer by Rev. Charles Townsend, Mrs. Charles B. Yardley of the Daughters of the American Revolution pulled the cords that unveiled the bronze. At the same moment, church bells began ringing and Markwith's Band (Professor Markwith in the center, arms raised) delivered "The Star Spangled Banner." (Photo courtesy the First Presbyterian Church.)

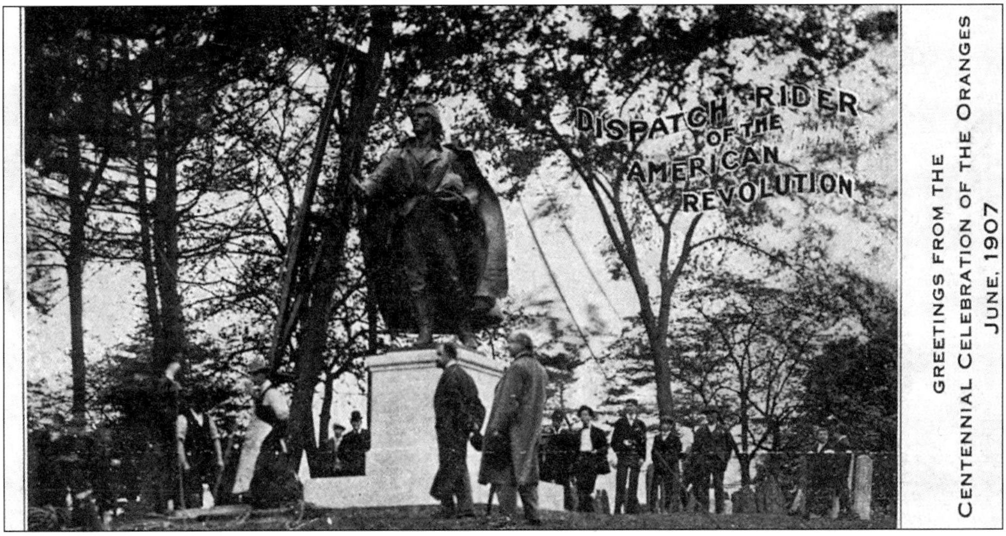

The "Dispatch Rider of the American Revolution" statue had its origins in May 1905, with the rehabilitation of the long neglected "Old Burying Ground." A Revolutionary Monument Association was formed and the idea of a statue proposed. It was designed by Francis Edwin Elwell, former curator of sculpture at the Metropolitan Museum of Art. The statue was erected at a cost of $5,000. Elwell's proposal won out over a number of other ideas submitted. The statue was modeled at Elwell's studio in Weehawken and cast in granite at the Gorham Works in Providence, Rhode Island.

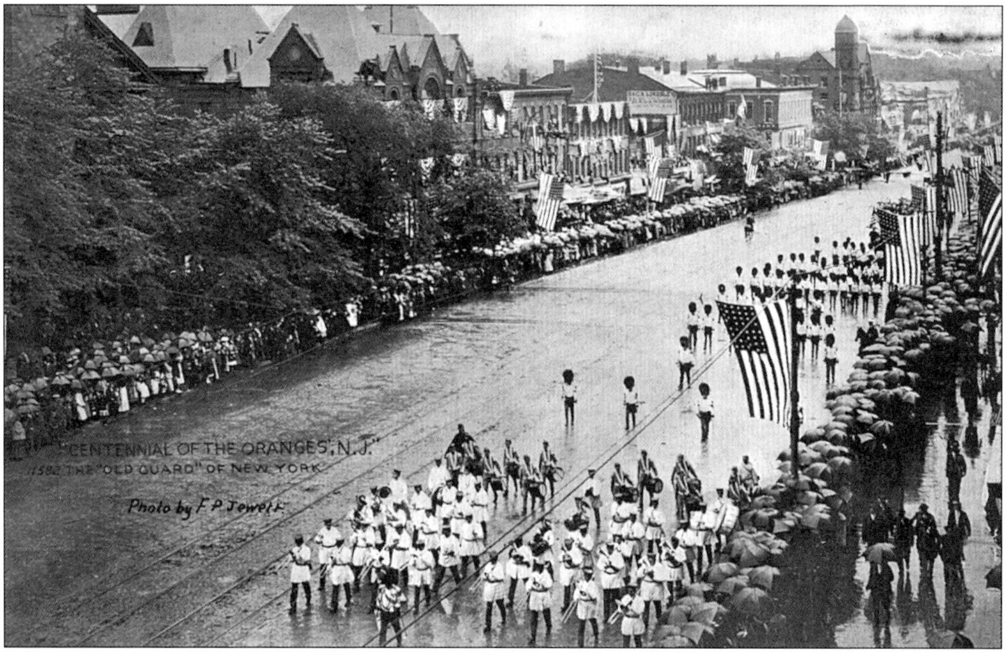

The parade began at the Parkway (Oraton) and Main Street in East Orange at 3 p.m. and passed in an unbroken line to the West Orange border. New Jersey Governor Caspar Stokes reviewed the procession at the Old Burying Ground. Colonel George P. Olcott was Grand Marshall, and the Old Guard of New York, pictured here, was the special guest of the day.

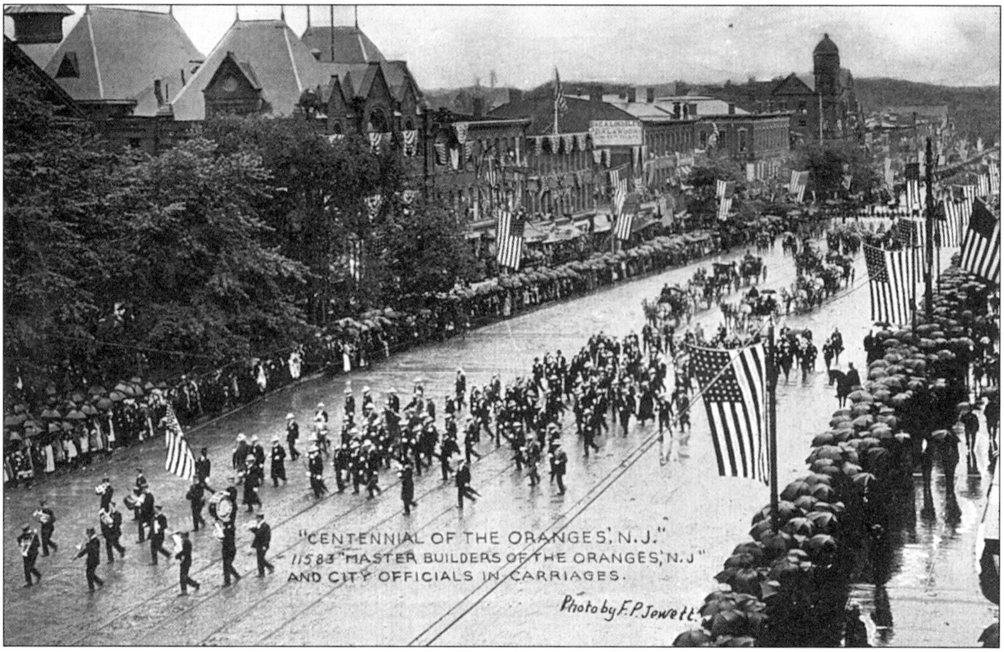

Photographer Frank P. Jewett stationed himself at the Drake College in the top floor of the Metropolitan Building to capture these views. Here, the Master Builders of the Oranges accompanies city officials of the Oranges, who rode in carriages.

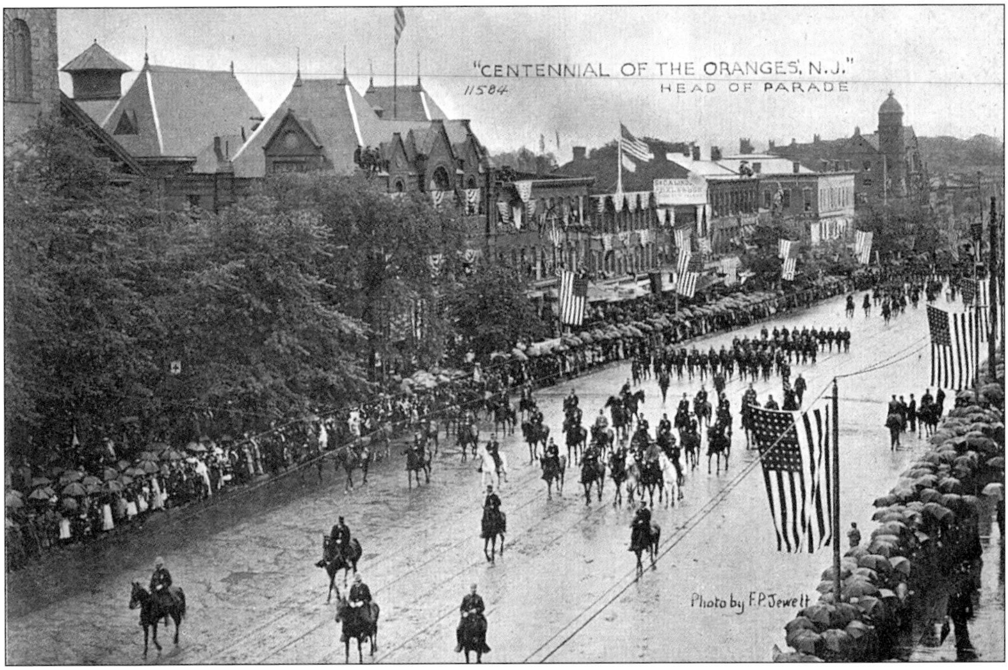

The head of the parade passes the Old First Presbyterian Church, and we might assume that the gentleman on the white horse in the center, surrounded by the cadre of police, is none other than Colonel Olcott himself.

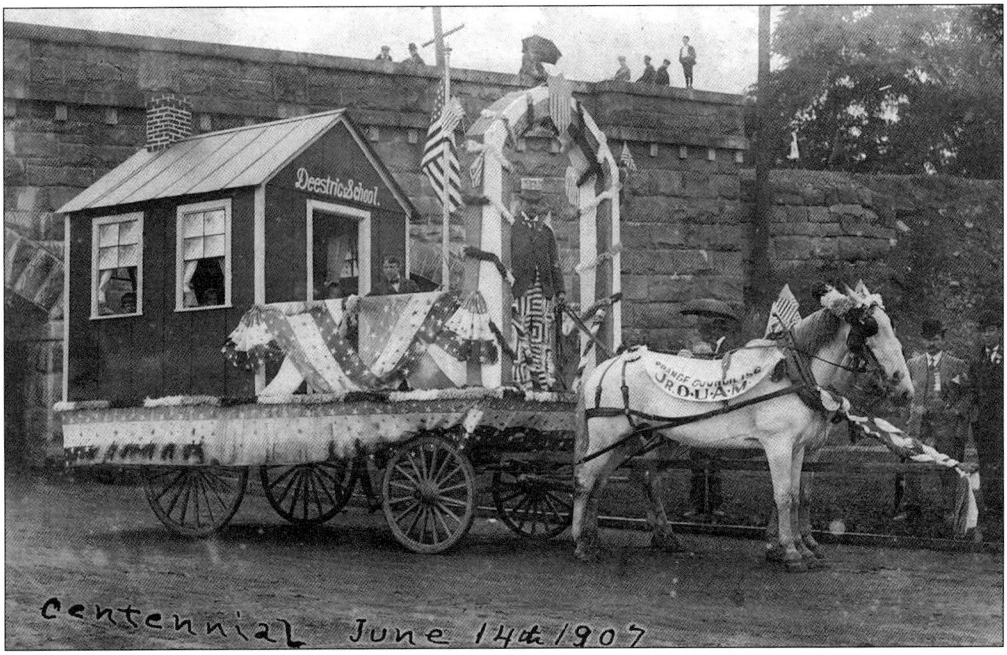

This is a close-up of the "Deestric School" float sponsored by Orange Council 156 of the Junior OUAM. The character under the archway bears a strong resemblance to "Uncle Sam."

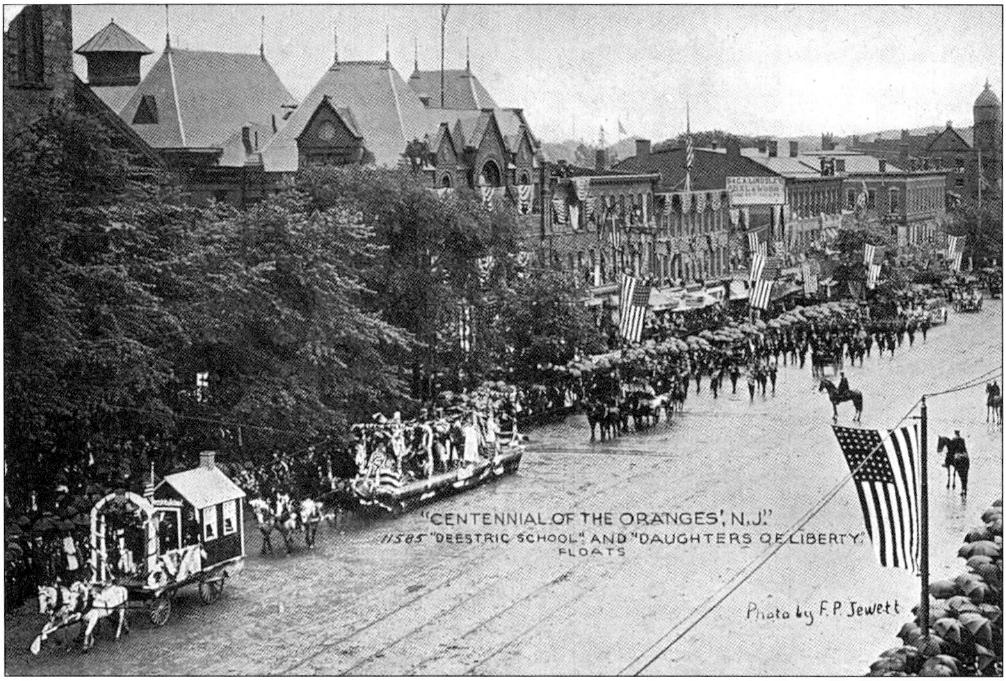

The "Deestric School" float passes the Old First followed closely behind by the wagon carrying the "Daughters of Liberty." Most participants in the parade are notably horse-powered. Even the Dispatch Rider statue was delivered on a horse-drawn dray and lifted into place with a mechanical crane.

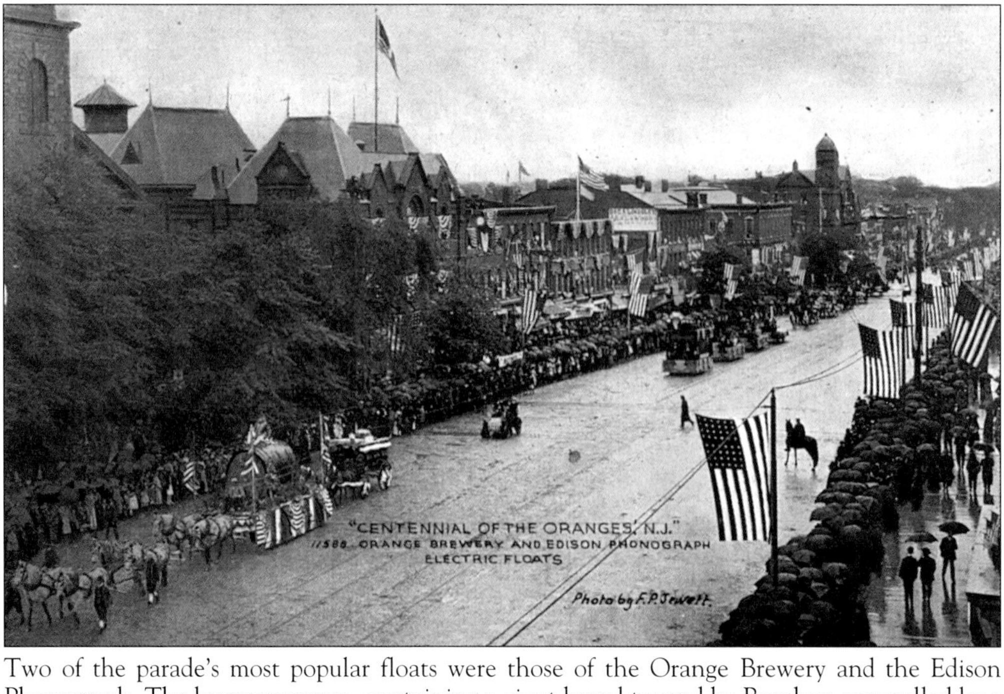

Two of the parade's most popular floats were those of the Orange Brewery and the Edison Phonograph. The brewery wagon, containing a giant barrel topped by Bacchus, was pulled by a three-team hitch. The giant phonograph concealed a full concert band inside.

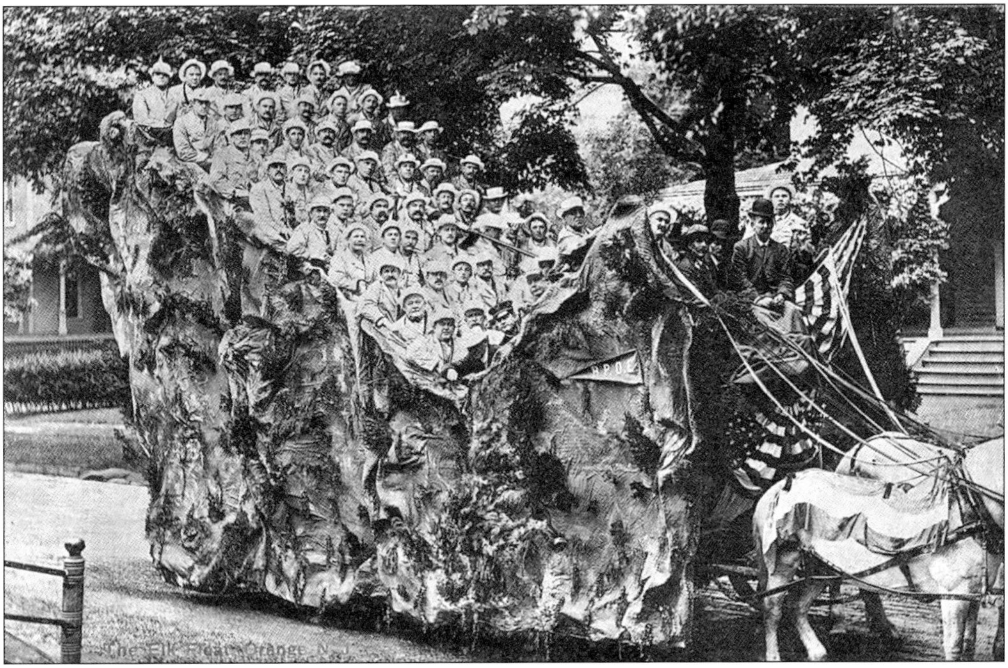

There are more than 60 members of the Benevolent and Protective Order of Elks crowded on this rather bizarre tiered float as it prepares to participate in the parade. The float was so high that the Elks on the top row had to hold their hats and duck every 50 yards whenever they approached a crosswire or flag.

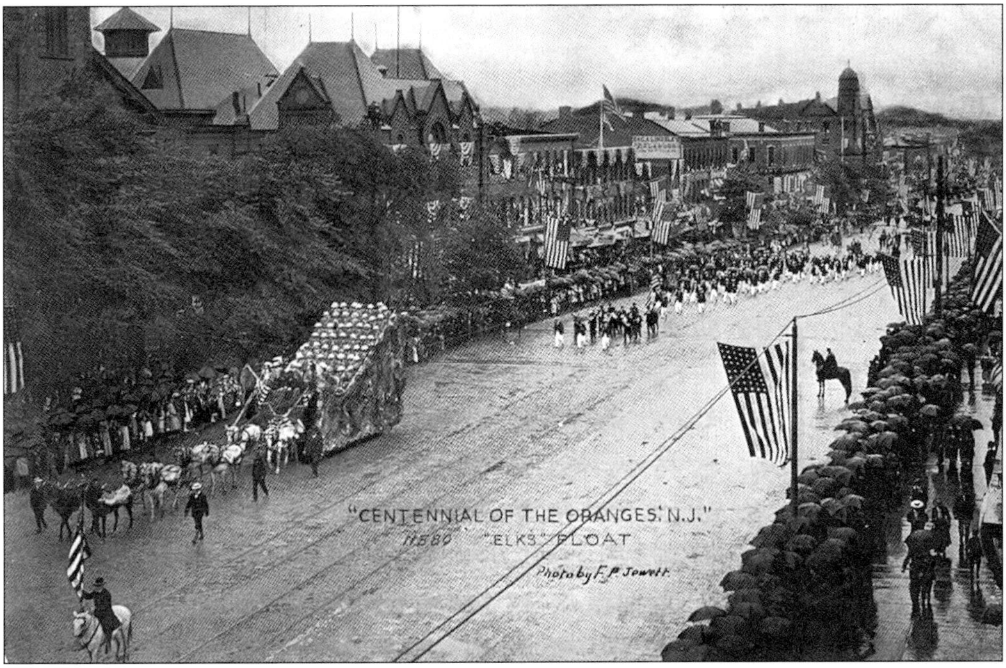

The Elks float passes Jewett's camera. When the float arrived at the reviewing stand, its riders broke out into a chorus of "Auld Lang Syne" and other selections. Too bad the days of videotape were still too far away.

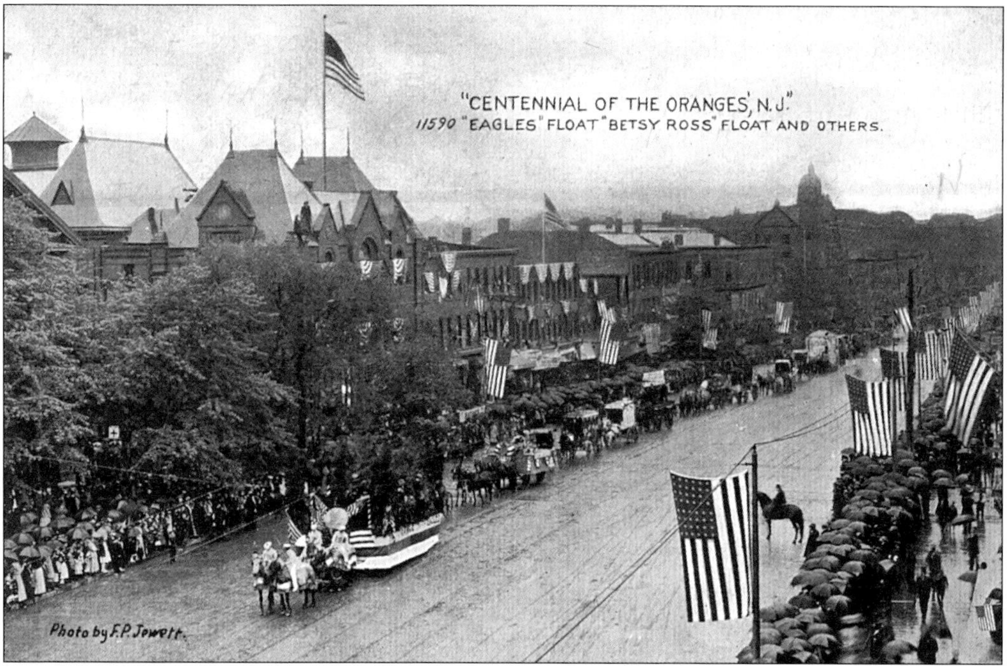

Under dark skies, the Fraternal Order of Eagles and the Betsy Ross floats pass by.

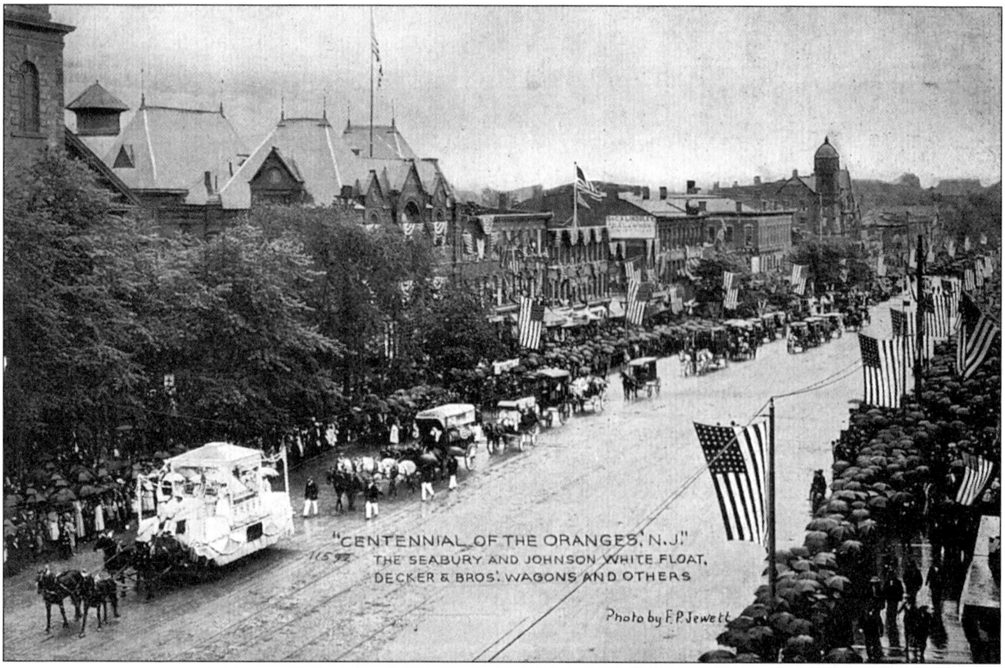

The Seabury & Johnson Pharmaceutical Company, which sponsored this white float, was located in East Orange on Glenwood Avenue near the Erie Railroad crossing. In June 1913, over $50,000 in damage was caused by a fire at their plant, which, thanks to the competent work of the East Orange Fire Department, was saved from total destruction.

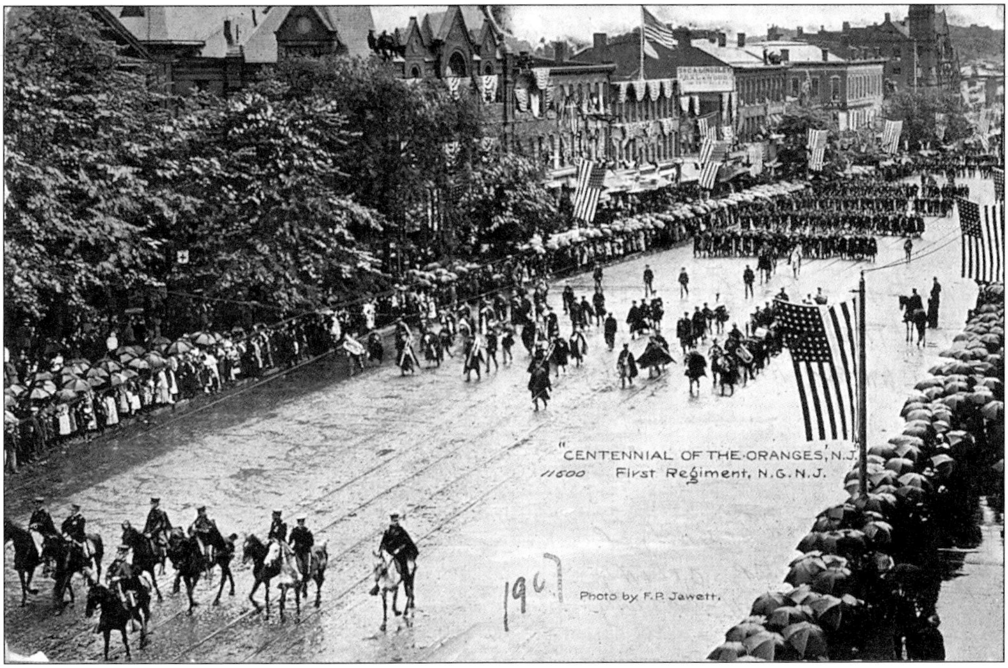

The New Jersey National Guard was represented by the First and Fifth Regiments, the Essex Mounted Troop, Battery A of the Field Artillery, and the New Jersey Naval Reserves. Here, the First Regiment passes in review.

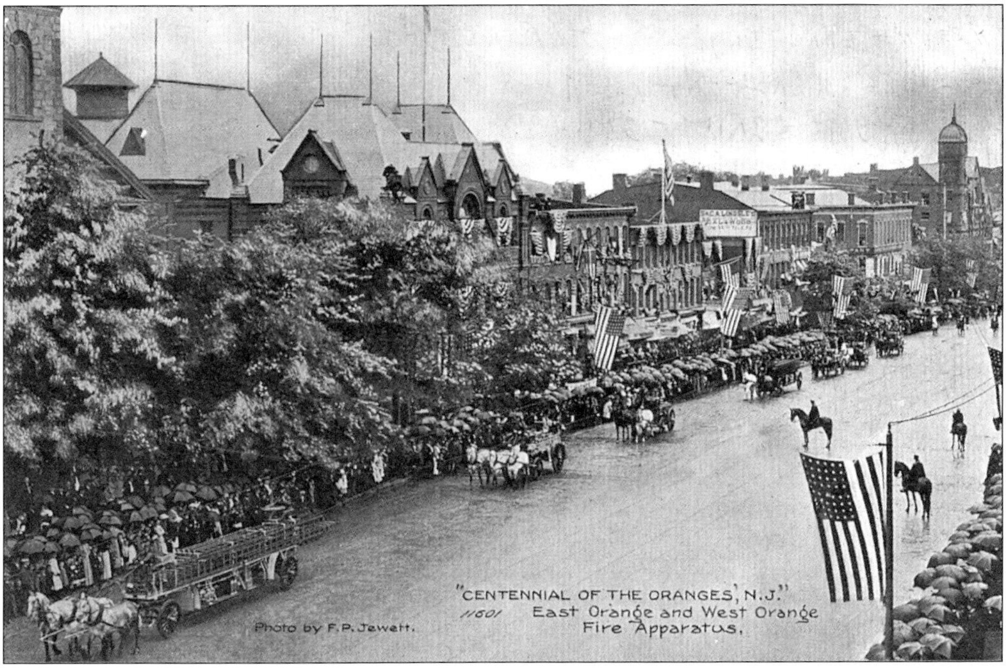

No parade would be complete without a display of fire apparatus. Here, the horse-drawn equipment of East and West Orange passes the cameraman.

MARIETTA DORFLINGER

ME-MET-MEAT-MEDAL-MANGER
AT-ATE-ATOM-ANGER-AILING
R.N.-RAM-REAM-REMIT-RANGER
IT-IRE-IDLE-IDLER-INMATE
E.R.-ERA-EARN-ELFIN-ERRANT
TO-TON-TONE-TONER-TARRED
TI-TIN-TINE-TRINE-TANGLE
AM-AIM-ANTE ANGLE-ANGLER

DR.-DOT-DOTE-DINGO-DANGL
OF-OFT-OMEN-O-RING-OARIN
N.M.-NOT-NOTE-NOMAD-NORMAL

BIBLIOGRAPHY

DO-DON-DING-DOING-DANGER
OR-ORT-OGRE-OTTER-OILING
RM.-ROD-ROAD-REIGN-RATING

Clark, Eleanor Sterling. *Orange, New Jersey 1806–1956*. Orange, NJ: The Orange Sesquicentennial Committee, 1956.

FL.-FAR-FARE-FLING-FILING

Hoyt, Rev. James. *The Mountain Society: A History of the First Presbyterian Church, Orange, NJ*. New York, NY: C.M. Saxton, Barker & Co., 1860.

LA.-LAD-LOAD-LINGO-LINGER

Orange Transcript. *Assorted articles on the Occasion of the 100th Anniversary of the Transcript*. Orange, NJ: Worrall Publications, 1998.

IN-ION-INRO-INGLE -INROAD

Our Lady of the Valley Church. *One Hundred Twenty Fifth Anniversary Booklet*. Orange, NJ: Privately Published, 1998.

NO-NEB-NEAT-NITER-NETTED
GA.-GAR-GRIT-GRIME-GANDER

Peabody, Reuben T., Chairman. *Seventy-fifth Anniversary, City of East Orange*. East Orange NJ: Souvenir Booklet and Historical Committees, 1938.

EN-EAR-ERNE-EAGER-ERRAND

Pierson, David Lawrence. *History of the Oranges to 1921*. New York, NY: The Lewis Historical Publishing Co., 1922.

RD.-RAG-REIN-REIGN-REFINE

Pons, Muriel, Ed. *250th Anniversary Book of the First Presbyterian Church in Orange*. Orange, NJ: The First Presbyterian Church, 1969.

Riordan, George. *Essay for the Sesquicentennial*. Orange, NJ: Unpublished 1956.